The Theater of Devotion

THE THEATER OF
DEVOTION

*East Anglian Drama and Society in
the Late Middle Ages*

Gail McMurray Gibson

THE UNIVERSITY OF CHICAGO PRESS

Chicago & London

The University of Chicago Press, Chicago 60637
The University of Chicago Press, Ltd., London
© 1989 by The University of Chicago
All rights reserved. Published 1989
Paperback edition 1994
Printed in the United States of America

98 97 96 95 94   5 4 3 2

Library of Congress Cataloging-in-Publication Data

Gibson, Gail McMurray.
The theater of devotion: East Anglian drama and society in the
late Middle Ages / Gail McMurray Gibson.
p. cm.
Bibliography: p. 233
Includes index.
ISBN 0-226-29101-4 (cloth)
ISBN 0-226-29102-2 (paper)
1. Mysteries and miracle plays, English—England—East Anglia—
History and criticism.   2. Christian drama, English (Middle)—
England—East Anglia—History and criticism.   3. Devotional
literature, English—History and criticism.   4. Theater—England—
East Anglia—History—Medieval, 500–1500.   5. Literature and
society—England—East Anglia—History.   6. East Anglia (England) in
literature.   7. East Anglia (England)—Church history.   8. East
Anglia (England)—Civilization.   I. Title.
PR644.E28G53   1989   89–4741
822'.0516—dc19   CIP

For John Baret and other ghosts

Contents

East Anglia in the 15th Century

Illustrations

Illustrations

Acknowledgments

In the long and gossipy progress of this shape-shifting book, there have been many good friends and scholars who aided and abetted the author (and were properly sceptical at the proper times) as I struggled to learn how to hear the voices of the theater I wanted to know. These are some of them: Kathleen Ashley, Donald Baker, Richard Beadle, Larry Clopper, John Coldewey, Theresa Coletti, Clifford Davidson, Alexandra Johnston, Stanley Kahrl, Alan Nelson, Milla Riggio, D. W. Robertson, Jr., Thomas P. Roche, Jr., Pamela Sheingorn, Stephen Spector, Peter Travis, John Wasson. All of these scholars have given me useful talk and still more useful example—and have never stopped asking me hard questions.

To V. A. Kolve, whose *The Play Called Corpus Christi* and whose prodigious talents as teacher galvanized me fifteen years ago to an abiding obsession with medieval theater, to John Fleming, who believed in this book when almost no one else did, to David Bevington, who has been a supporter of unstinting energy and kindness, and to Margaret Statham, who has shared her archivist's knowledge of Bury St. Edmunds with profligate generosity and has been as tough and exacting a critic as she has been a valued friend, I owe special thanks.

The Suffolk Record Offices at Bury and at Ipswich and the Norfolk Record Office at Norwich have rendered many good services, patiently answered short- and long-distance queries, and been generous hosts. David Dymond, Diarmaid MacCulloch, Peter Northeast, Clive Paine, and Norman Tanner all gave useful comments and corrections on matters of local East Anglian history. Sarah Brown and her staff at the National Monuments Record, London, helped immeasurably in the procuring of photographs for this book (and earned my undying gratitude for services above and beyond the call of duty). I am also grateful to the photographers and to the libraries and museums named in this book who allowed me to reproduce their photographs, and to Flora Jones and to Fraser and Mary Sutherland for patiently indulging my own zeal for photographing East Anglian parish churches.

Research for this book was begun with the gift of a year's leave from teaching at Princeton in 1979–80 as John E. Annan Bicentennial Preceptor, and the final draft was written during a leave of absence from Davidson College in 1986–87 made possible by a fellowship grant by the American Council of Learned Societies. My debt for both of those acts of financial and moral support is obvious and real. Neither could I have begun this book without what the English local-history collections of Princeton's Firestone Library and the Index of Christian Art taught me, nor could I have finished it without the hidden, phoneless, basement office that the staff of the Davidson College Library loaned me for a year, without the many kindnesses of the Davidson College Faculty Secretarial Services—or without the word processor that good friends like Trent Foley, Peter Krentz, Randy Nelson, and Karl Plank nagged me into learning to use.

Travel in East Anglia was made possible by summer research and travel grants from Princeton University and from Davidson College, but especially by my parents, Ginny and Sam McMurray, who have babysat over the years even to the limits of their own fond endurance. My children, Josh and Annie, who have grown *in* and long out of *utero* with this book, and my husband, McNeill, helped most by frequently voicing their exasperation with the whole project—and by reminding me by my bonds of love what mattered and still matters.

The Theater of Devotion

Chapter One
Fifteenth-Century Culture and the Incarnational Aesthetic

This book began as a book about late medieval habits of mind and the English mystery plays, but it soon became a book laboring with increasing vexation to connect the ceremonial spirituality and Marian iconography of the East Anglian N-Town cycle (long known by the misnomer inscribed in the manuscript by Sir Robert Bruce Cotton's librarian, *Ludus Coventriae*) with the late medieval cycles of biblical plays from York, Wakefield, and Chester. As I struggled to understand the compilation of religious pageants in the problematic Cotton Vespasian manuscript, I became more and more struck by the evidence that, except for the most superficial resemblances of genre and function, the N-Town cycle was a very different dramatic and devotional artifact from the drama cycles created by northern civic piety. Wherever its specific provenance in fifteenth-century Suffolk or Norfolk (the "Proclamation" introducing the plays of the Cotton Vespasian manuscript heralds their place of performance only as *N*, for *nomen*, name), it was late-medieval East Anglia that I needed to know in order to answer my questions about the N-Town cycle. I found my conviction shared by Arthur Brown in a thirty-year old, but seldom-heeded essay entitled "The Study of English Medieval Drama." "What seems to be needed now," wrote Arthur Brown,

> is a series of detailed studies of medieval drama as it appeared in single localities in [England]. This kind of study will consider the drama of a single locality not so much from the point of view of its resemblances to drama elsewhere, not so much as a single manifestation of the great spirit of religious drama in Europe in the Middle Ages, but rather as a local product, influenced to a great extent by local circumstances, reflecting local conditions and attitudes, produced and performed by local people, often tradesmen, regarded as a local responsibility.[1]

My study of the fifteenth-century habits of mind that shaped a text like the N-Town cycle has thus become an effort to reconstruct an accurate overview of fifteenth-century English religious culture—and then the way that East Anglian poets, playwrights, patrons, and especially the East Anglian people, fit with that context. The Suffolk and Norfolk of the N-Town cycle was also the home of a remarkable number of other dramatic texts and fragments, of much of Lydgate's devotional poetry, of the extraordinary *Book* of the mystic Margery Kempe. The fifteenth century was East Anglia's golden age, and in that age its thriving literary culture was dominated both by the old monastic spirituality and by the new lay piety, wealth, and patronage of rural cloth merchants. It is surely only because the eyes of literary historians have been focused so myopically on London and on the court literature there that the fifteenth-century literary climate has so often been characterized as stale and lifeless Chaucerian imitation. For Chaucer and for other court poets of the fourteenth century, the most viable literary models were in southern Europe, in the Italy of Dante and Boccaccio, or in the Paris of the polished French court poets. But for the thriving fifteenth-century culture of East Anglia, it is not the influence of the previous century's court poets which should be the focus of our inquiries; not to southern Europe but to Flanders and Germany we should look for continental models of religious thought as well as for influences on its flourishing drama, saints' lives and devotional texts, parish church architecture and stained glass. It is not Margery Kempe's travels to Italy, but her pilgrimage in old age to Germany which should stand as emblem in our mind as we seek to understand her time and place in fifteenth-century Norfolk.

As I proceeded to write this book, I saw that the critical bias which has all but ignored the important regional culture of East Anglia as a fact of the late Middle Ages has only been exceeded by the widespread prejudice against the English fifteenth century in general. It is necessary to say at the outset that this is not a book about the "medieval" context of literature in the way that word has too often been applied in literary studies, as a "medieval" age presented as a pastiche of thirteenth-century high scholasticism, the "Augustinian metaphysic," and Franciscan affective piety. The tendency to overgeneralize what is "medieval" is especially noticeable in many studies of the English vernacular drama texts, especially the so-called Corpus Christi cycles, which have nearly always been discussed as though they were traditional "medieval" texts which merely happen to survive in late manuscripts. The English religious drama of the fifteenth and even early sixteenth centuries was an integral part of the religious and social life of the time, but that time has rarely been faced squarely. It has been, in fact, only in the last few years, largely because of the ambitious efforts of the Toronto REED project,[2] that hard scrutiny of the existing dramatic records has begun to challenge the widespread general view of the cycle plays as texts whose real life was "medieval" (i.e., of the thirteenth and fourteenth centuries). Lawrence Clopper has convincingly argued, after an exhaustive study of the records at Chester, that there is evidence that the cycle play at Chester was not a "medieval" phenomenon at all, that the transformation of a single Passion play on the French model to an entire cycle of biblical history may even be a fact of Tudor history.[3] It seems that in the Chester cycle we do not have sixteenth-century manuscripts of moribund medieval plays, but rather texts whose shape and content are the results of contemporary social history, devotion, and politics. We may speculate about now-lost versions of earlier, more truly "medieval" forms of the Chester cycle, but to substitute such intellectual archaeology for the texts themselves is no more fair or useful than to approach *Beowulf* solely as the pagan folk tale which may have given it birth.

Our first task, then, before we can come to understand fifteenth-century East Anglian culture, is to understand the nature of the prejudice against the fifteenth century generally, that nearly unanimous censure and impatience with the times which has made us believe the fifteenth century to be a literary wasteland, a century all but lost to literary histories and to our collective consciousness of our literary past. "A vulgar interlude," Donald Hall calls the fifteenth century in his book on medieval pilgrimage. "In a century after Chaucer almost the only memorable book is Malory's *Morte d'Arthur,* itself not an original work."[4] One of the very few genuine literary studies of the fifteenth century, H. S. Bennett's tellingly-named *Chaucer and the Fifteenth Century,* lists half a dozen different "break-ups" and "declines" in the fifteenth century which, he argues, made that century "full of divided aims and lacking in much that encourages great literature."[5] David Knowles, in the standard study of English medieval spirituality, praises the "intellectual and emotional austerity" of the fourteenth-century English mystics like Walter Hilton and the anonymous author of the *Cloud of Unknowing,* but dismisses thusly the fifteenth-century English mystical tradition:

> There is some evidence that from the beginning of the fifteenth century onwards it [the spiritual climate] was contaminated by another current, that of a more emotional and idiosyncratic devotion, manifesting itself in visions, revelations and unusual behaviour, deriving partly from one aspect of the teaching of Ruysbroeck and Suso and the other mystical writers, and partly from the influence of some of the women saints of the fourteenth century, such as Angela of Foligno, Dorothea of Prussia, and Bridget of Sweden. The most familiar example of this type in England is Margery Kempe, whose spiritual experiences lie outside our province, and it seems to have flourished chiefly in individual groups in the more important towns.[6]

To these accusations of the "contaminations" and vulgarities of the age could be added other negatively-charged words which appear and reappear in descriptions of fifteenth-century culture written by literary historians, charges of "decadent sentimentalism"[7] and of naiveté in pictorial imagination.[8] Even from apologists we receive damnation by faint praise in the form of the argument that the fifteenth century can be valued as a "period of transition."[9] Although it is no longer true, as it was for many years, that the only available anthologies of English medieval drama are contained in editions which call themselves *Chief Pre-Shakespearean Dramas* and *Specimens of the Pre-Shakespearean Drama,* that teleological focus which O. B. Hardison exposed and challenged in our critical understanding of medieval drama doggedly perseveres in general critical attitudes to fifteenth-century culture.[10] The fifteenth century has traditionally been the subject of active and sympathetic enquiry only for historians of warfare and political conflict; with only a few and very recent exceptions, historians of the cultural climate of fifteenth-century northern Europe have continued to remouth, in language more or less negative, the working assumptions of Johan Huizinga, whose original Dutch version of *The Waning of the Middle Ages* was written more than half a century ago.[11] *The Waning of the Middle Ages* was a brilliant synthesis of fifteenth-century Northern European culture, and it takes its rightful place as one of the handful of genuine historical classics. Huizinga's sonorous prose, magnificent even in English translation, gave the world a fifteenth century with the "mixed smell of blood and roses," a time of childlike dependence on visual signs and rituals, of turbulent contradictions which eventually canceled themselves out in a noisy clash of warring and ultimately impotent wills.[12] Although Huizinga himself named the book the "Herfsttij" or "harvest-tide" of the Middle Ages, The English word "waning" more accurately reflects Huizinga's point of view toward the times. For fifty years historians and laymen alike seized Huizinga's words and revered them as primary texts, almost never reassessing his evidence or questioning his conclusions. Whenever even so great an historian of ideas as Erwin Panofsky, in another classic synthesis of the fifteenth century called *Early Netherlandish Painting,* turned from his dazzling decodifying of disguised symbolism in van Eyck to speak of actual human beings inhabiting the fifteenth-century world, he invoked those familiar stereotypes from Huizinga: "that childlike delight in everything that glitters and tinkles. People took to wearing little golden bells on their belts and collars and the very horses wore hundreds of medals, engraved or enameled with images or emblems, every one of which is now a museum piece."[13]

It is this charge of childlikeness more than anything else, I think, that reverberates in our collective thinking about fifteenth-century culture and arts and which hinders our fullest understanding of the mystery plays. This first chapter is an attempt to come to terms with those characteristics of fifteenth-century thought which have evoked the epithets "childlike," "naive," and "popular," epithets which have served to mask by patronizing stereotypes rather than to explain.

Perhaps the single most insistent characteristic of this troubling fifteenth century and its "childlike" mind was its tendency to formulate concrete images—in thought, in the arts, in wax *ex votos* draped on shrines, even in those hundreds of little horse medals which jingle in Panofsky's sketch of fifteenth-century man. There is no question that there had always been an important concrete element in the Christian religion. Coulton has even suggested that the abstract dogmas of the church fathers, the carefully nourished inheritance of the Greek philosophers, were throughout the medieval centuries in a kind of continual combat with the popular mind and its concrete expressions of worship. "A great many medieval ideas grew up from below, and were only adopted and defended by the theologians after the official church, having attempted in vain to eradicate them, had determined to adopt them and make the best of them."[14] Meyer Schapiro in his analysis of the English iconography of the Ascension of Christ suggested that the invention as early as the year 1000 of what was to become standard English iconography of the Ascension—the footprints of the disappearing Lord visibly present on the rock on which he had last stood—was a "vernacular achievement," an "essentially empirical attitude" to an abstract supernatural mystery.[15] In the case of Christ's footprints in the rock, this "empirical attitude" was formed as much by pilgrims' accounts of the rock of Ascension in the Holy Land as by a human need to assert the reality of Christ's earthly presence. Schapiro does not identify the "vernacular" here with the "popular" in a crude sense of that word but rather with the "freshness and spontaneity of the lyrical passages in Anglo-Saxon writings." Whatever we may think of the appropriateness of that analogy, Schapiro's words may offer a reminder useful for our purposes in analyzing the concrete mind of four centuries later. "We should remember," he cautions us, "that in the Middle Ages an intense religious individualism is often associated with an empiricist attitude: The mystics who repudiate logic, rites and systematized dogma for the higher evidence of individual religious experience are also drawn to the concrete and singular within the living world which correspond to their lyric mood and nourish it."[16]

One of the important social facts often overlooked about fifteenth-century religious culture is that those same buying of indulgences and establishing of perpetual chantries whose abuses were to change the shape of Christendom also served to foster an intense religious individualism. That is, such customs were ways for lay persons, at least lay persons of means, to take an active role in the mysteries of religion and of the soul's salvation. As we will see in chapter 4, the Last Will and Testament evolved in the fifteenth century into a means of establishing chantry and charity bequests in ways that were individually expressive and marked by a fervent and emotional religious individualism as much as by fear of death. The cult of saints and relics which had long characterized much of what was "popular" in medieval Christianity became increasingly in the fifteenth century focused on the individual and local realities of the saint. As Jonathan Sumption has observed, men looked on the saints "as individuals, no less immediate, no less visible and tangible in death than they had been in life."[17] Cult images, too, were accorded this local and immediate reality. When Isabella, Countess of Warwick, left bequests in her will of 1439 to the statues of Our Lady of Tewkesbury, Our Lady of Caversham, Our Lady of Walsingham, and Our Lady of Worcester, she was not naively confusing the identity of the Virgin with these local and singly named cult images, but rather acknowledging the individual reality of the ideas of Marian piety which each image represented. The great popularity of Books of Hours in the late Middle Ages, the emphasis on the use of private images for meditation and devotion were results of spiritual attitudes once contained in the cloister which had been absorbed into the lay world and which now shaped new private and individualistic expressions of piety.[18]

The fifteenth-century commitment to the particularity of religious experience—the adoration of Our Lady of Walsingham or a Madonna in a Book of Hours rather than an abstract Mother of God—is not so much, I would argue, an increasing secularization as much as a growing tendency to see the world saturated with sacramental possibility and meaning and to celebrate it. In fifteenth-century devotion, in the visual arts, in the religious drama, it is the Incarnate Son rather than the Godhead who is ever fixed before the eyes of the beholder. Instead of God the Pantocrator with his book of mysteries, the relevant central image for the late Middle Ages is a suffering human body racked on a cross; the book has become his body, its secrets red, fresh, and bleeding if still mysterious to the minds of man. And it is one characteristic of this fifteenth-century mind that the incarnational focus—the insistence on particular, corporal religious image perceived in the world—is extended as far as, quite literally, the human eye can see. The spiritual object of meditation is held earthbound for as long as human ingenuity (and pious curiosity) will permit. Thus it is the fourteenth and fifteenth centuries which first produced images of the Annunciation with the conceived Lord already visibly present to the human worshipper on fecundating beams of light sent from God's hands, or, less problematic theologically, images of the homunculus Christ visible within the windowed reliquary of Mary's womb.[19] Even in vision, Margery Kempe's conviction that her eyes can follow the ascending form of Christ "most semly, most bewtyuows, & most amyable þat euyr myght be seen wyth mannys eye" up to the very instant that the clouds of heaven receive him speaks eloquently for the imagination of her age. For Margery the visual experience of Christ's Incarnation extends beyond footprints in a rock to the very gates of heaven itself: "And a-noon, as he had seyd þes wordys, sche saw veryly how þe eyr openyd as bryght as ony levyn, & he stey yp in-to þe eyr, not ryght hastyli & qwykly, but fayr & esly þat sche myght wel be-holdyn hym in þe eyr tyl it was closyd a-geyn."[20] It is impossible to know whether it is more accurate to say that Margery's visual experience suggests the actual stage machinery of an Ascension play or whether Margery's habits of mind suggest how such a play would have been both devotionally and aesthetically possible.

The ever-growing tendency to transform the abstract and theological to the personal and concrete was not only the general characteristic of mind in the late Middle Ages, it was the center of raging controversy. Transubstantiation, like Incarnation itself, was abstract mystery become the concrete reality of flesh and blood. To those who supported and believed in the doctrine of transubstantiation there was no irreconcilable conflict between a concrete image—flesh and blood—and a mystery—the Mass. That there were others whose empiricism found it troubling gave the fifteenth century the constant protests of the Lollards, heretics who were to find politics on their side in the Reformation and who would turn the altar into a communion table and turn images back into the abstract words from which they had come. Queen Elizabeth I ordered sentences of scripture painted over the censored "pictures and other like fancies" in English parish churches. Those sentences sometimes survive today, like those in the little Suffolk church at Hessett, superimposed upon dimly visible saints and Crucifixions, the words and images fading into the limewash together in the modern light to remind us still of the transubstantiation conflict and its fundamental challenge to the late medieval habit of mind.[21] Many of the iconographical types which the fifteenth century produced could have been produced at no other time than in this age of the contested, and thus ever more insistently asserted, concrete image of devotion. To most modern eyes and tastes (and I would venture to say, to the eyes of a Wycliffe or a Huss) this German Visitation sculpture of about 1410 (fig. 1.1) presents the yet-unborn children in the wombs of Mary and Elizabeth in an almost obsessively physical way. The holy children are seen through wound-like slits as much reminiscent of *memento mori* tomb sculptures as reliquaries. The fetal John the Baptist, though much worn, can still be seen kneeling in humility before his Lord amid the sculptured bowels of his mother. The Messiah (fig. 1.2) waits not among detailed intestines but within a mandorla of glory on which traces of gold paint are still visible. Both prophet and Christ, though yet unborn, are as physically and concretely present in the composition as the mothers who bear them.

It is no accident that it is the late Middle Ages that gives form to such images, nor that Visitation images of this type, with insistently visible fetal Christ and St. John, were especially common in Bohemia and Austria, where the seeds of the Wycliffite heresy were presenting most challenge to the church. Helen Rosenau has made the likely suggestion that "a trend of thought directed towards the change from bread into flesh and from wine into blood gave the background for the vision of the unborn Child in the Mother's womb."[22] Such images, once invented, continued to exist in South Germany, even as late as the eighteenth and early nineteenth centuries in the peasant art of Austria and Bohemia. But the origins of these Visitation sculptures are not "popular" except insofar as all late medieval religious culture was marked by fervent lay participation and emphasis on the concrete and incarnational aspects of Christian mysteries. What has too often been confused with the naive and the childlike, or has been dismissed as crudely popular because it had an afterlife in succeeding centuries in the cultural residue left to peasant culture, was in fact a deliberate and conscious effort to objectify the spiritual even as the Incarnation itself had given spirit a concrete form.

The origins of this conscious effort can probably be traced to the Franciscans and to their emphasis in both piety and preaching upon the human nature of Christ, the Virgin and the saints, to their organized effort to "keep always before their eyes an image of the crucified Christ in vivid versimilitude."[23] What began for the Franciscan preachers as an Incarnational aesthetic sustaining their spiritual vision of the world, had by the fifteenth century turned itself outward and transformed that world. It matters not that by the fourteenth and fifteenth centuries many friars had betrayed the apostolic fervor of those early years or that "friar" had often become a word charged with hypocrisy and deception. The mental revolution which the Franciscans brought, however it was accomplished, most certainly was accomplished. The enormously influential *Meditationes vitae Christi,* written by a Franciscan follower of Bonaventure to guide the pri-

FIGURE 1.1. *Visitation of Mary and Elizabeth,* a devotional statue from Passau, Germany, c. 1410. Nuremberg, Germanisches National-museum (Marburg/ Art Resource, New York).

FIGURE 1.2. Detail of the fetal Christ from the *Visitation.* Nuremberg, Germanisches Nationalmuseum (Marburg/ Art Resource, New York).

vate and cloistered devotions of a Poor Clare, was in 1410 translated and adapted by Nicholas Love, a Prior of Mount Grace monastery in Yorkshire, to serve as an officially sanctioned gospel harmony and model for lay devotion.[24] It is probably fair to say that the Pseudo-Bonaventure's *Meditationes* was, with the sole exception of the Bible and apocryphal gospels, the single most influential literary text upon the vernacular English drama. That influence at times involves direct paraphrase or quotation and the borrowing of invented detail (especially in the case of the N-Town cycle which thoroughly exploits the language and themes of the Nicholas Love version[25]), but even more significant is the role of the *Meditationes* in providing a basic religious aesthetic for vernacular devotional literature. Simply stated, the *Meditationes* replaced the claims of traditional authorities with the claims of the heart, challenged the claims of historical veracity with the claims of the eye. Even time, the sacred artifact of God himself, could be bent by the *Meditationes* to the greater demands of empathetic effectiveness. "Although," wrote the Pseudo-Bonaventure,

> according to the belief of history, the cursing of the fig tree and the appearance of the adulteress in the temple are thought to have occurred after the arrival of the Lord Jesus on the ass in Jerusalem, it seems more convenient not to meditate on anything after this arrival except the Supper and the Passion and their circumstances. Therefore I thought of placing these two events here [with the events of the Ministry].[26]

Truth, as the writer of the *Meditationes* defined it, was sacred events "as they occurred or as they might have occurred according to the devout belief of the imagination."[27] It is the truth of imagination, of imaging, which is the fundamental truth behind late medieval lay spirituality and is the shaping aesthetic for the religious drama and lyric.

Any attempt to analyze this fundamental truth, this aesthetic, which shaped fifteenth-century culture and its arts must, of course, acknowledge the innate difficulty in the anachronistic word "aesthetic." Even with the beginnings of artistic personal identities in the late fourteenth century and in the fifteenth century—the emergence of names of English poets and painters to replace the customary anonymity of earlier centuries—it is still the case that most English religious art remained genuinely and not merely accidentally anonymous.[28] It is also important to realize that late medieval arts still largely represented the world's and not the artist's preoccupations. It was the patron or donor who controlled the images in the artist's imaginings, a patron whose attitudes were formulated by the communal assumptions of his time and place and class and whose preferences and specifications were often quite precisely detailed in the artist's contract.[29]

Fifteenth-Century Culture and the Incarnational Aesthetic

Just how much the patron was likely to control the artist's imagination we may see in a document like the remarkable will of Lydgate's patroness Isabella, countess of Warwick. Although we know nothing of the personal influence Isabella exerted upon the composition of the poem called *Fyfftene Ioyes of Oure Lady* which Lydgate translated from the French at her request (Schirmer has described the poem as "heaped-up invocations [which overwhelm] . . . the reader's senses in a manner similar to that employed by metaphysical writers like Crashaw"[30]), we must infer from the evidence of Isabella's will of 1439 that she was unlikely to have been a passive partner in the enterprise. In her will Isabella not only specifies the design, measurements, and iconography of the tomb monument she wanted constructed amid the other spectacular Warwick tombs at Tewkesbury Abbey, she even stipulates in that document, with considerable pragmatism and foresight, that her head-jewels be sold and the proceeds given to the monks to soften any objections they might have harbored about her personal tastes in tomb sculpture ("so they groche noȝt with my lyenge, and with such thyng as y woll have done a-bowt my body"[31]). If the fallen political fortunes of the Warwick family had not in fact consigned Isabella to a monumentless grave beneath the abbey's sanctuary floor, we might today be able to view a tomb sculpture envisioned by its patroness as a dramatic and affecting work of art. Surely only Browning's bishop ever ordered his tomb in language more self-revealing than this:

> And my Image to be made all naked, and no thyng on my hede
> but myn here cast bakwardys, and of the gretnes and of the fas-
> cyon lyke the mesure that Thomas Porchalyn hath yn a lyst, and
> at my hede Mary Mawdelen leyng my handes a-cross, and seynt
> Iohn the Evangelyst on the ryght syde of my hede; and on the
> left syde, Seynt Anton, and at my fete a Skochen of myn Armes
> departyd with my lordys, and ii Greffons to bere hit vppe; And
> all a-bowt my tumbe, to be made pore men a[n]d wemen In
> theire pore Array, with their bedys In theire handes.[32]

Isabella's will is remarkably useful not only for the knowledge it reveals about the tastes and visual expectations of the female aristocratic audiences which influenced many works of late-medieval court literature (we may recognize in Isabella's words more than a little of the affective imagery and pathos of Chaucer's tale of the long-suffering Custance, for example), but also for the confirmation it offers about the fifteenth century's incarnational aesthetic. The devotional identification of the countess with her patron saint Mary Magdalene, already evident in her founding of the Chapel of Mary Magdalene at Tewkesbury Abbey, was in the most concrete way possible to be given image in her tomb.[33] For the sepulchral image which the will describes, naked in its mortality, was to be adorned only by the loose and thrown-back hair which traditionally emblemized Mary Magdalene herself. St. John the Evangelist and Saint Anthony were to be sculpted in attendance at either side of Isabella's head, but it was the image of Mary Magdalene who was to cross the arms of the dead woman's image in the final gesture of supplication and peace.

If the vision of the medieval artist was shaped by a patron's will, either figuratively or literally, so too an artist's understanding of the function of his art was shaped by exterior argument. The incarnational aesthetic was not private manifesto, but communal adage. What immediately strikes the historian who would review the justifications for art in the Middle Ages is the conservatism and ubiquitousness of the received philosophical arguments. Beginning with Gregory the Great and continuing throughout the twelfth century, the primary justifications for Christian art were intellectual and didactic: art is a book, a *biblia pauperum,* a practical way of instructing humble souls about the God who had lived to insist that no soul was too humble for the mansions of heaven, that even the least of men might in the celestial paradox be the first. In actual practice, of course, the widespread conception of visual art as a book did not always apply to the needs of the unlettered. Such visual *biblia* were also produced for learned men who could have read and interpreted the texts and exegetical commentaries which gave them form. There is no question that the immediate social context of religious images decreed their form and nature more than philosophical justifications. For every simple narrative painting of the life of Christ in a parish church, there were also elaborate and sophisticated visual programs—those, for example, which survive in the stained-glass windows of Canterbury Cathedral, windows, which as Madeline Caviness suggests, were "bookish" in the restrictive rather than the communicating sense of that word: "The treatment is bookish and esoteric; the typological windows were less a poor man's Bible than an elaborate display of twelfth-century theology, which could only be fully understood by the literate." [34] In the case of the Canterbury windows, even the ordering of subjects was bookish; following the conventions of reading rather than of visual logic, the images are read from top to bottom and from left to right rather than upwards like their counterparts in French Gothic cathedrals. [35]

For the world of the Middle Ages, any potential conflict with the second commandment of the Decalogue had been resolved to the satisfaction of the Church, East and West, after the Iconoclastic Controversy of the eighth and ninth centuries. Gregory's old *biblia pauperum* argument gave authority to the defenders of religious images, but the most forceful argument for the Iconodules was theological appeal to the *visibilia* of the Incarnation itself.[36] The Mosaic Law had forbidden idolatrous images of the invisible Jahweh, but the coming of Christ in visible form gave sacred authority to image making. The Incarnation itself was the book made visible, the Word made Flesh. Just as telling as the rich tradition of Carolingian art, whose muscular and assertive linear images in manuscript illumination, ivory, and stone sculpture proclaim the triumphant vindication of the incarnational principle, are the poems of Rhabanus Maurus, one of the foremost defenders of Christian art in the iconoclastic struggles. Many of Rhabanus' poems in his Latin collection *De laudibus sanctae crucis* are devotional contemplations of the visible book of the Incarnation, *carmina figurata* or pattern poems in which correspondences and images are patterned to emerge from within the text of the poem.[37] Visual pattern emerges from words to assert the providential and mysterious orderliness of God's creation perceived by the human sight, and especially to assert the recurrent pattern of the Cross, that image upon which manhood and godhead are joined.

If we were to choose one devotional image which would best emblemize the meaning of religious art in the early and middle centuries of the medieval age, it might well be the image of God the Pantocrator, gazing down from the center dome of great Byzantine churches like Hagia Sophia, mysterious and all-powerful, the Beginning and the End, holding in his hand the visible book of his creation. In narrative art, too, to make the Word flesh is to insist upon the image as book, on the reality of the sacred letter. In the ninth-century *Utrecht Psalter,* for example, no line is too offhand, too rhetorical, too *bookish* to be made image. "Awake, why sleepest thou, O Lord?" (Psalm 43 (44):23) gives rise to a curiously literal, nimbed, male figure lying in a cradle bed.[38] It is an image which insists even at the expense of decorum on the incarnational possibility of each line of the sacred text. Medieval Christian art inherited from classical art a tendency to focus on a moment of crucial dialogue in the formation of narrative images.[39] But unlike classical narrative images in which conventional postures and gestures represented the general act of conversation, medieval narrative art is marked by a compulsion to show the exact words of the sacred dialogue which is the narrative's numenous center. Thus we have in medieval illuminations and paintings scrolls emanating from the mouths of characters in which the letters themselves are made image in philosophical conviction of the sanctity of the Word.

If we analyze the form and function of such visual books, we find that the dynamic and the transformational act lies in the letter itself. That is, early medieval art does not receive most of its energies from the transform-

ing of worldly *visibilia*—sleepers and cradles are not spiritually transformed in the *Utrecht Psalter* illustration by being yoked to a sacred text—
but rather from the devotional celebration of the text itself. The central
meaning of the Gospels for early medieval art is the Word itself; hence the
long-time tradition of illustrating the gospels solely by important full-page
evangelist portraits in which we see the evangelist in the very act of writing
the Word, the *biblia*. The controlling metaphor for most religious art,
therefore, as well as its standard theological justification, is the book. And
as is the case with any book, its true meaning does not lie in the carnal
medium of pages and jeweled binding, but in the invisible hidden in the
words. In devotion, in mysticism, in daily piety, the book of the sacred
image was like the book of all other kinds, a means to an *invisibilia*. St.
Bernard of Clairvaux, despite the sensuous and incarnational imagery of
his sermons, insists upon the overcoming of image to attain understanding. In Cantica 20:6, St. Bernard reminds men that image, like the incarnational mission of God, exists "in order to make it possible for those 'who
cannot love otherwise than carnally' to fix their affection on Him, and
hence gradually ascend to spiritual love."[40] Hence mental images, like visible ones, were to be understood as a kind of *biblia pauperum,* as a "book"
which is in theory, if not always in actual practice, the property of the
simple, the unlettered, the carnal.

But by the fifteenth century, the long-repeated *biblia pauperum* justification of (and hence theoretical understanding of) Christian art has taken
third place in a threefold justification of image whose ordering well reflects
new preoccupations in the religious arts, both visual and literary. Indeed,
it is now significantly enough the "Pauper" himself, the author's *persona*
in the English prose dialogue *Dives and Pauper,* who expounds on the
theoretical justifications for arts. This fifteenth-century "Pauper" argues
for religious images on three counts. The first of these, and I would suggest, the most fundamental for an understanding of fifteenth-century religious arts, is that images "steryn manys mende to thynkyn of Cristys in-
carnacioun and of his passioun and of holye seyntys lyvys."[41] The
Incarnation as book, as central argument against idolatry, has in *Dives and
Pauper* given way to the quite self-sufficient importance of the Incarnation
model itself. It is this particularity, this incarnational image of the holy,
both in Christ's humanity and in the *imitatio Christi* of his saints and believers, which has now become the primary justification for art, indeed,
the very model for art. The Word has become not book visible but flesh.
The sanctifying presence of God's image in the *world,* image in human
shape and likeness, now dwarfs in importance even that second argument
of "Pauper": "Also þey been ordeynyd to steryn mannys affeccioun and
his herte to devocioun, for often man is more steryd be syghte þan be

heryng or redyngge."[42] This argument is the emotional equivalent of the intellectual *biblia pauperum* argument, that is, simple men may "feel" (and the Franciscans of the thirteenth century had bequeathed to all Europe the conviction that it was important for pious men and women to feel deeply) from images what they are unable to feel from the letter of book or sermon. In this fifteenth-century "Pauper's" arguments for art, Gregory's standard answer comes last. Oft-repeated adage is here accorded the respect, and also, one might argue, the remoteness, of ancient law; "as þe lawe seyȝyt" images "been a tokene and a book to þe lewyd peple, that þey moun redyn in ymagerye and peynture þat clerkys redyn in boke."[43]

It was the extravagant weeping of Margery Kempe that was most noticeable and troubling to her contemporaries and which has continued to preoccupy modern critics; Margery's tears have evoked from both the same suspicions of hypocrisy and indignant or amused charges of excess. But what makes Margery Kempe's *Book* most revealing of its age are not those tears (whose literary antecedents are, in fact, with Franciscan devotional writings of the thirteenth century and the legends of continental women saints of the fourteenth century), but rather the extraordinarily concrete—the incarnational—nature of her language and imagery of devotion. The simple suggestion, for example, by the author of the *Meditationes vitae Christi* that the Poor Clare he addresses in that text imagine herself as Mary's handmaiden undergoes, as we shall see in chapter 3, an alchemical transformation in Margery Kempe's consciousness. Margery holds the Christ Child, swaddles him with white cloths, not in her soul but in her own hands, human hands whose reality has been forever sanctified by those hands stretched in agony upon the Cross. What Margery Kempe most desires and struggles for even at others' charges of vainglory is crucial to the meaning of fifteenth-century religious art and drama; she seeks not just the hot, close tears of compassion (for those come, she insists, unbidden) but the visible and tangible reality of her incarnate Saviour: "Sche was smet wyth þe dedly wownd of veyn glory & felt it not, for sche desyryd many tymes þat þe Crucifix xuld losyn hys handys fro þe crosse & halsyn [embrace] hir in tokyn of lofe."[44]

Although I know of no medieval image of the crucified Christ that could literally move its hands down from the cross and embrace the worshipper, records do survive of a celebrated crucifix, the Rood of Grace from the Cistercian Abbey of Boxley in Kent, which had been designed by means of "certain engines and old wires"[45] to nod its head, move its eyes, and to shed tears in response to the prayers of penitents. This statue was enormously popular with pilgrims; in 1510, the crowd of eager pilgrims to Boxley Rood included young King Henry VIII, who prayed and made an offering before the holy image.[46] Cromwell's commissioners who sought out, exhibited, and destroyed this Rood with special zeal decried "the false, crafty, and subtle handling" of the Boxley Rood, but as Julian Jaynes has observed in another context, we must be wary of assuming along with the propagandists for the Reformation that the sole purpose of the Crucifix was to deceive the unwary pilgrim.[47] It may well be wondered if the Boxley Rood, as well as a similar statue mentioned in a letter by John Hoker,[48] may not better be understood as the logical results of the late Middle Ages' intense focus on the fleshly reality of the Incarnation, of that same nearly hallucinatory concreteness we see in Margery Kempe's visions. Late medieval wills that list the Rood of Grace as a place of pilgrimage along with the renowned Marian shrine at Walsingham can testify only to the perceived holiness of the statue; they can offer no evidence about whether the Rood of Grace was considered a genuine miracle or a miracle of artfulness.[49] Either could well have been reason to single it out as a place of pilgrimage and meditation, since as the Lollard author of the *Lanterne of Light* tells us, medieval priests taught that "God's power in working of his miracles loweth down in one image more than in another."[50]

The greater sensory concreteness with which the central mystery of Incarnation was experienced in late medieval devotion has an interesting analogy in changes which occur in visual depictions of that paradigmatic and insistent believer in the sensory concrete, the apostle Thomas. The doubting Thomas of John 20:25 in earlier ages had existed as the paradigm of shame; he was the disciple unflatteringly compared to Paul, who had faithfully witnessed for Christ without even having known him in his physical person, much less having insisted on touching his wounded side.[51] But in the fourteenth century and increasingly throughout the fifteenth century, the doubting Thomas who demanded to touch Christ's wounds is surprisingly metamorphosed by late medieval piety into positive emblem. As one Middle English sermon explains, the other apostles may have been blessed because of their unquestioning faith in the Resurrection of their Lord, but Thomas is more blessed than any of them because through his doubts the doubts of others may be resolved: "Take we no(w) hede to þis gospell, and ȝe may see þat Seynt Thomas dud us more good þorowe is mysbeleue þan did all þe apostels þat beleued anoon. For be hym is putt awey all þe dowtes of oure feyȝth, we are made stabull in þe beleue."[52]

Far from forbidding curiosity about "Goddes privitee" or passively suffering the indignity of Thomas' groping hand, as the Christ of the earlier iconographical tradition had been portrayed,[53] the Resurrected Christ of late medieval art now often initiates the very sensory testing of his miracle which the Gospels had criticized. In this English example, a fifteenth-

FIGURE 1.3. *The Incredulity of St. Thomas,* English fifteenth-century alabaster relief, London, Victoria and Albert Museum, Hildburgh Collection (Courtesy of the Board of Trustees of the Victoria and Albert Museum).

century alabaster relief in the Victoria and Albert Museum (fig. 1.3), Christ quite literally seizes Thomas' hand and inserts it in his wounded side. "My woundes are yett freshe and wett as the first were," promises the Christ of the Chester play of the Doubt of Thomas, as he urges, even wheedles, the unbelieving Thomas to reach out his hand to touch Christ's bleeding wounds.[54] And at the conclusion of the N-Town cycle's play of Thomas' Doubt, Thomas turns to address the witnessing audience directly in a formal and very moving lyric which is also an emphatic argument for the importance of corporal image:

> The prechynge of petir myght not conuerte me
> tyll I felyd þe wounde þat þe spere dyde cleve
> I trustyd nevyr he levyd þat deed was on A tre
> tyll þat his herte blood dede renne in my sleve
> Thus be my grett dowte oure feyth may we preve
> be-hold my blody hand to feyth þat me Avexit
> be syght of þis myrroure from feyth not remeve
> Quod mortuus et sepultus nunc resurrexit.[55]

To feel Christ's arms reaching down in physical embrace from the Cross, to see Christ's heart blood "renne in my sleve," to see the Word made Flesh in the image of a moving statue or a player's feigned bloody hands—these are the concrete and incarnational devotions of the fifteenth century.

Chapter Two
East Anglian Religious Culture in the Late Middle Ages

East Anglian culture in the Middle Ages was distinctive and self-sufficient, impatient, even suspicious, of life and customs elsewhere on the island of Britain. Although geography and especially the North Sea at their north and east borders tended to keep Suffolk and Norfolk, the ancient kingdom of the East Angles, a natural and somewhat insulated unit, East Anglia seems to have retained its rather "obdurate singularity" by choice rather than necessity.[1] As W. K. Jordan observed of the county of Norfolk, it remained, despite easy access by road or sea to London, "notably self-sufficient, self-contained, and certainly somewhat self-satisfied."[2] Unlike Yorkshire, also stubbornly remote from the capital and court of London, East Anglia in the fifteenth century was not an economically depressed backwater, but the thriving center of the English cloth trade. A quarter of the late-medieval cloth production in England came from these two counties, especially from the Suffolk villages dotted along the Stour River and its tributaries. The village of Lavenham, near Bury St. Edmunds, had grown prosperous enough in the cloth industry to be listed with the twenty wealthiest towns in England in fifteenth-century tax rolls; by 1525, this rural Suffolk village would be the twelfth richest community in England—and the great Norfolk port of Norwich would be richer than London.[3]

The prosperous East Anglian cloth merchants and local landed gentry by the late-fifteenth century had so intermarried that a new landed merchant aristocracy of immense vitality and influence populated what had once been small, obscure ports and agricultural villages. As for the city of Norwich, it was the second largest city in all England in the fifteenth century. It functioned not only as the busy regional capital for Suffolk and Norfolk, but as a second and somewhat competing London, both for its huge, proud, and enterprising population and for the otherwise predominantly rural parishes that dotted the region.[4] When a prominent burgess of Norwich named John Smyth made his will in 1503 and requested a chantry priest to sing masses for him after his death, he specified that he wanted that priest to be young and honest, a secular man newly made priest, of wisdom and reason, and "noon owtlondissh man."[5] "Owtlondissh man" here almost certainly does not mean non-Englishman, but rather non-*East* Englishman.

Norman Tanner has suggested that much of the strained relationship in the Middle Ages between the city of Norwich and the Benedictine cathedral priory there existed simply because those monks were perceived as "aliens," that is, unlike the overwhelming majority of secular clergy in the churches of the city, they were not usually the sons and cousins of local families.[6] When East Anglian wills do make bequests to Norfolk and Suffolk religious houses, they are usually to small local foundations and nearly invariably mention personal friends or family enclosed there; in the last century before the Reformation, East Anglian monastic houses were still perceived as extensions of family piety, and close and affectionate ties were retained with local monastic institutions. Moreover, these local religious houses performed many extraparochial roles for the laity. As Tanner notes in his study of Norwich popular spirituality in the fifteenth century, the close connections with the friaries of the city gave the people, even in a city like Norwich which had an astonishingly high number of parish churches, places to hear sermons, say confessions, be buried, find executors for their wills.[7] Such functions were almost necessarily limited to local inhabitants, and will bequests rarely included religious houses which were not perceived as part of this immediate religious community, a community which for Norwich was readily extended to include neighboring Suffolk, but not outlanders.

There were really only four exceptions to this intensely local and loyal religious patronage. The sole distant religious houses which are named with some frequency in East Anglian wills were the Charterhouse of Mount Grace in Yorkshire (the monastery, by the way, which owned the only surviving copy of the autobiography of Margery Kempe),[8] the Charterhouse at London (where a number of the greater East Anglian nobility whose station had taken them to London asked to be buried),[9] and especially the two monastic houses founded by King Henry V—the Charterhouse at Sheen and the Brigittine convent of Syon. Norman Tanner observes that it is surprising that a Carthusian Charterhouse was never founded in East Anglia, since there is evidence of considerable local respect there for the three English Carthusian foundations at Mount Grace, London, and Sheen. He suggests that these Carthusian houses were popular recipients of charitable bequests because they were "recent foundations . . . whose monks led, or were thought to lead, austere lives."[10]

The convent at Syon, one of the places to which Margery Kempe of Lynn made her enthusiastic pilgrimage in the 1430s, was the only religious house in England dedicated to St. Bridget of Sweden, the fourteenth-century saint and mystic who had founded the Order of the Holy Saviour (or Brigittines, as they were more commonly known), and who seems to have had a remarkable influence upon East Anglian lay religious life. As we shall see in chapter 3, Margery Kempe wrote her *Book* consciously emulating (even competing with) St. Bridget, and both John Clopton and Anne Harling, exemplars of East Anglian lay piety who will be discussed in chapter 4, had been admitted to lay-confraternity membership in the Syon convent. The third representative of the East Anglian's drama's formative audience discussed in chapter 4, John Baret, professed in his will a special friendship with a pious Norwich widow named Margaret Purdans (or Spurdaunce), who we know owned one of the English copies of the *Revelations* of St. Bridget.[11]

The attraction of the Syon Brigittine convent seems to have been its very singularity; it was a unique center of devotion, a national shrine to a saint whose cult was burgeoning in the fifteenth century, especially among the new female literate public whose tastes and piety were so influential on vernacular English devotional prose. Syon was, however, a shrine that, unlike most famous monastic houses, did not possess the actual body of its patron saint, but rather possessed an intense concentration of prayer and fervor; it was a place where "the whole power of monasticism" was "concentrated with all its strength upon a single spot."[12] Much the same could be said of the Carthusian house of Mount Grace in distant Yorkshire, which despite its remote location, was perhaps the monastic house which along with Syon and Sheen best exemplified the kind of emotional devotion that so marked fifteenth-century popular piety, especially the Flemish-born piety of Northern Europe that in East Anglia freely mingled with the native English spiritual traditions.[13] It was at Mount Grace that Prior Nicholas Love translated and transformed the *Meditationes vitae Christi* of the Pseudo-Bonaventure, the text that was probably the single greatest influence on lay devotional life in England in the late Middle Ages.[14]

If there is paradox in asserting that East Anglian religious life was focused loyally on immediate and local monastic houses which were seen as extensions of the family or parish units, at the same time that so much fervor was directed at four distant monastic houses that housed orders— the Carthusians and the Brigittines—that were not even represented in Suffolk and Norfolk, greater paradox emerges in trying to characterize the spirituality of these East Anglian people. It is probably fair to say that Norfolk and Suffolk were at once both the most troublesome area of nonconformist thought in England in the fifteenth century, and at the same time the counties second only to Yorkshire as strongholds of the old-style Catholicism. Norfolk and Suffolk were famous for their great monastic foundations: the powerful and royally-favored abbey of Bury St. Edmunds; the virtual monastic center at Thetford (a smallish town on the Suffolk-Norfolk border that boasted no fewer than six major priories and friaries); the large and important group of monastic houses at Lynn and at Norwich; important noble foundations like the Austin friary at Clare; and the great monastic pilgrimage centers at Walsingham and Bromholm (Bacton) on the Norfolk coast.[15] Norfolk and Suffolk, though predominantly rural, supported a greater area density of churches than any other county in England, and the old piety that had been celebrated in those churches died hard.[16] In the sixteenth century, even in the seventeenth century, East Anglia had a formidable recusant population, especially among rural landed gentry like Roger Martyn, the wealthy squire of Long Melford, Suffolk, who was deprived of his position as churchwarden in the sixteenth century for his papist sympathies, and who subsequently wrote a fond and wistful reminiscence of the worship and ceremonial observed in his parish in the days of his Catholic boyhood.[17] Many were the "old gentle families who maintained a stubborn devotion to the ancient faith,"[18] but, as W. K. Jordan has written, East Anglia "also faced the North Sea, and the chill winds of heresy blew early across its shores."[19]

At the same time that East Anglia was renowned for the strength and conservatism of its monastic and lay piety, its towns, especially those coastal towns whose prosperity, trade, and commercial links with Flanders and the Low Countries made them hospitable to religious change, were widely known as breeding grounds for nonconformist religious thought and later for Protestant sectarianism.[20] Already by the time of Queen Elizabeth, Norwich had become a "Puritan stronghold."[21] The culture that these paradoxical attitudes shaped in the last century before the Reformation was one of astonishing variety and fervor, a vital culture that also clung tenaciously to its regional consciousness and character. That character was influenced increasingly in the fifteenth and early sixteenth centuries by East Anglia's close economic and cultural links with northern Europe; indeed Norfolk and Suffolk were in some ways closer allied to Flanders than to London. The only known English experiments with the Flemish *beguinages,* houses of lay nuns, were at Norwich,[22] a city that swarmed, like the other East Anglian ports, with Flemish merchants and sea captains and with continental pilgrims to Walsingham. A huge influx of Flemish weavers and craftsmen supported the thriving cloth industry, both in the larger towns and in the small, prosperous cloth villages along the Stour River that furnished woolen cloth for continental trade at the port towns of Lynn and Yarmouth and Ipswich.[23] London merchants, too, flocked to great East Anglian cloth fairs like famous Bury Fair, but East Anglia hardly needed to go to London; London came to her.

Out of this wealth, fierce local and regional pride, and the catalyst of

Flemish piety upon a spiritual climate which was already "of considerable richness and variety" came a religious culture which was as fruitful as it was self-sufficient.[24] The fifteenth century was the great golden age of religious architecture and art in East Anglia, and the artifacts that were created there almost without exception developed a distinctive, even idiosyncratic, local style, a kind of assertively vernacular dialect that had small need for the fashions of London or of other outlanders. A distinctive painting style in stained glass, which Christopher Woodforde has named the Norwich School,[25] created vividly colored, sweet-faced saints and donor portraits whose somewhat sentimental appeal was popular with the family-oriented burgesses of East Anglian towns and villages. Spectacular parish churches were built of mortar, rubble, and knapped flint, whose designs elaborately patterned the exterior walls and towers in stunning compensation for the virtual absence of block building stone in the East Anglian flatlands and fens. The famous wooden hammerbeam roofs of fifteenth-century Suffolk and Norfolk churches made dazzling virtues of the same necessity, eschewing stone-vaulted roofs for breathtaking demonstrations of the local carpenters' craft. Even the parish churches of small country churches had their great ribbed timber ceilings, gracefully arched like huge holy ships (and indeed there must have been considerable reciprocal influence between East Anglia's church builders and its busy crews of ship builders). The East Anglian hammerbeam roof gave way in the later fifteenth century to dizzying double hammerbeams, often populated with a rush of carved wooden angels, as at the beautiful little church at Woolpit, Suffolk (fig. 2.1) or at St. Mary's in Bury St. Edmunds (see chapter 6).[26] John Baret, a prominent Bury clothier who was one of St. Mary's most important patrons in the fifteenth century, spoke fondly in his will of "alle the werk of the aungellys on lofte wiche I have do maad for a rememberaunce of me and my frendys."[27]

The East Anglian baptismal fonts (fig. 2.2), characteristically carved with reliefs of the seven sacraments around their bases, also developed entirely local kinds of elaborately carved font covers—wooden fantasies of carved tracery and gilt reaching slenderly to the roof and manipulated by pulleys to raise and lower in place. One of the most spectacular of these, in the parish church at Ufford, Suffolk, so impressed William Dowsing, the Cromwellian trooper who was sent throughout Suffolk in 1643 to smash remaining evidence of popery and "superstitious images" from local churches, that he railed in his journal about that "glorious [i.e., vainglorious] Cover over the Font, like a Pope's Tripple Crown, with a Pelican on the Top, picking its Breast, all gilt over with Gold."[28] That vast canopied spire, carved in wood and reaching fully eighteen feet above the upper rim of the font, proclaims not only the flamboyance of the uniquely

FIGURE 2.1. The double-hammerbeam roof of the parish church of St. Mary, Woolpit, Suffolk (Royal Commission on the Historical Monuments of England).

FIGURE 2.2. The elaborate wooden baptismal-font cover in the parish church of St. Mary, Ufford, Suffolk. The tabernacle rises eighteen feet above the stone font and is crowned by a sculpture of a pelican piercing her breast to feed her young, a symbol of the Passion (Royal Commission on the Historical Monuments of England).

East Anglian form of the Perpendicular style, but also bears mute witness to an astonishing local mastery of craftsmanship; the entire carved font cover at Ufford is so made that it can telescope perfectly upon itself in a veritable tour de force of the carpenter's art.

Scores of beautifully built and furnished Perpendicular churches were erected in fifteenth-century East Anglia from the wealth the woolen cloth trade brought, churches that even today are referred to as "wool churches." So many timber roofs and rood screens were carved and painted, so many saints set in canopied niches and so much stained glass set in east windows and chantry aisles that W. C. Hoskins is probably right in claiming that in late medieval Suffolk and Norfolk "the building industry might well have rivalled the cloth industry in importance."[29] In Norwich almost every parish church in the city was extensively rebuilt in the fifteenth or early sixteenth century.[30] In thriving cloth villages like Long Melford, so thorough and so ambitious were the building programs of the parish cloth merchants that scarcely a trace of the earlier church structures remains today.[31] East Anglia produced nearly as many great masons and architects as cloth merchants; the great fifteenth-century architect Simon Clerk, master mason of Bury St. Edmunds abbey, was called away from Suffolk building projects only long enough to supervise the completion of the spectacular chapels of Eton College and of King's College, Cambridge.[32] Simon Clerk was only one in a virtual dynasty of great Bury masons like William Layer and like John Worliche (perhaps connected with the "Worlych" whose entrance cues are written in the margins of the N-Town cycle manuscript?[33]), who was master mason for King's College chapel before Simon Clerk's appointment in 1477.[34]

The straining church architecture of the East Anglian Perpendicular style has been called propitiating and slightly nervous, somewhat overconcerned with materialistic demonstration of a merchant's old piety and new wealth. Graham Hutton, in his commentary on Edwin Smith's beautiful photographic studies of English parish churches, dismisses the Perpendicular style of the great fifteenth-century East Anglian churches with this rather moralizing criticism:

> Perpendicular as a style has something of ambivalence, of paradox, about it. Possibly every stylistic climax has, since beyond that it is only possible to degenerate. One gets in the finest Perpendicular parish churches of the fifteenth and early sixteenth centuries a sense of impending doom; of strained self-assurance accompanying fear of the hereafter; offerings, of uneasy consciences over newly gained riches; indeed, of the approaching end of the long era of One Belief, One Faith.[35]

Hutton's assessment probably errs in attributing to the fifteenth century a conscious end-of-the-age anxiety, even given the uneasiness with which a few millenialists must have waited for the year 1500.[36] In fact, it is striking just how little prescience, even in the years immediately before the dissolution of the monasteries, the English will-making classes seemed to show about the possibility of change as vast and sweeping as the English Reformation was to be. "Perpetual" chantries were being founded right up to the very month of appropriation of chantry trust funds and lands; indeed the rate of such bequests probably actually increased during the last decades of the so-called medieval age of "One Belief, One Faith." Only two years before the Chantries Act of 1545 that would authorize the king's seizure of chantry funds, the Norwich city government saw nothing inappropriate about founding a civic chantry in which a priest was to "sing" in the Common Hall (which only a few years before had been the Blackfriars church) for the King and Queen, the Prince, the King's Council, for the members of the craft guilds of the city (both living and dead), and for the continuing prosperity of Norwich.[37]

And yet it must be admitted that there is evidence in East Anglian wills of men with anxious hearts, if not guilty consciences, about their worldly and prosperous lives. It would perhaps be somewhat surprising if the insistent late medieval doctrine of hell and purgatory had not induced guilt, at least last-minute guilt, in men who had attained such visible material comforts in this life. Walter Daniel, a prosperous merchant and former mayor of Norwich, specified in his will that he wanted three annuals of masses celebrated for the souls of the faithful departed, but especially for the souls of carpenters and other tradesmen whom he had "knowingly or unknowingly cheated" in the course of his business. Another Norwich merchant making his final accounting likewise ordered in his will two annuals of masses to be said for those with whom he had traded to make up for any sins or faults against them.[38] John Baret of Bury St. Edmunds wanted chantry masses sung for the souls of those whom "I have caused to lose silver," and seemed to have had an especially uneasy conscience over one Edmund Tabowre, because he indicated that in addition to special chantry masses for Tabowre he wanted "bothe my colers of silvir [i.e. silver livery collars], the Kyng's lyfre, be sold, and the money disposid in almesse for Edmu[n]d Tabowre soule and his frendys, to recompe[n]se broke silvir I had of his to oon of the colerys and othir things with othir stuff by syde wiche I took to my[n] owne vse."[39] Perhaps the most remarkable record of a guilty conscience appears in the 1438 codicil to the will of Richard Edy, alias Fermer, of Westacre, Norfolk, who with "sore ransakyng in my consciens," lists an incredible array of swindles, cheated inheritances, unpaid bills, and misappropriated goods for which recompense was to be paid after his death from the inheritance due his wife since, "margar, my wyf, is nowghte lovynge to me, ne to noon of my kynne, god knowyth the trewthe."[40]

But most of these wealthy East Anglian landowners and merchants wrestling with their consciences, their pocketbooks, and their driving need for memorial images and posthumous prayers were also consciously trying to add humility to those virtues of conspicuous piety and largesse that had built their spectacular parish churches. The fifteenth-century Suffolk clothier and entrepreneur Thomas Spring of Lavenham was one of the wealthiest men in all England; he was so rich his contemporaries frequently referred to him simply as "The Rich Clothier."[41] Out of that wealth, Spring financed a splendid tower for the Perpendicular nave his family and others had built for the parish church in Lavenham. That tower today still rises high above the flat Suffolk farmland, visible for miles—yet local tradition says that it was designed to soar even higher until the fatal fall of the tower's architect from the building scaffold. That fall was disturbing enough a sign of God's displeasure to halt even the pride of the Rich Clothier—and the height of his church tower.[42]

Thomas Spring's neighbor and rival, John Clopton, spent a great deal of his own considerable cloth fortune rebuilding the parish church of the nearby Suffolk cloth village of Long Melford (fig. 2.3). John Clopton gave fine velvet vestments, alabaster sculptures, and altarpieces to the spectacular Perpendicular church he helped finance; he had his own name and the names of his family and friends inscribed in huge flint letters around the facade of the church; and he filled the stained-glass windows with praying figures of his ancestors, kin, and prominent friends. Clopton's cloth fortune also built a separate Lady Chapel to the east of the church encircled by processional aisles for the admiring visits of pilgrims, and it built a private Clopton family chantry within squint's eye view of the high altar. And yet when John Clopton made his will he asked with apparent sincerity and with no discernible awareness of incongruity that there be no great "A-do" at his funeral in Long Melford church.[43] The tugging claims of the monuments of memory and the aggressive humility of late medieval aspirations to Christian virtue perhaps created some of those tensions which some have seen in the Perpendicular style or in its aptly-named continental counterpart, the Flamboyant.[44] But as we shall see, the social and religious implications of Perpendicular architecture—and of fifteenth-century devotional theater—in East Anglia are far more resonant and complex than the usual dismissals of the ostentatious piety of the late medieval age would suggest.

Also decidedly complex is the character of fifteenth-century lay or "pop-

East Anglian Religious Culture in the Middle Ages

FIGURE 2.3. The parish church of the Holy Trinity, Long Melford, Suffolk. This, one of East Anglia's most famous "wool churches," was rebuilt and an elaborate Lady Chapel added to the east of the church through the patronage of John Clopton and other prosperous local cloth merchants. The west tower is a replacement built in 1898–1903 to replace a fifteenth-century tower ruined by lightning (Photo by G. M. Gibson).

ular" spirituality in East Anglia. As we shall see more fully in chapter 4, the will of someone like John Clopton reveals intriguing evidence of both traditional and explorative means of reaching toward a closer relationship with the divine. Although the religion of John Clopton and his kind seems in many ways the epitome of the "power exchange" of late medieval Christianity[45]—in a spiritual climate in which the merchandizing metaphors of debt and payment and the materialism of holy images and relics formed the most coherent and consoling means of religious definition—it was a spirituality that embraced much more. John Clopton's religion was also one that revered the power of lay prayer and contemplation (a number of bequests in his will were, like those made by his contemporaries, to lay recluses and hermits), the power of the sermon (it was a sermon that John Clopton ordered for his burying day instead of much Ado) and even the importance of a vernacular Bible. In 1504, at a time when the possession of vernacular scripture was still damning evidence in heresy trials, Clopton bequeathed, without comment, "my Bible in Englisshe."[46] Since John Clopton was not only a successful merchant but had once served as sheriff of Suffolk and Norfolk, and since he left that Bible to the archdeacon of Suffolk (William Pykenham, who was also dean of the College of Stoke by Clare, a few miles from Clopton's Long Melford home), we must assume that John Clopton had received episcopal sanction for possession of an English Bible (and may indeed have been rendering it up to proper authority at his death).[47] But there were others who certainly had no official permission for their vernacular Bibles. In 1530 Bishop Nykke of Norwich complained in a letter about the constant influx into his diocese of "erroneous books in English" (among which he included the New Testament), and he noted that "merchants and those that lived near the sea were especially infected with them."[48]

But curiously enough, except for an extensive heresy prosecution in East Anglia during the bishopric of one of Nykke's predecessors, Bishop Alnwick, in 1428–31, the attitude of both secular and ecclesiastical establishment in East Anglia throughout most of the fifteenth century was one of remarkable tolerance and leniency, indeed almost of resignation, about the presence of Lollardry, a convenient label that was invoked for nearly any kind of religious nonconformity. There was tolerance, that is, if those nonconformists were discreet and if they presented no threat to the state. It was the lurking fear of treason, especially after the Oldcastle uprising of 1413, and the paranoia of a London court whose king was still only a child, that led to the extensive heresy trials at Norwich in the 1430s. These trials involved at least fifty-five individuals, both laymen and clergy; this was the largest number of accusations in a single campaign recorded in the fifteenth century.[49] Three lapsed heretics were handed over to secular authorities and executed, as required by law, and though all the rest abjured or were purged,[50] the results of the trials were to show that Lollardry, or more accurately Lollard-like individualism of religious conscience, was rampant in East Anglia at the time. After the Alnwick trials, the influence of new piety from the Low Countries and from Germany continued if not increased, and the number of Lollards must have multiplied, yet there is no record of organized episcopal opposition to heresy in East Anglia again for more than a century.

By the time of the heresy persecutions following the so-called Walsingham Conspiracy in 1536–37, changed politics had made the stubborn supporters of the old pilgrimages and cult images the new threat against King and Church.[51] The Walsingham plot, conceived by ringleaders who included the subprior from the famous Marian shrine at Walsingham and a minstrel named Ralph Rogerson who earned his living singing at Walsingham Priory, was foiled almost before it started. The public executions that were staged strategically at chief towns throughout Norfolk seem to have had the desired effect, although a few rumbles of discontent continued to be heard, as from Elizabeth Worde of Aylsham, who was accused of saying that "it was a pity the Walsingham men were discovered and that there never would be 'a good world' till blows were struck against the government."[52] It is important to observe that once again treason more than religious nonconformity was the motivating factor in the persecutions.

The spiritual climate of fifteenth-century East Anglia, then, seems to have been much clouded by the troublesome presence of unorthodox religious attitudes, attitudes whose very prevalence may have discouraged official retaliation. It is also important, however, to emphasize that East Anglian Lollardry was far from a deliberate sectarianism and that Wycliffian attitudes toward vernacular scripture or the Eucharist were often accompanied by entirely reverent attitudes toward masses for the dead, the communal benefits of monastic prayer, or the efficacy of cult images and relics, attitudes that a modern historian would be quick to consider most un-Wycliffian.[53] According to John Bale, Richard Caister, the saintly vicar of St. Stephen's in Norwich, was a Lollard sympathizer, and Caister's brief Latin will might add some credence to the charge, since that will left nothing for the soul masses, prayers, and images that usually preoccupied the clergy and pious laymen of the age. Except for a bequest of ten pounds to his parish church for antiphoners, everything Caister owned was to be given to the poor. But if Richard Caister was a Lollard, he enjoyed an exceptional reputation for holiness and after his death even became something of a local cult figure. Margery Kempe mentions going to his grave to pray, and Richard Caister's grave is mentioned as a pilgrimage site in several fifteenth-century Norwich wills.[54] The truth is probably simply that many East Anglian clergymen as well as laymen explored with intensity and sincerity a wide range of religious options. As Norman Tanner observes about the religious life of Norwich in the fifteenth century, the absence of formal accusations and definite evidence of Lollardry at Norwich during most of the century would seem to suggest that "the religion provided by the local Church was sufficiently rich and varied and sufficiently tolerant towards what might be called the left wing of orthodoxy to cater to the tastes of most of its citizens."[55]

This "rich and varied" East Anglian religious culture was to provide the stimulus for a remarkable flowering of religious and devotional literature, especially of the communal literature of religious drama. If the surviving manuscript evidence is any fair indication, East Anglia was one of the most important drama centers in England in the fifteenth century; it would not be difficult to argue that surviving manuscripts make it *the* most important dramatic center. These texts include the only two extant English saints' plays and all but one of the fifteenth-century English morality plays (the single exception, *Everyman*, whose earliest English text is a printed copy by John Skot, may in fact be only a translation from the Dutch play *Elckerlijc*).[56] Also East Anglian is the single surviving English miracle play, the Croxton *Play of the Sacrament*, which, as we shall see, not only contains local allusion but is a text uniquely suited to the charged religious climate of East Anglia, with its simultaneous censure and sympathy for the problem of Lollardry.

Just how much sympathy there could be in East Anglia for attitudes that Londoners were quick to label Lollardry can be seen in the N-Town Passion play, a two-day Passion play that was compiled into the East Anglian mystery play cycle known as the N-Town cycle (or by old misnomer, *Ludus Coventriae*) sometime in the third quarter of the fifteenth century. As Theodore De Welles has pointed out, the string of accusations that Christ's detractors make in that play are specific and topical charges of Lollardry, as if the playwright wished to protest that if Jesus of Nazareth were to preach in fifteenth-century England, he might well be charged with heresy.[57] The first Passion play even opens with Annas proclaiming his responsibility to search out and try all persons of heretical opinions, in what is a recognizable scene from a medieval bishop's heresy court:

> I Annas be my powere xal comawnde dowteles
> Þe lawys of moyses no man xal denye
> Hoo excede my comawndement Anon ȝe certefye
> Yf Any eretyk here reyn to me ȝe compleyn
> For in me lyth þe powere all trewthis to trye
> And pryncypaly oure lawys þo must I susteyn.[58]

The N-Town plays of Christ's trials and Passion signal, De Welles argues, "the playwright's uneasiness over the indiscriminate persecution of suspected heretics by the anti-Lollard faction—a persecution that frequently lumped together the righteous along with the reprobate."[59] Certainly, as Margery Kempe's experiences show, it was not uncommon, particularly in the aftermath of the 1414 Oldcastle rebellion, for any kind of religious eccentricity to be met with suspicion of heresy, accusation, and even arrest. Insofar as we can accept as history the rather self-serving evidence of Margery's *Book*, Margery seems to have found more acceptance in her native Norfolk for her idiosyncratic religious life than in, for example, Leicester, where she was immediately arrested when she entered the city.[60]

But in the N-Town Passion, I suspect that the accusations of heresy brought against Christ may be more a topical comment on power struggles with the episcopal establishment than evidence of fairmindedness—especially in the face of other evidence which seems to point to monastic provenance or sponsorship of those plays.[61] William Curteys, the abbot of Bury St. Edmunds during the East Anglian heresy trials, was incensed by what he viewed as the gross invasions of Bury's exempt spiritual jurisdiction occasioned by the trials at Norwich. Master Robert Bert, a chaplain at Bury who like all parochial clergy in the monastic borough of St. Edmund had been appointed by the abbot, was arrested by the episcopal summoners and brought before Bishop Alnwick accused of owning a copy of *Dives and Pauper*, a book which the accusors claimed contained numerous errors and heresies. Robert Bert was also accused of associating with other known heretics and of preaching that "tithes should not be paid to clerics in mortal sin or honour paid to images." Bert admitted to being an acquaintance of Sir John Poleyn, whom the bishop's court considered a heretic, but denied all knowledge of the heretical nature of the book and indeed denied all other charges. Master Bert was ordered to purge himself in the chancel of St. James church in Bury and was instructed henceforth to show all his books in English to the bishop.[62] Earlier heresy accusations against mere citizens of Bury had annoyed the abbot enough that he joined with the burgesses of the town to ask that the suspects be set at liberty until the time of their trial.[63] This public accusation against one of the abbot's own chaplains and Bert's required ceremonial purgation in a parish church the monastery itself owned—which was indeed even built within the monastery grounds—must have infuriated the abbot. As John A. F. Thomson observes, the bishop's campaign against Bury "may well have proved more trouble to the Bishop than it was worth."[64] It is interesting to note that it was precisely at this time, in 1431, that John Lydgate wrote for Abbot Curteys some emphatic verse propaganda about the jealously guarded "franchises" of the Liberty of St. Edmund, under the guise of a *Legend of Sent Gyle*. Lydgate's aureate verse life of St. Giles emphasizes the abbey that the holy hermit founded, an abbey that Lydgate says had been endowed with special freedoms by papal degree (freedoms which sound suspiciously like Bury St. Edmunds') and whose exempt status was memorialized in great carved cypress doors which St. Giles

> Kept in thy chirche ffor a memoryall,
> Tokene of ful graunt and confirmacioun,
> That thy menstre in Especyall
> Fraunchised was, for pleyn conclusioun,
> From all maner Iuredyccyoun,

Of foreyn power be thyn holynesse,
Prelat nor prynce of no presumpcioun
Thy lybertees nor fraunchise to oppresse.[65]

So, too, the N-Town Passion plays may memorialize in dramatic text the antagonism between monastic lord and bishop over the jurisdiction issues that accompanied the East Anglian heresy trials.

After the persecutions of 1428 to 1431, the campaign against doctrinal error in East Anglia found propaganda a more effective remedy than the bishop's court. Certainly the prevailing attitude toward nonconformist thought there seems to have been not to plot punishment but rather to "bring the offender back into the fold,"[66] as was, indeed, usually the intention of the episcopal trials elsewhere. There is documentary evidence that in at least one fifteenth-century heresy case, in Lincolnshire, the penance assigned to a convicted Lollard was to take part in a Corpus Christi procession, and John A. F. Thomson has suggested that such obligations may customarily have been imposed on offenders who had denied the doctrine of transubstantiation.[67] Participation in the communal affirmation of Corpus Christi plays, either as actor or witness, may well have served the similar purpose of ritually incorporating a troubling member of the parish or town community into the body of orthodox believers. This is, for example, quite transparently the purpose and polemic of the Croxton *Play of the Sacrament,* a play which though set in the exotic distance of Heraclea, Spain, is pointedly East Anglian in its topography of mind and purpose.

The unique manuscript of the *Play of the Sacrament* is East Anglian and was probably copied in the very early years of the sixteenth century. The play itself was presumably written soon after 1461, the year in which the reputed miracle of Heraclea is said in the prologue to have taken place.[68] The play is preceded in the manuscript by banns that announce that the play is to be performed on a Monday, at "Croxston," almost certainly Croxton, Norfolk, a small village two miles north of Thetford and fourteen miles from Bury St. Edmunds. As David Bevington has written, "Although a number of places named 'Croxton' have been found in the Midland area, local allusions to 'colkote [the "Tolcote" or tollhouse just opposite the friary near the North Gate of Bury] a lytyll besyde Babwell Mill'[69] make it clear that the play was performed near Bury St. Edmunds in Suffolk."[70]

The text of the *Play of the Sacrament* is followed in the manuscript by a list of dramatis personae and then by the note that "Nine may play it at ease."[71] This interesting scribal comment not only proves that role-doubling was used in medieval dramatic productions, but is also a comment that would probably have been unnecessary, as John Wasson has pointed out, "were the play written *at* Croxton *for* Croxton players."[72] Presumably we have in the *Play of the Sacrament* either a play commissioned by the village of Croxton but written elsewhere, or a manuscript copy of a play first performed in another town. Although there is no way to know with certainty where the Croxton *Play of the Sacrament* originated, both the local Bury allusions in the text and the staging requirements of the play have suggested independently to John Wasson and to me that the play might have been originally written for performance in Bury St. Edmunds, fourteen miles directly south of Croxton on the Thetford road. The large downward-sloping market square at Bury, now called Angel Hill, with the west gate of the abbey and St. James church opening directly upon the *platea,* fulfills the staging requirements of the *Play of the Sacrament*—a town setting with space for two scaffold stages for the houses of Jonathas and Aristorius, and, opposite the stages, a church ("Here shall þe merchant and hys prest go to þe chyrche and þe bysshop shall entre þe chyrche and lay þe Ost on þe auter, saying thus . . .").[73] It is significant that the theretofore rather congested market area in front of St. James church was widened in the fifteenth century to make an open space, which would have been as admirably suited for performances of dramas as for the busy regional cloth market conducted there.[74] The meaning of the initials "R. C." that are written beneath the note about the required number of players (on the botton of the final folio of the play text) is even more difficult to decipher than the other puzzles about the play's provenance, but I find it possible that the initials are those of Robert Cooke, the vicar of a village named Haughley (about twelve miles east of Bury St. Edmunds), who bequeathed to his brother in a will of 1537 "all my playbooks."[75] Unless there were many men with playbooks in this small East Anglian neighborhood in the early sixteenth century, the correspondence of initials is at least suggestive.

What is certain about the Croxton *Play of the Sacrament* is that it has some festival connection with Corpus Christi (celebrated annually in English churches after 1318)[76] and that it is a careful, polemical answer to Lollard heresy, staunchly if somewhat ingeniously affirming the miracle of the Real Presence and the importance of the sacraments and defending the efficacy of the priesthood. The "pagan" opposition to these doctrinal truths by the "Jews" in the play are, in fact, the familiar challenges of the Lollards:

Jonathas: Þe beleve of thes Christen men ys false, as I wene;
        For þe beleue on a cake—me thynk yt ys onkynd.
        And all they seye how þe prest dothe yt bynd,

And be þe myght of hys word make yt flessh and blode—
And thus be a conceyte þe wolde make vs blynd—
And how þat yt shuld be he þat deyed upon þe rode.[77]

Cecilia Cutts, who in 1944 first drew attention to the anti-Lollard propaganda of the play, wrote that the Croxton *Play of the Sacrament* was analogous to other "persuasive methods of combatting heresy by the recital or
picturing of miracles" prevalent in England in the fifteenth century, among
those "the St. Edmund Host miracles of 1464."[78] This was a miracle
claimed in the monastery's account of a disastrous fire that devastated the
abbey church at Bury in 1464. The fire burned fiercely all around the famous shrine of St. Edmund and in the vestry where the reserved host was
kept, yet was said to have left both shrine and host miraculously intact.[79]

In the Croxton *Play of the Sacrament,* the real setting for miracle is likewise East Anglia in the 1460s. The Christian merchant Aristorius is reluc-
tant to steal the sacred host for Jonathas and his sceptical experiments
because he is fearful of being reported to the bishop for heresy. That "Jew"
named Jonathas both proclaims familiar Lollard error and delivers an un-
witting orthodox Christian sermon as he explains to his fellows the "mer-
velows case" and the "heresies" of Christian doctrine. The strategy of the
playwright is to make the opponents of Catholic Christianity witness for
the mysteries of the faith in spite of themselves. The Jews somehow even
know the iconic emblem of the cult of the Five Wounds, for to test the
bread they prick the stolen host with four holes shaping the form of a
cross, then stab the center with the fifth mystical wound that causes the
host to bleed.[80]

Although the assertive propaganda of the Croxton *Play of the Sacrament*
and its apparent anti-Judaicism make it an unappealing play to modern
tastes, the play's technique of pervasive irony, its shaping of a deliberate
tension between what seems to be true in the forthright narrative of the
plot and what is true for its fifteenth-century enlightened viewer, is reminiscent of the technique of the Gospels themselves, especially of the ironic
narrative of the Gospel of Mark.[81] What is probably the cleverest part of
the play is the so-called interpolated episode of the comic doctor, which
enacts a sacral parody of Christ's healing that effectively utilizes both scriptural and local allusion to make its point.

Jonathas, who after his sacrilege against the host finds that sacred bread
stuck fixedly to his hand, calls for a doctor to heal him, but the quack
doctor who arrives, Master Brundyche from "Þe colkote . . . A lytyll besyde Babwell Myll" is rejected by both Jonathas and his fellow Jews.[82] The
Jews again affirm, even in their ignorance, Christ as the true Saviour. Part
of the local topical comedy of the scene lies in the Flemish nationality of

the money-grabbing physician who lives—not in a coal-shed as the line has erroneously been glossed[83]—but in a tollhouse. Resentment against the virtual commercial invasion of Flemings in late medieval East Anglia sometimes ran high. The prejudice against the Fleming in the play is, in fact, both more real and more repellent than the highly stylized characterization of what would have been for fifteenth-century Englishmen the exotic and unknown Jews—virtually nonexistent in the country since their expulsion from England by royal edict in the thirteenth century.[84]

But there is another resonant local context of the doctor episode that has gone unrecognized by drama scholars, and it, too, depends upon the allusion to the doctor's lodgings at Babwell Mill. The Croxton *Play of the Sacrament* assumes an audience who knew that Babwell Mill was not only near the North Gate tollhouse but near St. Saviour's Hospital (fig. 2.4), the most famous, even fashionable, of Bury's several hospices. St. Saviour's Hospital was owned and administered by the monastery of St. Edmund and was perhaps more a "hospital" in the modern sense of the word than any of the other abbey hospices. Staffed by an important resident community of physicians, St. Saviour's had since the twelfth century been famous for its care of the sick and infirm. It was so popular in the

FIGURE 2.4. Ruins of St. Saviour's Hospital, Northgate Street, Bury St. Edmunds. From Henry Davy, *Architectural Antiquities of Suffolk* (1827) (Suffolk Record Office).

fifteenth century, especially among the wealthy and nobly born, that applicants had to be placed on a waiting list for review and approval by a specially-elected committee of monks and town burgesses.[85] The coarse joking in the play over the failure of Master Brundyche's healing is comedy founded upon a kind of local inside joke, but it also serves a serious function in the play. For the local and knowing audience, the play's reference to a doctor near Babwell Mill would have evoked the name of the actual hospital there, the hospital of St. Saviour, even as the play exists to affirm the true physician. It will be St. Saviour himself, the crucified saviour of mankind, who will finally both heal Jonathas' hand and lead the false Lollard-Jews of the play to conversion and belief. The miraculous image speaks to order the "Jews" to "Ite et ostendite vos sacerdotibus meis" ("Go and present yourselves to my priests"[86]), the standard refutation to the errors of the Lollards.[87]

By the miracle of stagecraft, the speaking image of Christ the Savior is then transformed back into the host ("Here shall the im[a]ge change agayn into brede"[88]) to be borne by Episcopus "to chyrche with sole[m]pne processyon" as the play now merges with festival celebration of Corpus Christi.[89] The host is borne in triumph from the playing area to a church and then to an altar (fig. 2.5) where the "Jews" are formally reconciled into the community of believers as they kneel in contrition. It is important to observe that the Croxton *Play of the Sacrament* is not a play about judgment and punishment, but about penance and healing acceptance. It is a play that assumes the presence of doubt and is just as forthright about assuming the power of drama to restore from doubt. The mimetic conversion and baptism of the denying "Jews" ends with the bishop's charge to the audience to serve God with devotion and prayer and to keep God's commandments. The concluding hymn of praise, "Te Deum Laudamus," offers the final liturgical blessing upon the witnesses of this play. Lollard heresy and doubt have been formally acknowledged and triumphantly resolved.

If the Croxton *Play of the Sacrament* was first performed at Bury St. Edmunds, then it would have been produced by one of the numerous religious guilds of the town, and probably one whose members included clergy. The text reveals repeatedly the preoccupations of the priesthood and is as much concerned with the servants of God who administer the sacraments as it is with asserting the orthodox doctrine of transubstantiation. The guild-certificate returns from Bury St. Edmunds filed in 1389 tell us that already by that date there was a Corpus Christi guild worshipping at the abbey church whose function included providing a play (*interludium*) on the feast of Corpus Christi,[90] and it may be that the Croxton *Play of the Sacrament* has some connection with the Bury Corpus Christi

FIGURE 2.5. The altar of All Saints church at Croxton, Norfolk (Photo by G. M. Gibson).

guild. By the late fifteenth century there was also a large and popular lay confraternity in Bury St. Edmunds called "The Holy Name of Jesus," which met at a college founded for secular priests on Bernewell Street (now named College Street).[91] The final words of benediction by Episcopus in the Croxton *Play of the Sacrament* speak of special worship of the "name gloriows" of Jesus and may suggest there was also some connection between the play and Holy Name guild:

> . . . To the whyche blysse he bryng vs
> Whoys name ys callyed Jhesus,
> And in wyrshyppe of thys name gloryows
> To syng to hys honore *Te Deum Laudamus*.[92]

To seek to uncover the lost historical context of a medieval play is necessarily a search for plausibilities rather than certitudes, but, to summarize, something much like this may be the history of the Croxton *Play of the Sacrament:* The *Play of the Sacrament* was written in the latter part of the fifteenth century, very possibly in Bury St. Edmunds, and perhaps in the late 1460s like the N-Town cycle compilation which contains very similar banns, likewise spoken by "vexillatores." The *Play of the Sacrament* was a play performed on Corpus Christi Day, a play deliberately addressing the troublesome Lollard sympathies of the Suffolk-Norfolk border region, and it was probably a play produced by one or more confraternities of priests and pious laymen. In its original setting, it may have been performed in the open market square at Angel Hill, just in front of the parish church of St. James, which could have served as the church setting for the Episcopus scenes. In the early sixteenth century, a copy of the play was made for a performance at the small neighboring Norfolk village of Croxton, perhaps, as was so often the case in East Anglian villages, to raise money for the parish church.[93] This copy of the text was made by "R. C.," who noted helpfully the smallest number of players required to perform the play and who may have been Robert Cooke, a local vicar who by 1537 had collected enough drama manuscripts to refer to them in his will as "all my playboks."

What is significant about even such a hypothetical reconstruction of the life and times of a play like the Croxton *Play of the Sacrament* is that it can help us recognize the integral community function of that text, a text that was shaped by local church politics, immediate parish needs, and particular social expectations as surely as were the local parish churches and their altars and monuments. It is also important to see in a study like this one of a regional culture, the extent to which public literary texts like vernacular religious drama were not only shaped *by* local facts and expectations, but served an active function in shaping them as well. The incarnational drama of the late Middle Ages was transformed by the local likeness at the same time that it helped make that local community identity recognizable and coherent. Medieval community theater in this sense both defined the social structure and celebrated it. Indeed, Clifford Flanigan has even argued that English vernacular drama had become a kind of active and popular liturgy, which performed essential ritual functions for a lay society separated by rood screens and philosophical abstractions from what Flanigan calls the "alienated liturgy" of the altar.[94] Likewise Charles Phythian-Adams has written eloquently and persuasively of the "desolation" of the city of Coventry after the Reformation wrested from that city the resonant sequence of liturgical and sanctified ritual that had earlier defined both the church's and the city's year.[95] It is intriguing that the so-called Walsingham Conspiracy in Norfolk in 1536–37, a short-lived attempt to restore the old monasteries and the old faith, was led by a small group of men who included the subprior of the shrine of Our Lady of Walsingham, a minstrel who had been employed to perform in Walsingham Priory, an actor, and an organ maker.[96] The whole futile plot can stand as an eloquent symbol of the old religious aesthetic flailing against the new "desolated" community religion.

To say that East Anglian religious culture shaped a rich communal drama is not, of course, to say that the ritual function of that drama served only the ends of Christian orthodoxy. In Suffolk and Norfolk, as elsewhere in late medieval Europe, there was a dense connectedness between the drama celebrating and defining the sanctified year of the Christian liturgy and the popular seasonal play that paralleled and accompanied it. Any attempt to create division between "folk" or "pagan" ritual and the officially sanctioned ritual of late medieval Christianity is inevitably misleading.[97] Keith Thomas' astute observation about the medieval "peasant" seems to me essentially true of all but a very small elite of fifteenth-century laity, that is, that the Church "was important to him not because of its formalised code of belief, but because its rites were an essential accompaniment to the important events in his own life—birth, marriage, and death. It solemnised these occasions by providing appropriate rites of passage to emphasize their social significance. Religion was a ritual method of living, not a set of dogmas."[98]

What fired the popular imagination about late medieval religion was religion's focus on just these human rites of passage in the lives of Christ and his mother and his saints, events whose less holy but still recognizable patterns were revered and celebrated in their own lives. Although fifteenth-century culture is often described as a "secularization" of religion, it might better be described, as Donald Weinstein has described it, as the "religious legitimation of formerly worldly and temporal activities and institutions."[99] The fifteenth century in East Anglia brought not a loss of spirituality but rather an effort to sanctify the secular that found both philosophical and aesthetic justification in the Incarnation doctrine. The "ritual" drama of East Anglia was as much a celebration of the human concerns of its community as a manifestation of its ecclesiastical preoccupations.

A good example of the way East Anglian vernacular drama celebrated both "folk" ritual and "Christian" ritual—terms that we must use advisedly—can be seen in the play "The Killing of the Children," a drama about the Massacre of the Innocents that appears in the East Anglian Digby plays manuscript of about 1510. Although the prologue to the play in this manuscript asserts that this is a St. Anne's Day play, everything about the text suggests that its original ritual function was closely tied both to the liturgical events of the Epiphany season that is its subject and to the popular calendar observance of that event. In "The Killing of the Children," the dark horror of a stage massacre of the innocent children of Bethlehem is disrupted by a comic scene in which the furious mothers of the dead children assault Herod's bumbling messenger, Watkyn, who had hoped to prove his worthiness for knighthood by joining Herod's knights in the killings. Watkyn, who had earlier boasted of his valor with comic excess, suddenly finds himself in confrontation with the "Prima Mulier" who fiercely attacks him with her distaff:

> Fye vpon the, coward! Of the I wille not faile
> To dubbe the knyght with my rokke [distaff] rounde!
> Women be ferse when their list to assaile
> Such prowde boyes, to caste to the grounde![100]

Wielding the very emblem of meek womanhood, the "Prima Mulier" threatens to "game" Watkyn "with my distaff that is so round!" The scene disintegrates into broad, slapstick comedy as Watkyn, who is terrified by the melee of mothers and helpless before their distaffs, is beaten, then finally rescued by Herod's soldiers ("Here thei shalle bete Watkyn, and the Knyghtes shalle come to rescue hym.").[101]

What would have been recognizable and coherent to a late medieval audience about this scene of comic misrule between the sexes was not that it was some kind of comic interpolation or "comic intrusion"[102] (the nearly inevitable way modern critics have dealt with this episode), but that it juxtaposed the biblical event in Bethlehem with a familiar English event that took place every year on the day after Epiphany. As inevitable a yearly ritual as the commemoration of the events of Epiphany-tide in English towns and villages was the celebration on January 7th of St. Distaff's Day, the day that women returned to their spinning work after the holiday reprieve of the Christmas season. This turning in the rhythm of the Christian year was celebrated with traditional games and practical jokes, especially with mock battles between the sexes, as, for example, ones in which the men of the village set afire the women's flax and the women laughingly retaliated by dousing the flames and drenching the men with pails of water.[103] Even as late as the seventeenth century, the poet Robert Herrick, who was a country clergyman in Devonshire, wrote of the good-humored, traditional games of St. Distaff's Day, which were still part of his rural parish's social ritual as it defined the end of its holy season and prepared for the return to its necessary labors:

> Partly worke and partly play
> Ye must on S. Distaff's day:
> From the Plough soone free your teame;
> Then come home and fother them.
> If the Maides a spinning goe,
> Burne the flax, and fire the tow:
> Scorch their plackets, but beware
> That ye singe no maiden-haire.
> Bring in pailes of water then,
> Let the Maides bewash the men.
> Give S. Distaffe sport good-night.
> And next morrow, every one
> To his owne vocation.[104]

The traditional Yule processions at York prominently displayed the distaffs of women of the town "which sheweth," explained a broadside of about 1570, "that women laying aside their servile workes, must make good preparation for this solemne feast."[105] In East Anglia where the commercial prominence of the cloth industry made the distaff a resonant symbol not only of personal necessity but of communal need, the St. Distaff Day play and game must have performed an especially significant kind of ritual definition, as the society turned from Christmas sport and Christmas worship to its "owne vocation."

The Digby "Killing of the Children" thus performs two kinds of ritual function, which can only very artificially be designated "Christian" and "folk." As the play triumphantly affirms, the playful disorder of St. Distaff's Day was an inevitable part of the sanctified yearly remembering of the events that happened long ago in Bethlehem. The comic distaff fight between Watkyn and the mothers functions not only as the kind of purposeful anachronism that gave immediacy and relevance to the medieval religious plays, but as defining ritual that reveals the local, social "play" to be an integral part of salvation history.[106]

The Christian ritual theater of East Anglia not only embraced the St. Distaff's Days and Plough Mondays of the so-called secular year, offering its sanctifying blessings upon the ordinary and necessary distaffs and ploughs in the hands of its community, it also blessed the very lives—from conception to purgatory—of that community. The richness and coherence of the medieval ceremonial acknowledgment of the human life often had little to do with its philosophical or intellectual content, or even with its integrity as Christian doctrine. Since the time that Pope Gregory first sent Christian missionaries to the distant pagans of Britain, Christianity in Britain (as elsewhere) had frequently incorporated ritual practices that were syncretistic at best, sometimes openly "pagan." Pope Gregory's pragmatic advice to build Christian altars in the purged temples of idols, "that the people . . . flocking more readily to their accustomed resorts, may come to know and adore the true God,"[107] was in the evangelizing early Christian centuries a matter of deliberate ecclesiastical policy and practical necessity. By the fifteenth century there would have remained little consciousness about the pre-Christian elements which had been routinely absorbed for centuries. But again the modern polarity between "Christian" and "pagan" will serve our purposes of understanding East Anglian religious culture no better than the false dichotomy of "sacred" and "secular." It is enough to say that fifteenth-century East Anglia was in name and in communal agreement a Christian culture. No matter that the local Suffolk pilgrimage to the shrine of Our Lady of Woolpit was to a healing well in the same Woolpit wood where a few centuries earlier two celebrated green children right out of Celtic mythology had been found wandering. The twelfth-century historian William of Newburghe who reported the tale was far less interested in the Celtic mythological origins of green children from another land than he was in the comforting particulars of their subsequent history—that, for example, the green girl-child later married a rich man from Lynn and bore thirteen children, none of them green.[108]

Probably even more astonishing to modern expectations about medieval "Christian" culture is the famous procession of the white bull, a lavish public display of what can only be called "devotional theater" that was regularly enacted at Bury St. Edmunds at least as late as 1533. St. Edmund, whose body was enclosed in a splendid jeweled shrine in the abbey church, was widely invoked in late medieval Europe for help in conception and childbirth.[109] Although the origins of the custom are obscure, by the

fifteenth century the mediating assistance of St. Edmund had been formalized by a curiously "pagan" ceremonial procession in which a white
bull, garlanded with flowers and ribbons, was led by Benedictine monks
from the abbey meadow at Haberdon through the streets of St. Edmund's
borough. As the monks sang and as crowds of pilgrims and townspeople
joined in the procession, wives desiring offspring walked along beside the
great white bull, stroking its sides, until the procession reached the west
gate of the abbey at Angel Hill. Here the hopeful women left the procession and reverently entered through the abbey gate to the church of St.
Edmund, where they made their prayers and offerings before the golden
shrine of East Anglia's martyred king and saint. So important were the
white bull and the conception ritual that the abbey performed for the
barren wives that came to St. Edmund on pilgrimage, that several extant
fifteenth- and early sixteenth-century leases of the Haberdon meadow recorded by the abbey sacrists actually specify the obligation of any tenant
of that meadow to keep a white bull ready and available at all times for
this ceremonial use.[110] And according to a document quoted by the Suffolk antiquarian Edmund Gillingwater in 1804, apparently from the now-
lost sacrist's register of John Swaffham (1471–75?),[111] this procession and
ritual blessing of the womb could even be bestowed by proxy, as it was in
1474 "in relief of the desire of a certain Noble Lady" from Ghent:

> To all Faithful Christian People that shall inspect these Presents.
> John Swaffham, sacrist of the monastery of St. Edmund of
> Bury, an exempt Jurisdiction appertaining immediately to the
> Apostolic See, and Arch Deacon of the same place, Health on
> the Author of Health [sic]: We made known to you all by these
> Presents, that Father Peter Minnebode, a lay Brother of the Or-
> der of Carmelites, of the City of Gaunt, on the second day of
> the month of June, in the year of our Lord 1474, did in the
> presence of many credible persons, offer at the Bier of the Glo-
> rious King, Virgin, and Martyr St. Edmund, of Bury, aforesaid,
> ONE WHITE BULL, according to the ancient custom, to the hon-
> our of God, and the said glorious Martyr, in relief of the desire
> of a certain Noble Lady. Sealed with the Seal of our office.[112]

If we can look beyond the startling echoes of pagan fertility customs in
this ceremony performed at one of the greatest centers of monastic learning in medieval England, we may see that the white-bull procession of
Bury St. Edmunds is in essential ways the same as the procession of Corpus Christi—or as the "ritual" performances of late medieval vernacular
religious plays. All are communal, sanctifying dramas of immediate and
important human utility. The white-bull procession, like the great mystery

plays, used the theater of town and parish streets to shape a religious legitimation and solace for the perils of the dark human progress in the world—for lives that ached for infant children and heirs as well as for the mysterious gift of God's grace. As we shall see further in chapter 3, it is no exaggeration to say that much communal medieval art, literature, and public ceremonial in fifteenth-century East Anglia concerned the religion of childbed.

Chapter Three
St. Margery: *The Book of Margery Kempe*

Margery Kempe was the troublesome and pious wife of John Kempe, a burgess of the bustling Norfolk port of Lynn, and the daughter (born about 1373) of John Brunham, who had five times been mayor of the city. Margery Kempe was the mother of fourteen children. She had tried her hand at running a brewing business, then at milling corn. She was also a self-proclaimed visionary and mystic. It was Margery Kempe's cross to bear that, in her own time as well as in most modern scholarship, she would be maligned, misunderstood, and alternately charged with hysteria and with hypocrisy.[1] It would be far more accurate, however, to say that Margery Kempe of Lynn possessed an unswerving sense of devotional theater and that she embraced her martyrdoms deliberately and self-consciously.

The Book of Margery Kempe, in which Margery dictated to a sympathetic fifteenth-century scribe the litany of her tribulations in Norfolk and far beyond, is the first autobiography in the English language. Lost for centuries and only rediscovered in 1934, Margery Kempe's *Book* is also a calculated hagiographical text, a kind of autobiographical saint's life. Its rambling and conversational style should not distract us from the fact that its true literary as well as spiritual models were the *legenda*—lives—of late medieval saints, especially the fourteenth-century Swedish wife, mother, and mystic, St. Bridget, to whom Margery quite explicitly compares herself—and with whom she often competes. ("As I spak to Seynt Bryde [Bridget] ryte so I speke to þe, dowtyr," Jesus more than once assures Margery in her visions.[2]) There is no doubt that Margery Kempe was an audacious and feisty lady who made her fair share of enemies; but there is also documentary proof that a Margery Kempe of Lynn was admitted to membership in the powerful and prestigious Trinity guild of Lynn in 1438, at the very time that she was dictating her story of persecutions and rejections.[3] If martyrdom by sword was not available to qualify her for sainthood, martyrdom by slander was, and Margery's *Book* seems quite conscious of the validating implications of such suffering. When, for example, she finds herself imprisoned in a kind of casual house arrest by her uneasy accusors in Beverly, Margery Kempe reports that God reassures her that such inconvenience is more precious to him than actual martyrdom by sword: "Dowtyr, it is mor plesyng vn-to me þat þu suffyr despitys & scornys, schamys & repreuys, wrongys & disesys þan ȝif þin hed wer smet of thre tymes on þe day euery day in sevyn ȝer."[4] Such despisings are not only reported as proof of her future sanctity and triumph (indeed, Margery tells us that God has revealed that someday in her parish church in Lynn, Norfolk, she will be reverenced as a saint, that "I [God] xal ben worschepyd in þe"[5]), but also as the source of much of her privileged spiritual knowledge. In one of her intimate conversations with Christ, she is assured that because of her hardships "þu xalt knowe þe bettyr what sorwe & schame I suffyrd for thy lofe and þu schalt have þe more compassyon whan þu thynkyst on my Passyon."[6] An attentive look at the language in Margery's accounts of her sufferings and trials shows her pervasive verbal as well as typological indebtedness to gospel Passion narratives.[7] Margery's spiritual compassion is manifested by physical experience which mirrors Christ's own sufferings; if she cannot be, like St. Francis, actually imprinted with Christ's wounds, she struggles for her own version of the *imitatio Christi*. Like Christ's on the Cross, her body is wrenched violently to one side in the extremity of her weeping meditations on the Passion. Like Christ, she is spit upon and scorned by her contemporaries. In the triumph of her conviction, like Christ himself, she magnanimously begs forgiveness for those who know not what they do:

> Sum seyde þat sche had þe fallyng euyl, for sche wyth þe crying wrestyd hir body turnyng fro þe o syde in-to þe oþer & wex al blew and al blo as it had ben colowr of leed. & þan folke spitted at hir for horrowr of þe sekenes, & sum scornyd hir and seyd þat sche dede meche harm a-mong þe pepyl. . . . & þan wept sche ful sor for hir synne, preying God of mercy & forȝeuenes for hem, seying to owr Lord, "Lord, as þu seydyst hangyng on þe Cros for þe crucyfyerys, 'Fadyr, forȝeue hem; þei wite not what þei don,' so I beseche þe, forȝeue þe pepyl al scorne & slawndrys & al þat þei han trespasyd, ȝyf it be thy wille, for I haue deseruyd meche mor & meche more am I worthy."[8]

Margery's protestations of the public hostility she faced must thus be read in the context of her deliberate attempt to participate in the martyrdom pattern of Christ and his saints; indeed, her qualifications for sainthood depend upon that participation. It is largely, I think, because modern readers have been so quick to accept Margery Kempe's own words uncritically that they have also thoughtlessly characterized her piety as aberrant and eccentric, and have thus underestimated the usefulness of her *Book*, not as historical fact, but as an indispensable guide to fifteenth-century English lay spirituality.

In fact, what Margery Kempe's *Book* discloses is not "pathologically neurotic" or eccentric visions of her own invention,[9] but rather a life of extremely literal and concrete achievement of those very spiritual exercises which the thirteenth-century writer of the *Meditationes vitae Christi* had once urged upon the Franciscan nun for whom that devotional text was first written. Nicholas Love's enormously popular English adaptation of the *Meditationes, The Mirrour of the Blessed Lyf of Jesus Christ* (1410), had helped perform the transformation of this contemplative text into a model for the lay devotions of men and women who lived very much in the world. Margery's sacred conversations, her noisy and physical participation in sacred events, her restless hankerings and pilgrimages to shrines and relics and to the Holy Land itself, are all manifestations of her determined attempts to live out a series of homely and affective meditations which were originally addressed to a Poor Clare in Italy more than a century before her birth. That Margery's living out of these spiritual exercises has seemed to modern readers like personal and idiosyncratic mysticism is largely testimony to the zeal with which she seized for her own life and time these Incarnation meditations.

It is often when Margery Kempe sounds most like her inimitable self that she is, in fact, most the Pseudo-Bonaventure. When, for example, Margery is present in meditational vision when the resurrected Christ appears to his mother, Margery's report of the spiritual dialogue between Mother and son—Mary's solicitous questions about Christ's wounds, her grudging approval to Christ's request for permission to leave so that he can appear (in canonical fashion) to Mary Magdalene—all has the ring of Margery Kempe's own and unique imagination. But in fact, the whole scene and suggestions for mentally producing it existed in the *Meditationes vitae Christi,* in the authority of a revered text and not in Margery's own psychology. It was the author of the *Meditationes* who was first to invent this Resurrection meditation in which Christ appears to his mother. Obviously dissatisfied with the silence of the Gospels about the matter, the Pseudo-Bonaventure presented a sweetly moving scene in which the risen Christ and his mother "stayed and conversed together, mutually rejoicing" until Christ begs leave to appear to Mary Magdalene and so return to historical veracity.[10]

The Pseudo-Bonaventure's determination to leave the Virgin Mary out of no crucial moment of Incarnation history is everywhere apparent in the *Meditationes.* In fact, it might be argued that the primary devotional model offered by the *Meditationes vitae Christi* is *imitatio Mariae* instead of *imi-*

tatio Christi; that is, although the text renders the humanity and suffering of the life of Christ in lingering and loving detail, the paradigm urged upon the reader is the life of she who had defined her paradoxical exaltation by humility, by proclaiming at the moment of Annunciation, "Behold the handmaid of the Lord" (Luke 1:38).

It is as handmaid of God's handmaiden that the Franciscan nun to whom the *Meditationes* was first addressed is to meditate upon the Incarnation. Likewise, in Margery Kempe's *Book,* just as to proclaim Margery's martyrdoms is to proclaim her Christ-likeness, so to serve humbly as handmaiden is to be like Mary, the very Queen of Heaven. The domestic and housewifely services which Margery Kempe repeatedly performs for the Virgin Mary and the Christ Child in her visionary life are not naive or childish attempts at mysticism, as they have so often been interpreted, but rather deliberate and self-conscious emulation of the Marian model. The Poor Clare addressed by the *Meditationes* was urged to be handmaiden in her soul; so concretely does that advice live in Margery's visionary imagination that she serves in her soul with no less pragmatism, clarity, and domesticity than she will serve her bedridden husband in his old age. Indeed the point is precisely that there is not great difference for Margery in the two prayerful acts of service. To attend to her incontinent husband's diapers is just as much a spiritual exercise for Margery Kempe as to swaddle the infant Christ is an incarnational reality.

In the early pages of her *Book,* Margery tells how God directed her to think upon the birth and childhood of the Virgin Mary, and how in doing this she prayed to Mary's mother, St. Anne, that she might be "hir mayden & hir seruawnt" and so help care for the infant Mary."[11] Margery also reports overhearing Mary's girlhood wish that she could be worthy enough to "be þe handmayden of hir þat xuld conseive þe Sone of God."[12] Mary's longing is here reported not so much for its dramatic irony (as is the case in the *Meditationes* and in the N-Town play "The Presentation of the Virgin"[13]) as for the apt commentary it offers on Margery's own sanctity. Margery has been chosen worthy handmaiden by St. Anne herself; it is *she* who has fulfilled the longing of Mary to be handmaiden of God's handmaiden. Indeed, since exaltation comes from service, Margery has, in a sense, out-humbled and out-performed the Virgin Mary herself by being not just handmaiden but handmaid to the handmaiden, as in being chosen by Mary to carry the baggage when Mary and Joseph go on their family visit to St. Elizabeth.[14]

Such visionary participation in Incarnation history becomes ever more energetic and more concrete as Margery follows as literally as possible the devotional exercises outlined in the *Meditationes*. From the passive service of bearing the holy baggage, Margery assumes roles of active handmaidenship, as, for example, in the vision in which she acts as comforter to the Virgin Mary, distraught with grief after the burial of her son.[15] Margery does this, in her typical womanly way, by bringing Mary nourishing food. A delightful detail in her *Book,* it is not Margery's invention at all but a suggestion of the author of the *Meditationes,* who had urged the Franciscan nun meditating on Mary's sorrow to "serve, console and comfort so that she may eat a little."[16] It is, however, a telling difference between Margery's thirteenth-century devotional model and her practical and concrete fifteenth-century East Anglian spirituality that Margery's account of her vision actually names the food that she prepares and brings to the Virgin Mary's sickbed—a "cawdel," or mixture of warm spiced wine, egg, and gruel. Indeed it would not be surprising if the fragmentary fifteenth-century recipe (ground sugar and cinnamon are among its ingredients) that appears on the verso of the last folio of the Kempe manuscript was intended to be the recipe for Margery's wine caudle, a kind of spiritual chicken soup.[17] So completely has all human life been touched by Margery Kempe's conversations with the Holy Family that instructions for making sickbed food for Christ's grieving mother seem entirely reasonable and appropriate—and the restoring caudle seems a likely and convincing symbol, resonant with particularity, of the restoring food and drink of the Eucharist, of the body of Christ that will itself become spiritual food.[18]

Margery's service to the Holy Family more often involves being nursemaid than cook. But again, it is the Virgin Mary herself who offers the model: Margery tells how as she stood at her prayers in the Lady Chapel of the "Frer Prechourys" she saw a vision of Mary "holding a fayr white kerche" in her hand and inviting Margery to watch as she swaddled the infant Christ. The sight of the Virgin at her motherly task brings Margery such joy and spiritual comfort, she tells us, that "sche cowde neuyr tellyn it as sche felt it."[19] In another meditation, Margery herself begs Mary for the "fayr whyte clothys & kerchys" so that she, herself might swaddle the newborn Christ in her devotions, a task she performs not only with love, but with "byttyr teerys of compassyon, hauyng mend of þe scharp deth þat he schuld suffyr for þe lofe of synful men."[20] The late medieval preoccupation with juxtaposing the joyful Nativity event with forebodings of the sorrows of the Passion is here focused in Margery's imagination on the physical act of wrapping the Child's body. The fair white cloth she sees in her vision is at once swaddling cloth and shroud.

What is particularly interesting about Margery's vision of the swaddling clothes is that it is based not only upon the text of the Gospel of Luke but upon an actual relic which Margery had seen on her pilgrimage to Assisi: "Vp-pon a tyme as þis creatur was in cherche at Assyse, þer was shewyd owyr Ladys kerche whech sche weryd her in erth wyth gret lygth and gret reuerens. Pans þis creatur had gret deuocyon. Sche wept, sche sobbyd, sche cryed wyth gret plente of teerys & many holy thowtys."[21] This "kerche" or head veil of the Virgin Mary was one of the most venerated relics of the Lower Church of St. Francis at Assisi. It had been presented to the church in 1319 by Tomasso degli Orsini, who claimed to have obtained the veil from the Pasha of Damascus, an Islamic prisoner of war. It was further claimed that this was the very cloth Mary had swaddled the Christ Child with at the Nativity; the holy relic, it was said, had been stolen by the Pasha from a church in Jerusalem.[22] The real source of the Virgin's relic was almost certainly not a prisoner of war, but a revered text—again, the *Meditationes vitae Christi*. For it was the *Meditationes*, written some fifty years before the mysterious reappearance of the Christ Child's swaddling cloth, which explained and gave canonical validity to the relic. The Pseudo-Bonaventure had urged his reader to pay particularly close attention to his meditation on the Nativity "especially as I intend to recount what the Lady revealed and disclosed, as told to me by a trustworthy holy brother of our order, to whom I think it had been revealed."[23] This special revelation included the information that the Christ Child was born on a Sunday at midnight, that he emerged from Mary's womb soundlessly and painlessly, that the Virgin Mary embraced the Child, washed him with the sacred milk from her breasts, and then "wrapped Him in the veil from her head and laid Him in the manger."[24]

The Pseudo-Bonaventure's purpose in revealing the swaddling clothes to be the veil from the Virgin's own head was to emphasize, as he does throughout the Incarnation meditations, the poverty and humility of the Holy Family, a favorite Franciscan theme that distinguishes this swaddling scene from, for example, that in the Nativity revelation of St. Bridget, who reported that the Virgin had brought with her to Bethlehem "two small linen cloths and two woolen ones of exquisite purity and fineness" to serve as Christ's swaddling clothes.[25] But the Virgin's veil in the *Meditationes vitae Christi* is not only a sign of humility but a visual emblem linking the joyful maternity of the Virgin with her anguish at Calvary. With a terrible symmetry, the Virgin's head veil again appears in the Pseudo-Bonaventure's *Meditationes,* this time in the midst of the Crucifixion narrative:

> Again He is stripped, and is now nude before all the multitude
> for the third time, His wounds reopened by the adhesion of
> His garments to His flesh. Now for the first time the Mother
> beholds her Son thus taken and prepared for the anguish of
> death. She is saddened and shamed beyond measure when she
> sees Him entirely nude: they did not leave Him even His loin-

cloth. Therefore she hurries and approaches the Son, embraces Him, and girds Him with the veil from her head.[26]

Although it is difficult to know precisely where and when the medieval tradition originated that Mary's veil covered Christ's loins after he had been stripped for the Crucifixion, it seems to have been the *Meditationes vitae Christi* which invented, or at least popularized, that veil as an image linking Christ's Nativity to his Passion.[27] It would perhaps be more accurate to say that the Pseudo-Bonaventure's text popularized the head veil as an important symbolic detail of Incarnation history, for rhetorical juxtaposition of the Virgin's joy at swaddling the infant Christ and her anguish as she shrouded the crucified Christ had been commonplace in sermon meditation in the Eastern Church far before the thirteenth century.[28] Indeed, as we shall see in chapter 6, both at the Nativity and at the Crucifixion, Mary's use of her own veil to clothe Christ is literal manifestation of the ancient and widespread metaphoric explanation of Christ's incarnate body as a "garment" bestowed upon him by his human mother. The poor frail cloth of humanity is what actually swathes the Christ Child in the *Meditationes vitae Christi* and in devotional texts like the fourteenth-century English lyric in which Mary sings

Iheus, suete, be nout wroth,
I haue neiþer clut ne cloth
Þe inne for to folde;
I ne haue but a clut of a lappe,
Þerfore ley þi feet to my pappe,
And kep þi from þe colde.[29]

Whatever the historical and symbolic explanations of the veil tradition, for the purposes of understanding Margery Kempe's meditations on the swaddling clothes it is sufficient to note that the cloth's significance lies in its substitution for an abstract theological concept—Mary as the mother who clothes the Logos in fleshly mortality—of an extremely concrete image for the Incarnation mystery. It is probable that Margery Kempe's veneration of the famous veil relic on her pilgrimage to Assisi reinforced a devotional image already familiar to her and to her English contemporaries, not only through Nicholas Love's translation of the *Meditationes vitae Christi,* but also through popular sermons like those in John Mirk's well-known anthology of vernacular sermons for parish priests.[30]

The veil image was conveyed especially strongly through the visual arts. One of the most ubiquitous devotional images in the fourteenth and fifteenth centuries was a type of Virgin and Child portrait in which the Christ Child reaches up to touch the Virgin Mary's head veil or to pull the veil around his body, in what Dorothy Shorr has noticed in her icon-ographic catalogue of Italian Madonna and Child paintings, is visual al-lusion to the " 'kerchiefs of the head' in which the Mother wraps the new-born child as well as the body of the dead."[31] The Passion symbolism of the head veil is sometimes only hinted at by the Child's casual or affection-ate placement of his hand on his mother's head veil. In Italian paintings the significance of the veil is sometimes made ominous and explicit, as in a painting by a Tuscan follower of Daddi in which the Christ Child tugs on his mother's veil with one hand while his other small hand reaches out for a Cross offered to him by an attending angel. It is, however, in a German memorial painting of 1431 from Nuremberg (fig. 3.1), under an epitaph inscription for Konrad Winkler and his two wives, that we can see most clearly the kind of popular, merchant-class icon that influenced Mar-gery's swaddling-cloth devotions: as the small, praying memorial portraits of Konrad, Kunigunde, and Adelheid Winkler look up solemnly, four at-tending angels help Mary wrap the Christ Child in a long white winding-cloth identical to the veil under her crown—a crown that is prominently marked with the cross of Christ's Passion.

The nearly wholesale destruction of such devotional panel paintings in England by Anglican, then Puritan, iconoclasts makes it necessary to seek the English iconography of the Incarnation veil in illuminated manu-scripts like the *Holkam Bible Picture Book,* a Southern or East Anglian pic-ture Bible of the early fourteenth century, which illustrates the Deposition from the Cross with an image of Mary wrapping her kerchief around the dead Christ's hips.[32] An even more evocative illumination is to be found in British Library Ms. Arundel 83, an East Anglian psalter fragment of about 1300 or 1320 which was given by Robert de Lisle to his daughter Audere in 1339 and which contains a full-page portrait of the Madonna and Child seated triumphantly on a canopied throne (fig. 3.2). The Christ Child clutches in his left hand, as he does in many Italian Madonna and Child portraits, the goldfinch that symbolizes his foreordained death and resurrection.[33] And with his right hand, Christ grasps the Virgin Mary's head veil, linking by the prominent gesture the joyful Madonna to the Virgin of Sorrows, wringing her hands in grief, who appears on the facing folio in the psalter.

Certainly the evidence of Margery's own *Book* suggests that her devo-tional preoccupation with the swaddling cloth of Christ went beyond the specific claims of the Assisi veil relic. In fact, Margery Kempe's difficult pilgrimage to Aachen in her old age took her to view the Assisi relic's principal rival. Margery tells us only that on St. Margaret's Day she saw at Aachen "Owr Ladys smokke & oþer holy reliqwis."[34] Those Aachen relics, exhibited to pilgrims only once every seven years, were a shirt worn by

FIGURE 3.1. *The Virgin Mary and Angels Swaddling the Christ Child,* a fifteenth-century German memorial painting (epitaph) for Konrad Winkler and his wives (Nuremberg, Germanisches Nationalmuseum).

FIGURE 3.2. *Madonna and Child with Goldfinch,* from the Robert de Lisle Psalter (BL MS. Arundel 83, fol. 131b), illuminated in East Anglia about 1320 (By permission of the British Library).

FIGURE 3.3. *Nativity with Midwife and Joseph Making Swaddling Clothes,* a panel from a diptych painted in the Meuse-Rhine region about 1400. Antwerp, Mayer van der Bergh Museum (Marburg/ Art Resource, New York). © A.C.L.

the Virgin Mary, the cloth that received the body of Christ at the Deposition from the Cross, the cloth that had held the severed head of John the Baptist, and the treasured and famous *Josefshosen*—stockings of St. Joseph—which from the fourteenth century the cathedral of Aachen had claimed were used by old Joseph at Bethlehem to wrap the Christ Child from the cold. The German swaddling cloth, like the rival Italian relic at Assisi, served as homily on the poverty and humility of the Holy Family, but, also like the Assisi swaddling cloth, proclaimed a wider symbolic meaning.

It is again to painted images that we must go to understand the late medieval devotional associations of the *Josefshosen*. There is a German painting of about 1400 now in the Museum van der Bergh in Antwerp (fig. 3.3) that depicts the kind of domestic Nativity scene which Margery Kempe may well have known in Norfolk or have seen on her journey to Aachen, or even have witnessed in mystery plays.[35] V. A. Kolve in his *Play Called Corpus Christi* drew attention to the Antwerp Nativity painting as an example of what he called the medieval drama's depiction of Joseph as "Natural Man":

> A fourteenth-century Nativity painting in the Museum at Anvers [Antwerp] shows a midwife tending the infant Jesus while Mary in blue robes lies resplendent on cloth-of-gold spread out on the hillside. High above, God holds a planet in his hand and looks down upon the scene, while in the lower left corner, Joseph with one boot off, is busy cutting open his leather sock with a knife. His feet have been hurting him, and though Christ has just been born, this is his chief concern.[36]

In fact, this seemingly "natural" act by natural man—an aged Joseph pulling off shoes and stockings to relieve tired, aching feet—is the same kind of religious symbolism concealed in domestic, even apparently comic, detail which Kolve has so brilliantly shown us in the English vernacular drama's Advent feasts and wrestling matches and in the singing contests of the mystery-play shepherds.[37] The truth is that Joseph removes his shoes and stockings in the Antwerp Nativity painting, as he does in a number of other German and Flemish paintings and vernacular plays of the fourteenth and fifteenth centuries, in simple, concrete action which emblemizes the twofold nature of the Incarnate Christ.[38] First, Joseph's removal of his shoes was understood as a typological fulfillment of Moses' gesture before the burning bush (Exodus 3:5); as a Middle English sermon explains, so must we all remove our shoes "as Moyses enformeþ vs" whenever we stand before the awesome mystery of the Virgin Birth.[39] And as for the stockings, as the Aachen relic testifies, Joseph actually rips his stockings not because of sore feet, but because he needs rags to warm the newborn baby suffering in the cold. "Mary, take my hose and wind your dear baby in them" ("Marie nym dy hosen min und wint dar in din lybes kindelin") proclaims a scroll above Joseph's head in a Nativity painting of about 1400 or 1420 from a parish church at Lezignan.[40] The simplicity and directness of the vernacular piety is reminiscent of Margery's own conversations with the Virgin, the swaddling gesture the same kind of handmaid's devotion that motivates her whole *Book*.

Margery's "eccentric" personal experience of Christ's swaddling clothes, then, encompasses popular texts and devotional images as well as two major relics of major pilgrimage shrines of late medieval Christendom. Margery tells us only briefly of the reverence she felt for the Assisi veil, she does not even mention the *Josefshosen* explicitly by name, yet her *Book* is compelling testimony to their importance in the devotional theater of her visions. So important were such relics to her incarnational aesthetic that she would have been baffled by the vehement reaction to come in the sixteenth century; by the response, for example of the English reformer Thomas Rogers who railed against the *Josefshosen* in his "Exposition on the Thirty-Nine Articles": "They [the Papists] have canonized for a saint the chains which bound St. Peter: to say nothing of the adoration they give unto the hair, milk, smock of the blessed Virgin . . . unto the breeches of Joseph . . . and unto many other things which of modesty I will not mention, but do overpass."[41] Margery Kempe's human and humanizing spirituality of handmaidenship was perfectly at ease with holy kerchiefs and stockings, but it is a telling commentary on the differences between Margery's fifteenth century and the apologetic mood of the Counter-Reformation that in the sixteenth century the church at Aachen changed the official name of the Joseph relic from *hosen* to the far safer and vaguer "swaddling clothes."

Margery Kempe's handmaidenly meditations, her imaginative focus on the Christ Child's swaddling clothes, can lead us to a second area of inquiry. Just as I have argued that much of what seems personally idiosyncratic in the *Book of Margery Kempe* can be traced to popular late medieval texts and images and to relics sanctioned by the Christian orthodoxy of her time, so it is also important to see that Margery's visions are linked to traditions of "folk" ritual magic that are also essential contexts of the age of the mystery plays. The first disclaimer, however, must be to acknowledge again both the difficulty and the danger of attempting artificial separations between religious piety and practice associated with Christian clergy and those which arose from the laity. Natalie Zemon Davis in a thought-provoking essay entitled "Some Tasks and Themes in the Study of Popular Religion" has argued persuasively against such artificial fragmentation of rites, symbols, beliefs, and institutions, which whether "magical" or Christian represented serious efforts to mediate human relationships with the sacred.[42] The important questions, the essential questions, to be asked, she insists, are not which manifestations of spirituality are officially sanctioned and which are magical or "pagan" manifestations of a human being's efforts to order and explain his world, but rather *how* these things provide ordering and "what feelings, moods, and motives do they encourage (or try to repress)."[43] Keith Thomas' *Religion and the Decline of Magic* has taught us that magic is redefined by each new era of believers as the employment of what it now sees as "ineffective techniques to allay anxiety when effective ones are not available."[44]

Clearly Margery Kempe's own human experience as a woman who had undergone the perils and pains of bearing fourteen children is as essential to the meaning of her spiritual visions of nursemaiding the Christ Child as her experiences with swaddling-cloth relics and the *Meditationes vitae Christi*. There is frequent suggestion, I think, in the *Book of Margery Kempe* that Margery's fascination with the holy event of Nativity involves her own intimate knowledge of the rites of conception and childbirth. The Lollard voice in this fourteenth-century poem protesting the tactics used by the drama to attract credulous female spectators should remind us that Margery Kempe's preoccupations were those of many other women in the mystery-play audience:

> . . . þe lulling of oure Ladye þe wymmen to lyken,
> And miracles of mydwyves & maken wymmen to wenen
> Pat þe lace of oure ladie smok liȝteþ hem of children.[45]

This Lollard poem, *Pierce the Ploughman's Crede,* speaks out not only against the vernacular drama's concerted efforts to stage scenes of appeal to laywomen but also against that very incarnational fixation that the drama shared with late medieval piety generally. The Lollards, as the first English reformers, were prophetic of what was to come: they were the first modern historians, the first modern scientists—stalwart empiricists insistent upon Gospel accuracy and decorum instead of the folklore of Joseph's stockings and of Mary's smocks and veils that shaped the vernacular drama, the paintings, even the sermons of late medieval spiritual life. The author of *Pierce the Ploughman's Crede* rejects not only plays about apocryphal midwives but also relics venerated as protection against the perils of childbirth. We should recall that the Nuremberg swaddling cloth painting shows the merchant Konrad Winkler reunited with his first wife, who probably died in childbirth, as well with his second wife. It is important to observe that the yearly renewal of the sacred feast of the Nativity, enshrined within the Church's liturgical calendar, was paralleled by the near-yearly occurrence of childbirth and by its prodigious physical risk for many late medieval women. Indeed, since in many parts of Europe local custom forbade burial on holy ground to women who had died in childbirth before their ritual churching and purification,[46] childbirth was a terrifying spiritual as well as physical danger. The relationship of that danger to medieval affective piety for the maternity of Mary is essential to our full understanding of the fifteenth-century plays of Incarnation—and of their worried womanly audience.

One of the most striking facts that emerges from a study of fifteenth-century social documents like letters and wills is the significant and sustained belief in the use of holy images and relics in the human rites of conception and childbirth. Even as late as 1530, Sir William Clopton of Long Melford, Suffolk, bequeathed to his oldest son "my crosse of gold which I where dayly abowtte my necke" and instructed that this crosse be given in turn to his son's own male heirs "upon the condicion that they and every of them dow lenne this same crosse unto women of honeste being with child the tyme of ther laboure and immediately to be surely delivered unto hours ayen."[47] The frequency of such references to heirlooms associated with childbirth and the high seriousness with which their uses, loans, and safekeepings are detailed in medieval wills suggests that the transferral of images of God's Incarnation to the uses of human beings conceived in God's image may have been supported at least as much by a self-conscious participation in the Incarnation model as by the customary rituals of folk magic. And it is not always possible or even useful to make distinctions between the two motives. Was it Christian piety or part of a family traditional ritual of childbirth, for example, that prompted one of the Paston women, Elizabeth Poyninges (née Paston) to specify in her will of 1487 that her daughter be given for her dowry "a tablet with the Salutacion of Our Lady and the iii kingis of Collayn"?[48] All we can observe with certainty is the appropriateness of such iconography for the practical purpose of aiding the daughter's successful conception and safe childbirth.

It seems significant, then, that just such an alabaster sculpture as Elizabeth Paston describes, hallowed by an age at least a century greater than the Suffolk parish church which secreted it, was discovered hidden under the chancel floor of Holy Trinity church, Long Melford, by workmen in the eighteenth century (fig. 3.4.)[49] The origin and early history of the Long Melford alabaster is not recorded, but we can know how it escaped destruction when the church was being stripped of its images and ornaments in the iconoclasm of the sixteenth century. A sales inventory of 1548 lists the sale of "the altr of Alebaster in our ladys chappell" to a "Mr. Clopton," almost certainly William Clopton—a churchwarden of Holy Trinity, the grandson of the Sir William Clopton who had bequeathed the

FIGURE 3.4. *Nativity with Midwife and the Adoration of the Magi,* English alabaster panel of the second half of the fourteenth century, Holy Trinity church, Long Melford, Suffolk (Photo by G. M. Gibson).

heirloom cross, and a descendant of the wealthy clothier John Clopton who in the fifteenth century had been the principal patron of Long Melford church.[50] A "Mr. Clopton" also purchased in 1548, says the Long Melford inventory, "the tabyll of Allebaster" in the Clopton family chantry and "a lytell tabyll in sent Annys Chappel."[51] The Holy Trinity church images were taken back to the Clopton family chapel at Kentwell Hall, then restored to the church in 1555 with the return of Catholicism under Queen Mary. When iconoclasm raged in England again after Mary's brief rule, maybe it was expectation of less iconoclastic times, maybe it was simple filial piety, or maybe it was an act of semimagical devotion that caused someone, perhaps William Clopton himself, to hide under the floor of his ancestor's church a holy image of the Virgin Mary in childbed, attended by Joseph and the apocryphal midwife and adored by the Three Kings. I suspect that it is not coincidence that the single sculpture saved from destruction at Long Melford was of a subject charged both with the meaning of sacred iconography and the holiness of family rites of passage.

If human life was saturated with sacramental possibility for the late Middle Ages, so too the Christian sacraments were blessed by the powers and mysteries of human life. There are moments in the *Book of Margery Kempe* when the magic of popular rituals of conception and childbed and the practices of Christian devotion seem inseparable. One of the most fascinating passages in Margery's account of her Italian pilgrimage is her description of an image of the Christ Child carried about in a chest by a woman and two Franciscan friars journeying to Rome. Little is told us about either the woman (perhaps a Poor Clare) or about her Franciscan companions except that "non of hem cowde vndirstand [Margery's] language," but what we *are* told is that whenever that company "comyn in good citeys," the woman would take out the image of the Christ Child "& sett it in worshepful wyfys lappys. & þei wold puttyn schirtys þerup-on & kyssyn it as þei it had ben God hym-selfe."[52] Margery Kempe in her characteristic way is overcome with emotion at seeing the reverence with which the women fondle and kiss the Christ Child's statue; Margery must finally be led away from the place and comforted. Her anecdote is illuminating for the evidence it provides about Franciscan encouragement of the Christ Child's cult, and it also provides suggestive evidence about the close connection in Margery's time between Christian piety and sympathetic magic. The gesture of placing the statue of the infant Christ in the laps of pious wives suggests a ritual blessing of the womb to ensure fruitfulness and protection from the dangers of childbirth as much as opportunity for visual contemplation of the Nativity of Christ. Indeed, Christiane Klapisch-Zuber has argued that the doll-like effigies of the Infant Jesus that appeared in the trousseaux of fifteenth-century Italian brides and nuns functioned as both ritual objects for adoration and as magical effigies that bestowed the power of "visual impregnation" upon young women who were going to their terrestrial or spiritual spouses.[53] It is certain that the ancient and nearly universal appeal to human effigies to ensure fertility was encouraged and validated by the incarnational forms of late medieval devotional iconography. We might point, for example, to the donor portrait of Mary, Duchess of Guelders, which appears in Staatsbiliothek Ms Cod. Germ 42, folio 19 vers. This illumination places Mary of Guelders, like her holy namesake, in a *hortus conclusus,* the enclosed garden that emblemized the womb of the Virgin Mary. Just as in paintings of the Annunciation God the Father sends down to Mary of Guelders his blessing and the dove of the Holy Spirit. As Erwin Panofsky has suggested, the image seems not so much portrait as propitiating prayer for offspring. In a Book of Hours that was probably a wedding gift, the painting is an act of visual sympathetic magic not unlike the fondling of trousseau Christ Child statues or the participation in St. Edmund's procession of the white bull. (It was a prayer, however, which failed to be granted; despite her figural identification with the mother of Christ, Mary of Guelders remained childless.[54])

Perhaps the most famous Christian aid to fecundity and childbirth in the late Middle Ages was not an image or a saint's shrine, but the relic which the magnificent cathedral of Chartres was built to honor—the chemise of Our Lady of Chartres, which was said to have been worn by

Mary at the Annunciation when she conceived Christ.[55] Whenever the monks of Chartres were informed of a royal pregnancy, a tunic of white and gold was prepared for the expectant queen or dauphiness and ritually placed in the crypt upon the holy reliquary of Mary's shift for nine days. Special masses imploring safe delivery were celebrated, and the tunic was then presented to the pregnant queen or princess by four of the monks.[56] Even as late as the sixteenth century, Henry III and Louise of Lorraine, dressed in sackcloth, walked barefoot fifty miles every winter to Chartres to pray before the holy shift, albeit fruitlessly, for children.[57] More happy results were achieved by Elizabeth of York, whose privy purse expenses mention the six shillings and eight pence paid to a monk who brought to her chamber at Westminster the girdle from a cult statue of the Virgin to help ensure her safe delivery.[58] Such relics were, like the Clopton heirloom cross, so hallowed by sacramental associations both Christian and human that they defy categorization. They preside as wordless and omnipresent over late medieval spiritual and physical life as St. Margaret, patron saint of childbirth, whom Jan van Eyck painted into his famous "Arnolfini Wedding Portrait" as a sculpture on a chair beside the marriage bed.[59]

To this truth of the sacrament of human life, Margery Kempe's *Book* bears ample witness. There is considerable evidence in Margery Kempe's extraordinary autobiography that Margery the self-styled saint was especially a self-styled Saint Margaret. Margery's very parish church in Lynn, that church where God promises her future sanctity, was dedicated to her namesake, St. Margaret. Margery takes care to inform her readers that her special place of devotion there was "a chapel of owr Lady, clepyd þe Iezyne."[60] The Gesine Chapel (from Old French "gesine," "childbed") was named for a cult image of the Nativity kept there, an image which may have been much like the Long Melford "childbed" alabaster. We know that officials of the prestigious guild of the Holy Trinity bore this gesine image in procession through the streets of Lynn on feast days, and we know that Margery Kempe was a member of the Trinity guild.[61] These facts we may verify; what we cannot so easily verify is the extent of Margery's self-conscious identification with the holy mysteries of the Gesine Chapel. To what extent did Margery Kempe, visionary handmaiden, mother of fourteen children, also see herself as Margaret, patron saint of childbirth?

If we cannot know the answer to that question with certainty, it is at least possible to point to what is certainly the central "miracle" of Margery Kempe's *Book,* her account of her magical healing of a woman mad from childbirth. Margery tells us that it was in the church of St. Margaret as she was at her customary devotions that she encountered a man in great distress. This man tells Margery that his wife "was newly delyueryd of a childe & sche was owte hir mende."[62] Margery at once leaves her meditations and goes with the distraught husband to the woman's bedside. There, precisely like Christ casting out demons, she brings miraculous calm to the woman, although "whan oþer folke came to hir, sche cryid & gapyd as sche wolde an etyn hem & seyd þat sche saw many deuelys a-bowtyn hem."[63] Margery's patient visits and intercessory prayers at last succeed in restoring the woman's mind, so that she can be "browt to chirche & purifijd as oþer women be."[64]

This healing is proclaimed by the scribe to whom Margery dictates her story as "a ryth gret myrakel." The special appropriateness of such a miracle to the namesake of St. Margaret is not proclaimed, but is, I think, just as clear. What is also evident is that Margery has come full circle by this miracle. For the Margery Kempe we first met in her *Book* was a woman who was herself tormented in mind and body from the hard labors of a difficult childbirth, Margery herself who raged "owt hir mende," tortured by fears of damnation, by visions of devils and echoes of demonic voices.[65] Margery's madness had been healed by a vision of Christ in his humanity, "in lyknesse of a man, most semly, most bewtyouws, & most amyable" seated upon her bedside. Now Margery has extended the incarnational likeness; she has herself performed the healing act and blessed with a human, womanly hand. This time it is the likeness of Margery Kempe sitting on the bedside, and Margery, by triumphing over the perils of childbirth has both enacted her qualifying miracle of sainthood and fully asserted her own spiritual health.

Chapter Four

In Search of East Anglian Devotional
Theater: Three Lives

One of the central problems in trying to know the vernacular medieval drama is the problem of its audience. The contract, implicit and explicit, between play and spectator was at the heart of the social and religious pragmatism of that drama. All justifications of drama against the objections of its detractors insisted upon the practical, social function of the plays to teach and preach, and move to penance and rightful action. But who were these spectators? How did they see and think and gain instruction, coherence, and entertainment from the devotional-play texts they have bequeathed to us? Although I have curiosity about what members of Chaucer's audience at court thought as they listened to Chaucer joke about turning the leaf and avoiding the churlishness of "The Miller's Tale," it pales beside my overriding curiosity to know what reasonably attentive citizens of York or Chester or N-Town thought about the biblical pageants they witnessed each year. That very curiosity is, in fact, at the center of this book. But especially at the heart of this book is the conviction that to understand the medieval audience it is necessary to assume—as fifteenth-century men and women did themselves—an extended definition of the devotional theater of their lives.[1]

Sources of information about fifteenth-century laymen are, of course, scanty, and about fifteenth-century laywomen, scantier still. But they are not impossible to find. We all know the famous letters of the famous Pastons, that busy, hankering, litigating East Anglian family that saved letters with the same seriousness with which they engaged in social climbing. But we may also hear the voices of the Paston's neighbors if we seek for them, especially in those documents in which life is stilled, observed, and rendered intelligible between the lines and the legal formulae—the Last Will and Testament.

To the objection that death-hour bequests are curious documents to use to assess attitudes toward life and toward dramatic art, I can answer only that the will of the late Middle Ages is an extant, lay, and often vernacular act, supervised and structured by clergy and by custom—as was the religious drama. The practical necessity of preparing for purgatory and heaven made the late medieval will as much preoccupied with posthumous

Chapter Four

acts of charity and with the endowing of chantries and masses as with the bestowal of earthly possessions. So, too, the constant context of medieval religious drama is the practical necessity of spiritual preparation for death. In medieval English drama we have biblical histories that end by encompassing present time and company in the play of the Last Judgment, we have plays of the martyrdoms and subsequent salvation of saints, and we have morality plays of deathbed reckonings like *Everyman* and *The Castle of Perseverance*. The message of a play like *Everyman* or the York "Last Judgment," or the N-Town "Death of Herod" is that its audience should always live *in extremis,* never knowing the hour or the day that God's messenger, Death, will approach and the reckoning be taken. The Last Will and Testament is a closely related literary and social act.

The earliest known Middle English will was made in 1387, within nine years of the first recorded performance of the York Cycle.[2] There can be little doubt that the emergence of the vernacular will and/or the vernacular drama are both results of growing English self-consciousness—national, civic, and personal. Nor can there be doubt that the element of lay participation which is the very hallmark of the English religious drama is also a significant element in the formulation of vernacular will documents. The will was a practical, legal, and literary means by which men and women were able as they believed, personally and actively to influence the future salvation of their souls. This was accomplished both by establishing acts of Christian charity (various late medieval wills bequeath funds for new roads and almshouses, for the care of idiots and poor and prisoners) and by giving gifts of "remembrances" to friends and relatives, whose gifts in exchange would be prayers for the testator's soul. Many wills make that mutual charitable obligation quite explicit. The will of Anne Harling of East Harling, Norfolk, a wealthy heiress who died thrice-widowed and childless, states at its close that "I requyre myn exers to desire all suche personys as I have in this my testament geven eny thinge, that they of theire charite pray to Almighty God for my sowle and for myn auncestres' sowles."[3]

Men and women of means—prosperous grocers, wool merchants, and clothiers as well as nobles—used the will to effect still more active lay participation in the mysteries of salvation, by their endowment of chantries and chantry priests. They used the will as a means of setting the stage for the saving ritual in perpetuity if they could afford it, or, if they could not, of making arrangements for commemorative masses and prayers for the first years or months after their demise. Sons bequeathed to their own sons hereditary obligations to endow chantries, provide for their upkeep, furnish vestments and chalices, and provide lodging and living for chantry priests. Indeed, since the giving away of actual property and land was largely controlled by common law and custom rather than by individual volition, it is probably fair to say that the business of establishing post-humous charities and masses was the most important aspect of fifteenth and early sixteenth-century wills. Frederick Furnivall as early as 1882 recognized the crucial importance of will texts to the understanding of medieval social history ("They let you into the state of every home"[4]) but despite his philological enthusiasm for the medieval London wills he edited for the Early English Text Society, he was hardly a sympathetic observer of late medieval attitudes. Furnivall's Victorian horror at the popular spirituality those will documents reveal says a great deal about the long and hard-won coming of understanding about the spirituality of fifteenth-century literary texts like the mystery plays:

> But the most surprizing [sic] and regrettable [sic] thing in these wills is the amount of money shown to hav [sic] been wasted in vain prayers, or orders for them. Fancy one man ordering a million masses to be said for his soul; another 10,000; another 4,400; another sending Pilgrims to Spain, Rome, Jerusalem, &c. for the good of his soul! I only hope some sensible Executors handed over the money to the Testators' wives and children or the poor.[5]

Most early wills were probably written down by parish priests,[6] and even where there is certain evidence that the testator did not dictate it but wrote the document in his own hand,[7] the ecclesiastical context of the Last Will and Testament is clear. The fact that church courts held jurisdiction for wills (as late in England as 1858)[8] resulted, for example, in the establishing of a confession of faith in the doctrines of the Church as a formal preamble to the document.[9] These preambles tended to be formulaic declarations of belief in Christ, Mary, and the saints, but they could also involve personal affirmations of belief, like that which a wealthy Hull merchant named John Dalton prefixed to his will of 1487. John Dalton's testament preamble subsequently was adopted as a kind of Dalton family tradition, for the same long preface was affixed to the wills of two later members of his family.[10] The Dalton will ceremoniously begins thus:

> I John Dalton of the Kingis town opon Hull, merchaunt, and of the parishe of Saint Trinitie kyrke in the said towne, considering and remembryng, thinke in my hert that the daies of men in this mortall lyfe be bot short, and the houre of deith is in the hand of Almighty God; and that He hath ordeyned the termes that no man may passe: remembryng also that God hath ordeyned man to dye, and ther is no thing more certayne than deth, and nothing more uncertayn then the houre of deth, I

seyng daily dye prynces and grete estates, and men of all ages
endes ther daies; and at deth giffes noo respit certayn to levyng
creature, but takis thaym sodaynly; for that consideration, I,
beyng, in my right witte and mynde, loved by God, hole and
not seke, besekyng Almighty God that I may dye the true
soone of holikirke, of hert truely confessed, with contricion and
repentance of all my synnes that ever I did sith the first houre I
was born of my moder into this synfull world onto the houre of
my deth, of the which offences I aske and beseke Almighty God
of pardon and forgifnes. And in this I beseech the blessid Vir-
gyn Marie, and hir blissed sone Jhesu, our Saviour, that sufferd
payne and passion for me and all synfull creatures, and all the
holy company of Paradise to pray for me, etc. For thies causes
afforsaid, I dowtyng to dye intestate, I beyng of lyve, of hole
mynd and memorie, loved by God, I dispose and ordeyne suche
gudes as God hath lent me, moveabill and immoveabill, my testament devise and ordeyne of this my laste wille in the fourme
and maner that folowith.[11]

Such testament preambles are one of the surest barometers of change in
religious convictions during the troubled transition to Reformation. Ida
Darlington, in a study of early London Consistory Court wills, notes that
new religious ideas began to appear in those documents after 1536 and
points to the 1539 will of Henry Walton, "citezein of London," as the first
of the London wills to use recognizably Lutheran formulae in the preamble.[12] Even earlier, the Suffolk will of William Shepard of Mendelsham
declares in staunchly Protestant terms his belief in Jesus as the sole media-
tor between God and man, his conviction that the powers of Pope are
usurped, and that good works are fruitless without faith and grace. This
will, though the testator styles himself "rude and unlernyd," reads like a
personal and considered apologia written in controversial times ("I also
forsake the Bysshoppe of Romes vsurpt power wherin he caused me to
trust").[13] The difficulty, however, of generalizing about lay religious convictions in Suffolk in the 1530s is strikingly illustrated by other Suffolk
documents like the will of Anne Buckingham of Bury St. Edmunds (written in 1539, although not proved until the year 1546) which counters William Shepard's reformer's zeal with a traditional late medieval bequest for
a chantry priest and masses for the dead, for a penny to a poor man to say
"the vii psalmes with the letany" every Friday for a year, for a penny to a
"poore bodie" to say the psalter of Our Lady every Saturday, and for a gift
to Buckenham manor chapel of "my table of alabaster with the imageries
of the Trinitie, Sainte Peter, and Say[n]te Nicholas."[14]

It is not only the declaration of faith which makes the late medieval will
invaluable as a source of knowledge about lay spirituality. Some of the

In Search of East Anglian Devotional Theater

most useful facts for a drama historian that can be gleaned from fifteenth-century wills are those which can be used to understand the visual imagination and habits of mind of the testator. If we do not have the kind of primary information we long to have about what medieval audiences actually saw before their eyes on a mystery-play stage or pageant wagon, we can use other kinds of primary documents to reconstruct the visual expectations of that audience. Just as the contemporary fifteenth-century visual arts are crucial in fleshing out the laconic lines of drama texts we try to reconstruct, contemporary will documents can help us understand the dramatic audience's habitual patterns of thought and response, the visual and iconic images in the mind's eye. Some of those fifteenth-century will documents are even self-revelatory in ways that give us sudden, surprising contact not just with an audience—but with a human heart.

Any scholarly theorizing, for example, about the attitudes of York citizenry as they viewed and acted in the city's pageants of saints and prophets and patriarchs ought to take into consideration the evidence of a will like that of a middle-class widow named Jane Chamberleyn. In her 1501 testament, Jane Chamberleyn instructed that at her death her wedding ring, her gold and silver girdle, and a pair of coral rosary beads be given to "the blessed ymage of saynt Anne" in St. Mary's Abbey, just outside the city. Furthermore, her will continues, "the rynge, the day of my bureall, be putt on hir fynger, the gyrdyll abowt hir, and the baydes in hir hand." [15] These words argue for an extraordinarily concrete identification between at least one member of the York lay audience and her patron saint. It can be said, in fact, that Jane Chamberleyn's will sets the stage for her own funeral theater, a drama in which on the day of Jane's burial, a cult statue of St. Anne was to "play" Jane Chamberleyn. St. Anne was to wear Jane Chamberleyn's ring, girdle, and beads not only in a visible, public sign of the testator's lifetime devotion to her, but in a final memorial image which co-identified the bodies of saint and supplicant in a moving and hopeful funeral drama. It is important to see this kind of "theater" as visual spectacle controlled by ideas as much aesthetic (if we mean by that anachronistic word, "perceptual") as pious.

It is also important to understand such will documents—as indeed the very phrase "Last Will and Testament" proclaims—as self-conscious and volitional documents. It might be argued that not only were will-makers *not* coerced and controlled by deathbed circumstances, but that perhaps no fifteenth-century layman ever was more in control than in that moment, usually in sight of death, when he tried to order and influence the deeds and memories and people he would leave behind. The social restraints on women and their actions probably made the female testator's will even more a document recording, sometimes for the very first time, her own self-identity, her sense of priorities, her convictions, and affirmations of her significant personal, family, and institutional relationships.[16] Sometimes these volitional documents involve, in both senses of the word, a contest of wills. Hence, it is interesting, for example, that Jane Chamberleyn of York, as a great benefactress of St. Mary's Abbey, orders that she be buried in the abbey church before the altar of St. Ursula. This despite the fact that her husband, who had died twelve years before, had stipulated in his own will that she was to be buried in *his* tomb in the monastery of the Holy Trinity at Kirkham.[17]

John Baret of Bury: Funeral Theater

Since our particular quest is to know the East Anglian devotional theater, let us now turn to a Suffolk will document that we may fruitfully study in some detail as a source of information about specific, local attitudes and habits of mind. I will argue in chapter 5 for the likelihood of Bury St. Edmunds, Suffolk, as an important center of the East Anglian dramatic tradition, but whether or not we assume a Bury provenance for several of the East Anglian play manuscripts that are linked to that town, it is certain that Bury St. Edmunds offers a particularly useful typological setting for the study of the East Anglian drama. Bury St. Edmunds is a focal point in this book about East Anglian lay spirituality, because of the manuscript evidence and trace records of dramatic ceremonial observed there, but especially because it was an important fifteenth-century town that mirrored two of the most significant influences on East Anglian regional culture— the monastery and the cloth merchant. In the case of Bury, the monastic influence was the ancient and powerful Benedictine monastery of St. Edmund, which controlled the town as well as much of the rest of western Suffolk, but which ever vied for authority against the growing wealth and power of the thriving merchants of the Suffolk cloth trade. We have in the extraordinarily revealing will of John Baret of Bury a document with ties to both worlds. More importantly, we have in the will of John Baret a document which eloquently proclaims its own kind of devotional theater.

John Baret, who died in 1467, just one year before the year inscribed in the N-Town cycle manuscript, was a wealthy clothier and property owner who performed an office of some kind for the monastery of St. Edmund. He may have been, as the Bury antiquary Samuel Tymms suggested, a lay treasurer of the abbey.[18] His town house, still existing though much remodeled and fronted in gray Georgian brick, was built directly across Church Govel Street from the abbey's Norman gate in what is now called Checquer Square—apparently a corruption of Escheker (Exchequer).

Baret referred to himself in his will as a "geyntlman of my lord abbotte," and he gave gifts for a "tokne of remembraunce" to the abbot and prior and to the monks of Bury, but he was also mindful in his will of the "spynning hous" where his workers labored.[19] Baret, though a self-styled "gentleman," was in fact one of those wealthy monastic patrons who were increasingly in the fifteenth century successful merchants and lawyers instead of old nobility. Lay-confraternity status conferred by monastic houses like St. Edmund's forged alliances with the merchant classes that are as significant in assessing the context of late medieval culture as the evidence revealing their competition for influence. And such alliances suggest that the saturation of worldly life by religious thought and imagery in the fifteenth century can to some extent be explained by the fact of direct reciprocal influence of monastery and laity. In the case of John Baret, his long and personal testament—over thirty pages long in Tymms' edition—offers an unusually full and revealing look at the piety and habits of mind of the kind of rich and pious tradesmen who were so important to the existence of the vernacular English drama.

Baret's will contains a conventional but no less instructive preamble, identifying the date (as did all pre-Reformation wills) not by calendar time but by reference to the liturgical year. The church year that structured the dramas of biblical history in the streets of England's towns also shaped the worldly time of its audiences and their legal documents. Thus John Baret identifies the date as "the Satyrday next folwyng the feeste of the Natiuite of oure Lady, the yeer of oure Lord Cryst 1463." Formulaic convention continues into the customary bequest of the testator's soul "to oure Lord God Almyghty and to oure Lady Seynt Marie and to alle the Seyntes." It was also conventional to provide next, as Baret does, for the interment of his body. He is to be buried by the altar of St. Mary in St. Mary's church in a pit under "my graue," "the body put in as neer vndyr my grave as may be wythoute hurt of the seid grave."[20]

What Baret calls his "grave," already in place in his parish church as an object of contemplation when his will was being written, was a stone tomb with an effigy that, five hundred years later, still jolts a casual visitor to St. Mary's church (fig. 4.1). Above a small stone relief portrait of John Baret in the garb of a successful cloth merchant reclines a life-size stone corpse, emaciated and horribly decayed. Baret's tomb is less a monument to the dead than a dramatic moral lesson to the living. Like Mors in the N-Town "Death of Herod," Baret's effigy is gnawed by worms, and, like Mors, it delivers an admonitory sermon about the world's false pomp and riches.[21] Verses carved round the base of the Baret monument offer both commentary and didactic lesson, urging the beholder to "se hys ownyn merour a[nd] lerne for to die."[22] A book called *Disce mori* (probably Thomas Hoc-

Chapter Four

cleve's poem by that name) is mentioned in Baret's will and no doubt influenced the commissioning of John Baret's tomb,[23] but so too must John Lydgate, poet and monk of Bury, have been an influence on Baret's *memento mori* portrait. It was Lydgate who, as the prologue to his poem *Danse Macabre* explains, rendered into English the verses accompanying famous paintings of the Dance of Death on the charnel house walls of the Paris church of the Holy Innocents.[24] Lydgate was credited with thereby popularizing in England visual allegories of Death's inexorable call—especially after his verses were painted around the ossuary and charnel chapel of St. Paul's Cathedral.[25] There can be no doubt that Baret knew Lydgate; Baret mentions in his will owning a copy of the popular Lydgate narrative *Siege of Thebes*,[26] and he was probably one of the wealthy patrons for which fine presentation manuscripts of *Siege of Thebes* were made.[27] Even more conclusive proof of their connection is to be found in Lydgate's pension documents, which show that in 1439 Lydgate wrote to King Henry VI requesting that half his royal pension be given to "John Baret squier". The reason for Lydgate's request and the precise nature of his

FIGURE 4.1. John Baret's tomb monument in the south aisle of St. Mary's church, Bury St. Edmunds, Suffolk (Photo © A. F. Kersting).

connection with Baret are no longer known. The only certain facts are that Baret was by no means in need of money and that Baret continued to receive half of Lydgate's pension for at least ten years, or until 1449, the year of the last recorded payment and apparently of Lydgate's death.[28]

What is also certain is that Baret, a cloth merchant, and Lydgate, a poet-monk, shared many of the same devotional preoccupations. Judging from the Baret will, for example, Baret's intensely fervent devotion to the Virgin Mary must have rivaled that of Lydgate, the poet whose *Lyf of Our Lady* is the most ambitious, (certainly, at 5,932 lines, the longest) *vita* and hymn of praise to the Virgin in the English language.[29] Baret's will leaves funds and detailed instructions for placing on one of the gates to the town "an ymage of oure lady, sittyng or stondyng, in an howsyng of free stone, and rememberaunce of me besyde."[30] His will is much preoccupied with instructions for creating a chantry at St. Mary's altar (fig. 4.2); there are bequests for a new painting of the Virgin, for chimes for the Mass of Our Lady, for a new crown for the Virgin's statue in the reredos, and most remarkably, for a painted altarpiece showing "the story of Magnificat" (the Visitation of Mary and Elizabeth). "And in the enner part of ye lowkys wtinne there be wreten the balladys I made therefore."[31] John Baret's "ballads" for a Visitation altarpiece are one of the most intriguing riddles of the will. Whether these verses he "made" were crude and self-serving versifyings (Baret instructed that his "pardon" or indulgence from purgatory was to be inscribed on the altarpiece also) or poems that he commissioned from Lydgate, or whether the Magnificat "balladys" are evidence that Baret was a poet as well as a cloth merchant, a literary disciple as well as patron of Lydgate's, we cannot know.

What we can know from the pages and pages of careful instructions and bequests in the John Baret will is a man both intensely pious and pragmatic. His town house is to be repaired and readied as the dwelling place for the parish priest of St. Mary's church, for example—but solely on the condition that he "prey for my soule at eu[er]y meel, mete, or sopeer, and yif he gynne gracys and sey *De profundis,* he to reherse my name, John Baret, opynly, that they yt here may sey, *God haue mercy on his soule,* wiche greetly may releve me with here devout preyours."[32] Baret's concern for practical detail extends to his elaborate orders for the keeping of chantry masses and the careful observing of his weekly death day and anniversary day. He remembers to leave money to the sexton to keep the chimes at his chantry altar in good condition and to keep his tomb clean; he even instructs that a new key to the rood-loft be made for the priest who will perform his death masses.[33] The same obsessive concern for detail that made Baret a successful merchant in life is focused in his will upon preparations for death—and for afterlife. But there is some guilty negotiation

FIGURE 4.2. The roof vaulting the area of the south aisle of Bury St. Mary's where John Baret's chantry chapel once stood is still embedded with small star-like pieces of mirrored glass and inscribed with Baret's motto, "Grace me governe" (Photo by Theresa Coletti).

too. Generous bequests are left for annual observances of Baret's death by the two most prestigious confraternities of Bury St. Edmunds, Candlemas guild and Dusse guild, and for lighted tapers at the Easter sepulchre,[34] but those rituals are to be undertaken not just for John Baret himself, but also "for the soulys whoos bodyes I have causyd to lese sylvir in ony wyse in my lyve at ony tyme."[35] And as we have already seen in chapter 2, John Baret had particularly uneasy feelings about one Edmund Tabowre, for his will explicitly instructs the chantry priest to sing for Edmund's soul, and Baret, remarkably, orders that his prized silver Lancastrian collar be sold and the money given in alms "for Edmund Tabowre soule and his frendys, to recompe[n]se broke silver I had of his to oon of the colerys and othir things with othir stuff be syde wiche I took to my owne vse."[36] To the readers and executors of Baret's will, this confession would have bestowed special irony to the staging of Baret's funeral, a ritual whose spiritual and visual effects Baret had also carefully planned and directed by this will. For

In Search of East Anglian Devotional Theater

FIGURE 4.3. John Baret's motto, "Grace me governe," is displayed on his tomb by a small carved portrait of Baret wearing the Lancastrian collar of *SS* which had been awarded to him by King Henry VI (Photo by G. M. Gibson).

as Baret's mourners gathered at his moralizing tomb they would have seen carved in relief, below the sculpted corpse, the portrait of Baret in his former prominence and prosperity, the "me" from Baret's inscribed motto "Grace me governe" clearly pointing out the fashionably dressed and coifed late-medieval gentleman who stands beneath Death's grim handiwork—wearing this same ill-gotten Lancastrian collar around his neck (fig 4.3).

John Baret's last will and testament reveals the omnipresence of such evocative visual language as survives in his tomb monument. Frequent and knowing references to the devotional images and icons that were a daily and concrete part of the life Baret is preparing to leave fills the pages of his testament. Many of these references are useful for reconstructing some sense of the richness of the now-lost visual art of East Anglia's medieval past, and they are useful as well for reconstructing something of the iconographic experience and expectations of the patrons and audiences who performed and watched the plays on East Anglian streets and stages. We can learn, for example, something about the once-rich visual imagery in St. Mary's church from Baret's instructions that a chantry door was to be constructed soundly enough to bear the weight of the beam "there the iii kinges be, and the Jesse set vndir our lady with the virgenys afore hire."[37] The numerous meditative and devotional images of Baret's own household are also instructive, and they are enumerated in his will with a businessman's precision: a favorite niece is left a cloth painted with the "Coronation of oure Lady," another niece is to receive a cloth with "the seven ages of man."[38] An image of the Trinity adorns the gold ring which is, remarkably, Baret's only bequest to his wife,[39] while a certain "Dame Margarete Spurdaunce" of Norwich is to receive both the rosary and the crucifix from his bedchamber, as well as an inscribed gold and ruby ring "for a rememberaunce" says Baret, "of oold love vertuously set at alle tymes to the pleseer of God."[40] Baret's high admiration for Dame Margaret Spurdaunce (or Purdans) was shared, among others, by Richard Ferneys, the famous and pious hermit of Norwich, who also named the widow Margaret prominently in his will and who, like Baret, there pairs her with Julian Lampett, the renowned anchoress of Carrow.[41] (Margaret Spurdaunce's own will of 1481 can tell us that Baret's old love seems, in fact, to have been a lay contemplative and a member of what Norman Tanner has called the "recluse society" of fifteenth-century Norwich.[42] Nearly all of Margaret Spurdaunce's own bequests are to Norwich hermits and anchoresses, who are given her painted altarcloths and religious images and her vernacular devotional books; perhaps most interesting of Margaret's bequests are "an English book of St. Bridget" and "a book called Hylton," apparently the Middle English mystical text *The Scale of Perfection*, by Walter Hilton.[43])

Devotional images for pious laity like John Baret and Margaret Spurdaunce went beyond pictures painted on church walls and altarcloths. In the charged spiritual culture of the fifteenth century, the human body itself could function as icon, as image and reminder of the incarnate Christ. Margery Kempe wept and wept when she saw at Norwich a statue of the Virgin Mary clutching the dead Christ in her lap,[44] but even the sight of a poor woman suckling her child could recall the Crucifixion to her mind:

> An-oþer tyme, ryth as sche cam be a powr womanys hows, þe powr woman clepyd hir in-to hir hows & dede hir sytten be hir lytyl fyer, ȝeuyng hir wyn to drynke in a cuppe of ston. & sche had a lytel manchylde sowkyng on hir brest, þe whech sowkyd o while on þe moderys brest; an-oþer while it ran to þis creatur [i.e., to Margery], þe modyr syttyng ful of sorwe & sadnes. Þan þis creatur brast al in-to wepyng, as þei sche had seyn owr Lady & hir sone in tyme of hys Passyon, & had so many of holy thowtys þat sche myth neuyr tellyn þe haleundel [the half], but euyr sat & wept plentyvowsly a long tyme þat þe powr woman,

In Search of East Anglian Devotional Theater

hauyng compassyon of hir wepyng, preyd hir to sesyn [cease],
not knowyng why sche wept. Þan owr Lord Ihesu Crist seyd to
þe creatur, "Thys place is holy."[45]

The intense religious sensibility of a Margery Kempe, that could see
Christ's human form and likeness in a small child distracted from his
breastfeeding, is a remarkable example of the incarnational focus of late
medieval habits of mind, but it is not an aberrant example, as a document
like John Baret's will makes clear. For John Baret, too, assumes the human
body itself to be an evocative image of Incarnation; his will's lengthy di-
rectives for his funeral service include the order that at his funeral mass
and burial there be "v. men clade in blak in wurshippe of Ieh[s]us v.
woundys and v. women clad in whith [white] in wurshippe of oure ladyes
fyve joyes, eche of them holdyng a torche of clene vexe [wax]."[46] Those
five men clothed in black garments were to function as both symbols and
devotional images of the five mystical wounds of Christ and as actors in
the dramatic ritual of Christian burial. That Baret would seek symbolic
coherence in such a way—and especially that he could expect that those
human images of the Five Wounds and of the Virgin's Five Joys would be
articulate to his mourners—is perhaps the most useful knowledge of all
that we can bring from his instructive will, a knowledge that should help
shape our understanding of medieval devotional theater, in which ideas
are played "in worship" by their human images.

2. John Clopton of Long Melford: The Piety of Kinship

The human life—and death—as devotional image is likewise proclaimed
by the will of John Clopton of Long Melford, who was Baret's kinsman
by marriage as well as the man whom Baret had named chief executor of
his own will.[47] John Clopton was, like John Baret, a prosperous and successful clothier who had achieved a social prominence possible only to the
nobly-born before the fifteenth century. Clopton was appointed sheriff of
Norfolk and Suffolk in 1452–53,[48] and his list of will executors reads like
an East Anglian who's who. One of his executors was James Hobart, a
Suffolk lawyer who sat on the Suffolk Commission of the Peace, who in
1486 was named Attorney General, and then became a prominent member
of the council of Henry VII.[49] For Hobart's service as will executor, Clopton bequeathed him "my rynge with sayntes that I were daily" and "a grete
ryng that Seliard yave me whanne he was made sergeant."[50] This "Seliard"
was probably John Sulyard, another prominent Suffolk man who had
made a successful legal career, being appointed Sergeant-at-Law and later
justice of the King's Bench.[51] The chief executors of Clopton's will were

no less than the earl of Oxford, who owned numerous Suffolk estates, and "Maister Willyam Pykenham," who was a doctor of canon and civil law, dean of the College of Stoke-by-Clare, and archdeacon of Suffolk.[52]

John Clopton's involvement with such great men and high politics had very nearly cost him his head in 1461, when he was arrested along with other notable Suffolk Lancastrians and accused of treasonable correspondence with the ousted queen, Margaret of Anjou, and of plotting to overthrow the Yorkist government. The other Suffolk gentry arrested with Clopton—John, earl of Oxford, and his son Aubrey de Vere; Sir John Montgomery; Sir Thomas Tuddenham; and William Tyrell—were all beheaded for treason at the Tower of London, but Clopton was somehow acquitted and allowed to return to his village of Long Melford.[53] There he seems to have lived a life which was rather more quiet after his hasty political realignment (Yorkist white roses appear conspicuously in the stained-glass windows he gave to Long Melford church). Despite Clopton's uneasy politics, if being named will executor is any fair indication of Clopton's reputation for honesty and efficiency, he continued to be very highly esteemed indeed, for his name is listed as chief executor over and over again in the wills of eminent East Anglian merchants and gentry.[54]

John Clopton's name also appears repeatedly in the inscriptions recording the ambitious rebuilding he financed of Long Melford church from the 1460s to 1495. The splendid Perpendicular-style church of the Holy Trinity is one of the most famous of the Suffolk "wool churches," and it majestically presides over the village of Long Melford even today as a visible sign of John Clopton's patronage and piety (fig 2.3). Inscriptions urging the prayers of passersby for the soul of John Clopton and his family and friends still run prominently around the exterior walls of the church; carved in huge letters on the mortar and flint of the north porch is the plea to "Pray for ye sowlis of William Clopton, Margy and Margy his wifis, and for ye sowle of Alice Clopton and for John Clopto', and for alle thoo sowlis' yt ye seyd John is bo'nde to prey for."[55]

In the north clerestory windows of Long Melford church are other reminders of John Clopton and of the souls he was "bound to pray for," a remarkable group of donor portraits from the Norwich stained-glass workshops that have managed to survive the ravages of time and iconoclasm that has thinned their number. Beginning at the west end, the lower windows once contained stained-glass portraits representing John Clopton's ancestors and relations, culminating in a portrait of John Clopton and his sons and daughters. The upper window contained portraits of John Clopton's associates, some of them kinsmen by marriage, some of them eminent friends and acquaintances as densely connected as kin in the power alliances of this close East Anglian neighborhood. Literary patron-

In Search of East Anglian Devotional Theater

FIGURE 4.4. St. Edmund, patron saint of the abbey of Bury, and Abbot Richard Hyngham in a fifteenth-century window in the north aisle of the parish church of Holy Trinity, Long Melford, Suffolk (Photo by G. M. Gibson).

age was as local and densely tangled: the Benedictine monk who appears below the looming figure of St. Edmund in a north aisle window in Long Melford church is Abbot Hyngham of Bury[56] (fig. 4.4), the same "Monk Hyngham" who is thought to have owned the East Anglian drama manuscript containing the Macro plays.[57]

According to detailed descriptions of the Long Melford windows and their inscriptions compiled by a seventeenth-century rector of Long Melford church, at the place of honor in the eastern, culminating window of the clerestory were originally placed images of those same holy women who figured so prominently in Margery Kempe's visionary life—the Virgin Mary with the Christ Child in her arms, St. Elizabeth with the infant John the Baptist, and, of special significance to the Clopton's, Mary's mother, St. Anne.[58] John Clopton's own family chapel at his nearby manor house of Lutons was dedicated to St. Anne,[59] and Clopton's will singles out the "Saynt Anne's aulter of Melford Church" to receive a bequest of a fine red vestment.[60] John Clopton's half-sister, Katherine Denston, was the patroness who commissioned a Middle English life of St. Anne from the Suffolk poet Osbern Bokenham, an Augustinian friar from nearby Clare Priory.[61] Indeed, the cult of Anne, the holy matriarch, was, as the St. Anne plays in the N-Town cycle bear witness, an important fact of local East Anglian devotion and patronage. We might pause to consider its implications for the Clopton family and their kind.

The evidence of St. Anne altars at Long Melford church and at Lutons is a useful reminder that though the official recognition of the cult of St. Anne in England was not until 1382 (when on the occasion of King Richard II's marriage to Anne of Bohemia, Pope Urban VI ordered that the feast of St. Anne be observed in the English church), and although the feast of the mother of the Virgin was not to be required for the universal Catholic church until the time of the Counter-Reformation (in 1582), St. Anne had possessed since the twelfth century influential champions in East Anglia. Abbot Anselm of Bury (1121–48) was credited with being the first in England to celebrate the feast of Anne's Immaculate Conception, and his contemporary, Osbert of Clare, wrote letters and treatises from the Augustinian priory at Clare urging special reverence for the mother of the Virgin and arguing for universal observance of the feast of Anne's Immaculate Conception.[62] By the fourteenth century, there were guilds of St. Anne at Bury and Lynn; by the fifteenth century there were dozens of St. Anne guilds,[63] and her feast day was deemed an important day for communal celebration and spectacle in East Anglia[64] and in Lincoln to the northeast (where there was an elaborate annual procession on St. Anne's Day[65]).

St. Anne's Day, July 26, was a feast set square in the middle of summer, when good weather and long daylight hours could be counted on for outdoor spectacles and performances. Surely such practical considerations, as well as the pious wish to honor the mother of the Virgin, are part of the context of St. Anne's Day plays like the East Anglian biblical plays preserved in the Digby manuscript. Although the prologue celebrates "Anna/In whos worshippe this fest we honoure,"[66] the subjects of the Digby "Killing of the Children"—the massacre of the Innocents and the Purification of Mary—are only indirectly related to the cult of St. Anne. Indeed, St. Anne nowhere appears in these plays unless the unusual emphasis on "Anna prophetissa" and her attendant virgins in the Purification play is to be explained as a kind of complimentary reference to St. Anne. Where St. Anne herself does appear prominently is in a group of texts, once apparently a separate quire, bound into the interesting fifteenth-century commonplace book compiled by Robert Reynes from the Norfolk village of Acle, eleven miles east of Norwich. Like John Clopton, Robert Reynes was an important patron of his parish church with a proprietary interest in the affairs of his local parish and community, and, like Clopton, he had close ties to a local monastic house. In Reynes' case, the monastery was Weybridge Priory, a small house of canons regular that had been founded at Acle by the Bigod family and which was the meeting place for the Acle confraternity of St. Anne.[67] Robert Reynes' *Commonplace Book* contains a series of entries concerning St. Anne that appear to be a register of texts for public recitation at guild festivities;[68] the most important of these is a poem of 460 lines on "þe worchepe of sent Anne in thys tyme of ȝeere." The Acle poem presents for the edification of "this gylde"[69] the same kind of redemptive prologue traced from the womb of St. Anne to the womb of Mary that we can see in Osbern Bokenham's *Vita S. Annae* or in the N-Town Contemplatio plays or in Lydgate's aureate hymn *An Invocation to Seynte Anne*.[70] All of these texts are wondering celebrations of a miraculous redemption that has been directed backward beyond the holy Child in Mary's womb to the conception of Mary herself. But, significantly, there are two other preoccupations in the Acle guild poem that may help explain the importance of St. Anne plays and altars and guilds in late medieval East Anglia—and offer a gloss on that St. Anne window once prominently placed before the Cloptons and their kin in Long Melford church.

First of all, the popular cult of St. Anne in East Anglia was an undisguised celebration of family ties and relationships of kinship. After its first call for silence, the Reynes poem begins to tell the complicated and somewhat gossipy story of Anne's family tree ("Summe wyll askyn of Sent Anne who was her ffadyr"[71]) and the improbable medieval legend of her three husbands—she marries Cleophas and Salome in turn after Joachim's death—and her trinity of daughters, all named Mary.[72] Three other entries in the Robert Reynes *Commonplace Book* also concern the lineage of Anne (including a Latin line which seems to be a mnemonic device for recalling the names of Anne's parents: "Est tuus Anna pater Izakar, Nazaphat tua mater"[73]). Far from being what Rosemary Woolf has termed "learned Latin notes," the marginal notes in the N-Town manuscript detailing the geneology of St. Anne and Joachim[74] reflect popular fascination with this subject that has its parallels in the dogged verse in the *Reynes Commonplace Book* and in surviving East Anglian painted glass[75] and rood screens.[76] Family patriarchs like John Clopton would have understood and approved the litany of such family connections.

And second, what the Acle guild poem rather ingenuously makes clear is that Anne and her husband Joachim are a merchant's saints par excellence. These were "ryght ryche folke," the writer tells us approvingly, transforming the poverty themes of the Gospels by an enthusiastic bourgeois piety.[77] This is no St. Anne of Franciscan humility but a St. Anne who with her multiple husbands and daughters appears in this poem like a rich pious widow on a fifteenth-century tomb monument, her prosperous and well-dressed family lined up with clasped, praying hands beside her. The Acle poem closely follows the account of the life of St. Anne in the *Golden Legend,* but adds elaboration and emphases that make Anne a model East Anglian matron, tending to her tithes, her almsbasket, and her prayerbook. She lives a busy, comfortable, and pious life and endures only the temporary martyrdom of her childlessness, a childlessness that will be wholly transformed by the miraculous conception that makes her mother of Mary and grandmother of God's own Son. It is difficult to imagine a saint with more obvious bourgeois appeal. The St. Anne invoked at the altar that John Clopton's cloth trade bought at Long Melford or on St. Anne's Day at Acle was a trusted and familiar matriarch who could be confidently invoked to "bryng vs to þe blys þat lestyth withowtyn ende."[78]

More evidence of Clopton's devotional life and its preoccupations survives at Long Melford in the beautiful Lady Chapel he had built as an adjoined but separate chapel to the east of Holy Trinity, for special worship of the Virgin Mary (fig. 4.5). John Clopton's will, written in 1494, refers to the Lady Chapel which he had "new made in Melford Churcheyard"; in a memorandum added to the will in 1497, the year of his death, John Clopton left the huge sum of one-hundred marks for "the garnysshyng of oure Lady Chapel and of the cloister ther abowte."[79] This "cloister" is a wide ambulatory surrounding the central sanctuary on all four sides; an ambulatory that G. H. Cook has called "without parallel in parish church planning."[80] Cook's likely suggestion that the Long Melford Lady Chapel was a pilgrimage shrine and was so designed to permit the easy flow of pilgrims is confirmed by a Long Melford inventory of 1529, which refers to a cult statue of the Virgin Mary housed in the Lady Chapel and which lists an astonishing array (and weight) of rings, jewels, silver spoons, and

FIGURE 4.5. The Lady Chapel (completed 1496) from the ambulatory, Holy Trinity church, Long Melford (Royal Commission on the Historical Monuments of England).

FIGURE 4.6. Detail of the Clopton chantry roof and cornice, painted with verses from John Lydgate's devotional lyrics, in Holy Trinity church, Long Melford (Photo by Theresa Coletti).

buckles that were affixed "upon the Apron of our Lady," apparently as votive offerings.[81] The decorative hand and unfurled scroll motif that runs around the cornice of this chapel may once have been painted with devotional lyrics or hymns of praise to the Virgin. (No trace of writing now remains on the cornice or elsewhere in the chapel, except for an ancient multiplication table painted on the far east wall; the Long Melford Lady Chapel was used as the village school from 1670 to 1840 and was stripped of reminders of its papist past with even more than the usual iconoclastic zeal.[82])

Identical cornice scrolls in John Clopton's chantry chapel at Long Melford, adjoining the north wall of the chancel, are painted with verses (recently restored) from John Lydgate's poem *Testament* and from his Marian lament, *Quis Dabit Meo Capiti Fontem Lacrimarum?* (fig. 4.6).[83] Lydgate may have been poet laureate to the Lancastrian kings, but he was also a monk of Bury abbey and an East Anglian poet whose local identity and connections bound him to the Cloptons as they had bound him to John Baret. Since the monks of Bury St. Edmund not only owned the advowson of Long Melford church, but were frequently in residence at their country estate at Melford Hall, we can assume there was a direct link between Lydgate's abbey and the verses inscribed on the Clopton chantry walls. Indeed, as J. B. Trapp has observed, since Lydgate's *Testament* is immediately followed by the *Quis Dabit* poem both on the chantry walls and in the manuscript collection of lyrics (Harley MS. 2255) that Lydgate made for his abbot, William Curteys, the monastery's own anthology of Lydgate's lyrics may have served as the text for the inscriptions.[84] It would not be surprising, however, if the Cloptons also owned a manuscript of Lydgate's devotional poems. Certainly John Clopton, who was about twenty-seven when Lydgate died at Bury St. Edmunds in 1449 or 1450, would have known Lydgate personally. John Clopton's father was Lydgate's contemporary as well as a patron and lay brother of Bury abbey,[85] and the Clopton family estate was just on the other side of the churchyard from the entrance to the abbot's country retreat at Melford Hall.

John Clopton mentions his "lytell chapell" in Long Melford church in his will of 1494; the Lydgate verses were probably already in place by then. Not only were the verses painted upon specially designed wooden scrolls decorating the cornices of the chapel walls, but they seem to have been carefully chosen for their chantry setting. Beginning with the twenty-ninth stanza of Lydgate's *Testament,* the Clopton Chantry verses lament the sins of misspent youth and implore mercy and forgiveness, in an appropriate prologue for the penitential purpose of the chantry and its prayers. Lydgate's *Testament* verses plead that "one request in especiall," may be granted, that while he is "here a-lyve" that he may have ever printed in his mind "The remembraunce of thy woundes fyve."[86] Devotional meditation upon Christ's wounds and upon the name of Jesus then merge in the poet's fervent prayer that "This word Iesu my .v. wittes tenlumyne,/ In length & brede like a large wounde."[87] With near-hallucinatory intensity, Lydgate's visual imagination invites the meditator to make the word flesh, to transform the very word *Jesus* into a gaping wound that assaults all the bodily senses—and embues that meditator with remorse for human sin.

Other verses from Lydgate's confessional *Testament* are painted on the cornice directly above the altar, where there must have once been a crucifix or a devotional image of Christ as Man of Sorrows, displaying his wounds in much the same manner as the surviving Long Melford pietà in stained

FIGURE 4.7. *The Virgin Mary Embracing Christ, the Man of Sorrows,* a fifteenth-century window in Holy Trinity church, Long Melford (Royal Commission on the Historical Monuments of England).

glass (fig. 4.7), in which Christ's bloodied body implicates the worshipper in emotional response. Here the Lydgate verses speak in the persona of Jesus himself, exhorting the beholder to "Beholde, o man! lyfte vp thyn eye, and see," to behold Christ's flowing wounds, his bloody face, and the selfless love that paid mankind's ransom. And ever more insistently the words urge the worshipper to make such images part of his devotional life, to "Emprente thes thynges in thyn inward thought" until the incarnation of the word is indelibly marked in the mind and will of the penitent who is prayerfully contemplating in the devotional theater of the poem—and the chantry chapel.[88] The final verse from Lydgate's poem *Testament* is painted as culminating stanza above the Clopton altar. It is a sober directive that explicates both the ideal spiritual focus of the Christian life and the meaning and purpose of the chantry prayers sung before this altar:

> Tarye no lenger toward thyn herytage,
> Hast on thy weye and be of ryght good chere,
> Go eche day onward on thy pylgrymage,
> Thynke howe short tyme thou hast abyden here.[89]

So Lydgate's devotional poetry defines the true home and God's own "herytage" in this chapel founded for the contemplation and the prayers of Clopton kin. In language equally uncompromising about the transitory nature of human worldly bonds and the worldly pilgrimage, John Clopton's own will and testament proclaims the same sermon:

> In Dei nomine Amen, by whome all kinges reyne, and all princes have dominacion, and every creatoure leveth, I John Clopton, knowing my selfe mortall, remembring also and daily havyng in mynde the uncerteyne of this transitory liffe, and that dethe is certeyne to me and to all mankynde, and the houre of it is moost uncerteyne, willing therfore that dethe commyth sodenly as a thife fynde me not unpurveied to die, therfore besheeling [*sic*] the Fader, the Sone, and the Holy Gost, of whom Allmyghty wisdome and grace procedith, at this tyme to geve me grace and wisdome to make my testament to the pleasure of God, and my discharge of the goodes of fourtune that he hathe geven me, and that it may take suche effecte to my merytte, that when I departe oute of this present pilgremage and the unstabull liffe, that I may come to the hevenly blisse where I may geve laude, honour, worship, and praysing to my Maker and Redemer impertetuite.[90]

As both Lydgate's and Clopton's testaments reveal, the Last Will and Testament is not so much final legal document as test of the Christian life, a measure of how well the testator can use the "goods of Fortune"—and an instructive and intimate spiritual text, revealing the drama of the interior will as well as providing for volitional public and social acts of charity.

Lydgate's verse *Testament* is a text negotiating between genuine autobiography and familiar echo of literary and biblical precedent and expectation. (We are not surprised, for example, to find there Lydgate's original childhood sin, stealing apples and grapes from other men's gardens, singled out for condemnation any more than its famous confessional prototype, the symbolic pear-stealing episode, in St. Augustine's *Confessions*.[91]) But so, too, is the legal testament of John Clopton, East Anglian layman, a text that defines the symbolic meaning of the self, a revelatory document that also has its negotiations to make between social expectation and convention and the interior human will.

The old man, John Clopton, in writing his will also writes his autobiography. Although John Clopton was John Baret's friend, kinsman, and neighbor, and although both were wealthy Suffolk clothiers, their wills reveal with the clarity of photographic portraits two very distinct human beings. John Baret, dying without progeny and with only one token bequest to his wife, is far more concerned with his own life's memory than with the kin he leaves behind him in the world.[92] Although Baret is careful to arrange for comfortable living quarters for a favorite niece, and although he names his nephew Jeffrey his heir (and carefully provides for several other contingency heirs), his will is otherwise almost entirely preoccupied with his parish church and chantry bequests, with the details of his elaborate funeral, and with personal remembrances to the dozens of people who are charged with remembering his death-day and praying for his soul. John Clopton, too, was a generous church patron (indeed his gifts to Holy Trinity in Long Melford exceeded Baret's extravagant patronage to St. Mary's in Bury St. Edmunds), but Clopton emerges in his will, despite its talk of life's transitory pilgrimage, as a man who seemed to view himself foremost as patriarch of a large, powerful, extended family, whose elaborate networks of relationships by birth, marriage, and friendship he cultivated and memorialized in his will—even as he had memorialized them in inscriptions and stained-glass portraits in Holy Trinity church.

John Clopton's will leaves his youngest daughter a "greate goblete" which his father-in-law ("my fader Darce") had given her mother; a former son-in-law and his second wife are left a "blak notte of silver and gilt."[93] In a complicated world of multiple marriages and of frequent intermarriage that made family lines tangled, close, and sometimes stormy, Clopton makes his intricate will and seemingly leaves no family tie or family friend unremembered. And although Clopton remembers with a businessman's precision, remembrance for him is always more than a coin in a purse. The whole Clopton will proclaims an extraordinary concern with family heirlooms, with material objects hallowed by age, sanctity, or simple family association, that John Clopton bestows and that he commands be handed down in the "blode of Clopton." Such is the stipulation, for example, that accompanies Clopton's bequest of his "owche [brooch], with the iii perlis and iii stones" to his daughter-in-law; she must leave it in turn to his grandson Fraunces "or to some issue male of my sonne Willyams, so that it may contynewe in the blode of Cloptons."[94]

Perhaps the most precious of all Clopton's bequests, a "relik of the peler of oure Lorde," entrusted to his oldest son and heir, William, is only given on the condition that he "leve it alwey in the blode."[95] But, unless the Clopton family owned more than one relic of "the Pillar that our Saviour Christ was bound to," Clopton's son, in fact, presented the relic to Long Melford church, for it appears in the 1529 inventory of the church's possessions.[96] Indeed, at first glance, John Clopton's son, who became Sir William Clopton, seems a more practical and pragmatic, certainly a less pious, man than his father. William bequeathed to his own son John (the Clopton family heirs were alternately named William and John for five generations) "the stuffe of my chapell" in the same breath with a bequest of his kitchen implements,[97] and William paid off his own will-executors with simple and efficient bequests of twenty shillings instead of with religious relics.[98] But even William gave a suit of vestments to Long Melford church, only on the condition that it be provided to his male heirs at "suche tyme as schall fortune to be any marige at my saide place."[99] And, as we have already seen in chapter 3, William Clopton left an heirloom cross to his own heir with the most intriguing evidence of all of the Clopton respect for the kinship rites of birth and marriage:

> Item, I gyve unto the aboue writen John Clopton my soone, my crosse of gold which I where dayly abowtte my necke after the deasse [sic] of my wyffe; and after the decesse of this same John Clopton my sonne, I wil this same crosse schall remane unto the heyres males of the body of this same John Clopton lawfully begoten . . . upon the condicion that they and every of them dow lenne this same crosse unto women of honeste being with child the tyme of ther laboure and immediately to be surely delivered unto howrs ayen.[100]

It was presumably similarly strong feelings for the power and sanctity of family possessions that led one of the Cloptons, probably John Clopton's great-grandson William (d. 1562), to buy back the alabaster panels that had been given to St. Anne's altar in Long Melford church by Clopton ancestors. It was a "Mr. Clopton," according to the Long Melford churchwardens' accounts, who in 1547–48, when Holy Trinity was being stripped of its images, bought several alabaster tablets including "a lytell tabyll in Sent Annys Chappell and all the gere therin."[101] And it may well have been this same Mr. Clopton who hid the small alabaster panel of Mary in childbed, adored by the Magi, under the floor of the Holy Trinity chancel, where it lay in secret until it was found by workmen repairing the church in the eighteenth century.[102] John Clopton's great-grandson also bought at the Long Melford Reformation sale "a Sent Nycholas' cote and woode [coat and hood] greatly eatyn wyth moth" for three shillings and four pence[103]; we cannot know whether this purchase of a moth-eaten old coat was motivated by affection for the old boy-bishop festivities or because it was his ancestor who had supplied the costume.

We do know from John Clopton's will that he provided both costumes and stage set for at least one important event in the devotional drama of his parish—the yearly ritual of Christ's Resurrection, enacted at the Easter sepulchre: "Also I will that suche clothes of velvet, with all maner braunches, flowres, and all maner oder stuff that I have set abowte the sepulture at Ester . . . as well the grene as the red, I yefe and bequeth it alwaye to the same use of the sepulture."[104] John Clopton could not know that within fifty years of his death the changed religious climate would make the symbolic "burial" of host and crucifix and its joyful Resurrection *elevatio* on Easter morning a forbidden part of the papist past. Except for the brief return to Catholicism under Mary Tudor in 1555–56, when the churchwardens' accounts once more list payments for the sepulchre watch and for making timber frames for the sepulchre canopy cloths,[105] the Long Melford Easter sepulchre ritual, which John Clopton had deemed important enough to provide for formally in his last will and testament, passed into history. The liturgical drama of the Long Melford Easter sepulchre now survives only in the text of the fond and wistful reminiscence of Roger Martyn, a Long Melford recusant and former churchwarden whose mid-sixteenth-century account, "The State of Melford Churche and of Our Ladie's Chappel at the Easte End, as I, Roger Martin, Did Know It," provides an eyewitness account of a liturgical Palm Sunday procession with a boy prophet singing atop the north turret (fig. 4.8)—and of the appearance of the Clopton Easter sepulchre in the years just before the Reformation:

> In the Quire was a fair painted frame of Timber [the *tenebrae herse*], to be set up about Maundy Thursday, with holes for a number of fair tapers to stand in before the Sepulchre, and to be lighted at Service time. Sometimes it was set overthwart the

Quire before the Altar. The Sepulchre being always placed and finally [*sic*] garnished at the North End of the High Altar, between that and Mr. Clopton's little Chappel there, in a vacant place of the wall, I think upon a tomb of one of his ancestors: the said frame with the tapers to be set up, all along by Mr. Clopton's Ile, with a door made to go out of the Rood loft into it.[106]

As both the Martin reminiscence and John Clopton's will tell us, this Easter sepulchre was also John Clopton's tomb. The "sepulture at Ester, over my grave," is the way old John Clopton referred to it in his will, and this marble tomb still survives today, set in the recess built for it in the wall opening between the Clopton chantry and the chancel of the church (fig. 4.9). Very faded mourner portraits of John Clopton's wife and children are painted around the sepulchre, and on the underside of the vault arching above the tomb, visible only to someone kneeling before the sepulchre, is a fairly well-preserved fifteenth-century painting of Christ's Resurrection (fig. 4.10). In the Clopton arch painting, Christ steps forth from his tomb bearing a Cross and a stave of victory; a white cloak is wrapped about his bleeding body and overhead an unfurled banner proclaims, "omni qui vivit et credit in me non morietur in aeternum"—"All who live and believe in me will not die eternally."

If we no longer have an extant fifteenth-century scaffold stage or a surviving English pageant wagon, we do have in the Long Melford sepulchre and its painting another kind of stage set, no less important to its witnesses and participants, and in John Clopton's will we have the record of a man who was not only an influential East Anglian patron, but who was in a somewhat extended sense both director and player in the devotional theater of his Suffolk village. For it was the bones of John Clopton, family and parish patriarch, as much as the reserved host wrapped in its symbolic gravecloth, that enacted the death of Christ upon the Easter sepulchre at Long Melford. Each year, until Reformation halted the play, John Clopton was "buried" and was "resurrected" again in the hopeful Christian drama that was both personal and communal expectation. That liturgical ceremony was the culminating act of a kind of theater recreated in stone, in image, and in verse on the devotional stage that John Clopton's cloth fortune bought, a devotional theater that ranged from the rueful confession of sin in Lydgate's *Testament,* to the saving image of the crucified Saviour, and to the triumph of Resurrection. And omnipresent as main characters were those mothers of mercy who were invoked for intercession and begged for grace—St. Anne listening at her altar, the Virgin Mary crowned and enshrined in the chapel that bore her name. The plot is sin,

FIGURE 4.8. In pre-Reformation Palm Sunday processions, a choir boy costumed to represent a prophet sang from the top of this fifteenth-century brick turret on the north side of Long Melford church. After the congregation processed around the churchyard to accompany the Sacrament to the south porch and into the church, the boy prophet entered the church through a tower staircase that led to the rood loft. (See David Dymond and Clive Paine, *The Spoil of Melford Church: The Reformation in a Suffolk Parish* (Ipswich: Salient Press, 1989], pp. 5–6.) (Photo by G. M. Gibson).

FIGURE 4.9. The Clopton chantry and (on the left) John Clopton's tomb, built into the arch between the chantry and the chancel of Long Melford church to function as the parish Easter sepulchre (Photo by G. M. Gibson).

FIGURE 4.10. *The Resurrection of Christ,* a painting under the arch of the Clopton tomb in Holy Trinity, Long Melford (Photo by G. M. Gibson).

redemption, restoration, and a promise spelled out upon a painted banner. The life—and the death—of John Clopton of Long Melford does not just reveal the devotional drama's preoccupations, it reveals the play.

Anne Harling of East Harling: Dame Anne's Children

Like John Clopton and like John Baret, Anne Harling of East Harling, Norfolk, was an important East Anglian patron who left a compelling self-portrait in her last will and testament. And like theirs, her own life's devotional theater both enriches and challenges our understanding of East Anglian drama. Anne Harling was the only child of Sir Robert Harling, a Norfolk knight who died in battle in France in 1435, and of Jane Gonville, sole heiress of the eminent Gonville family (who had endowed Gonville College, Cambridge). Anne Harling was orphaned at the age of nine, had her wardship sold to the highest bidder (Sir John Fastolf, her father's uncle by marriage), and was married off at sixteen to Sir William Chamberlain, a hero of the French wars who was at least fifteen years her senior. As heiress of both the Harlings and the Gonvilles, however, Anne Harling inherited both immense wealth and power. She owned and supervised nineteen manors and five advowsons in Norfolk and a number of estates in Suffolk and Essex, which made her a political as well as economic force in both of those counties.[107] She always retained her own Harling coat of arms.[108]

Anne Harling was a woman exceptional in her own time, and she would be exceptional in ours—for her great wealth and influence, but also for her learning and her piety. She was a literate and learned member of the country aristocracy, a member of the bookish East Anglian circle presided over by Alice Chaucer, Duchess of Suffolk (and granddaughter of Geoffrey Chaucer).[109] John Paston II's inventory of English books mentions that Dame Wingfield (née Harling) had borrowed his *Book of Troilus*[110]; her own list of books, in her will, names books both in French and in English, as well as "a Premer [lay mass book] whiche Kynge Edward gauffe me" (perhaps when her second husband, Sir Robert Wingfield (d. 1480) was controller of the household to Edward IV).[111] Her name emerges in a letter from William Paston in 1487 describing King Henry VII's plans for a royal progress to Norwich, which would take him to Ipswich, Bury St. Edmunds and "þan to Dame Anne Wyngfeldys."[112] The Pastons had some special interest in this visit since years before an unsuccessful effort had been made to marry her to one of the more ambitious Paston sons.[113] Anne Harling was, however, way out of the Pastons' league. She married three great lords, each one more notable than the one

In Search of East Anglian Devotional Theater

before; she was three times widowed. She died in 1499, shortly after her last husband, Lord Scrope of Bolton, Yorkshire.[114]

These are the external facts of the life of Anne Harling. But if we wish to know something of the woman behind these facts we must look at the extraordinary text, written August 28, 1498, that is her last will and testament. Anne Harling, now Lady Scrope, was in 1498 seventy-two years old; her third husband had died twenty days before, and she was herself in failing health. Since her will emphasizes that she signed and sealed it with her own hand,[115] but does not say that she wrote the will herself (as some fifteenth-century lay wills do), we should probably assume that the text of the will was dictated rather than drafted by her. And yet that will is a long, vigorous, and remarkably intimate document, full of personal asides and detailed lists of keepsakes, possessions, and household goods to be given to friends and goddaughters and daughters of relatives of her three marriages (many of whom were her namesakes, in testimony as much to the respect accorded this old woman as to the strength of the St. Anne cult in fifteenth-century East Anglia).

And through this all, the voice of Anne Harling of Harling Manor emerges with strength and clarity. Not unlike the great merchants Baret and Clopton, Lady Anne seems to have been both indomitable and sentimental, intensely religious and rigorously practical. Her will bequeaths a symbolic gold heart centered with a diamond to the "roode of Northdor" (probably a crucifix in the Harling chantry, which was built to the north side of the chancel of East Harling church and which had a private, north-door entrance).[116] Anne Harling carefully arranges in her will for her own gold and crimson rosary to be divided into four equal strands and bestowed at her death to four great pilgrimage shrines—Our Lady of Walsingham, Our Lady of Pity at Ipswich, St. Edmund of Bury, and St. Thomas of Canterbury.[117] These gifts, and especially the tactful division of her rosary beads, make an eloquent statement about her relationship in life and in anticipation of death to these holy places of East England and to their spiritual intercessors.

Lady Anne's charitable bequests include gifts to numerous monastic foundations, including both old Benedictine houses and houses of preaching Franciscan friars and Dominicans. All of these are local Norfolk and Suffolk houses, except for the influential center of new spirituality at Syon, near London, an important convent of Brigittine nuns founded by Henry V.[118] Anne Harling's will notes that at five of these monasteries, including the royal convent of Syon, she is a lay sister.[119] Other East Anglian wills repeat such a pattern of lay-confraternity affiliation with local monastic houses, and, as we have seen, they also frequently mention Syon, which was the major center in England for the dissemination of the spiritual style of St. Bridget of Sweden and other North European mystics. John Clopton's will mentions the "graunte of broderhodde" that entitled him to funeral dirges and masses at the Suffolk monastic houses at Sudbury, Clare, and Babwell, but also at the Brigittine convent of Syon ("I will that the house of Sion have xiii s. iii d. and that they sey dirige and a masse for me according to theire graunte, consideryng that I am a broder of the place"[120]); the pious widow Dame Margaret Spurdaunce, who figures prominently in John Baret's will, actually owned an English translation of St. Bridget's mystical revelations.[121] Margery Kempe's pilgrimage to Syon, like many other aspects of her much maligned *Book,* is thus probably far more characteristic of fifteenth-century East Anglian devotional life than has usually been acknowledged. Indeed, the emotionally-charged lay spirituality of the late Middle Ages represented not only an extension to the laity of religious meditational practices and spiritual attitudes once deemed the monopoly of the cloistered elite, but, in East Anglia at least, an actual alliance between the noble and merchant lay classes and the monasteries. Certainly in noble and rural life as well as in town life in East Anglia, the hybrid spirituality signaled by lay sisterhood and brotherhood memberships in monastic houses is one of the most distinguishing characteristics of the age.

Just as Anne Harling's will affirms her social relationships and family ties, so it affirms those numerous monastic alliances and sisterhoods. Both the social and the institutional relationships are part of important and explicit contracts. Anne Harling gives her gifts in death as she had given her patronage and friendship in life, in full expectation of an equal exchange in spiritual commodities. That mutual responsibility is bluntly spelled out in the close of her will: "I requyre myn ex[ecutors] to desire all suche personys as I have in this my testament geven enything, that they of their charity pray to Almighty God for my sowle and for myne auncestres' sowles."[122]

If the merchandising metaphor is an operative one for understanding the social contracts affirmed in this text, so too is the maternal metaphor. Despite the difference of class and gender, Anne Harling, much like the head of the Clopton clan, uses her last will and testament as an occasion to assert the importance of family relationships and political ties. The main difference between Anne Harling's matriarchy and John Clopton's patriarchy is that in Anne Harling's case, local politics more often was also national politics, and her self-conscious parental role was, as we shall see, more symbolic than real. But certainly it is as matriarch that Anne defines herself and her relationship to those whose names appear in her will. She appoints her second husband's nephew, Robert Wingfield, her chief executor, and at the same time deftly reminds him of his filial duty: "I name

In Search of East Anglian Devotional Theater

. . . my neveu Robert Wyngefeld esquyr, which I have brought up of a childe sythen he was iii yeres of age."[123] The line implies a reciprocal contract, filial duty owed for maternal love and care.

Despite the current fashion among social historians to proclaim maternal affection a luxury of the post-industrial age (which does not have to steel itself against appallingly high infant mortality rates),[124] nothing that I know about the audience for medieval drama nor about the plays themselves would seem to support this thesis. It is hard to imagine any text more wrenchingly manipulative of the sentimental feelings of parents for young children than the Brome *Play of Abraham and Isaac,* a touching play for the extended family of an East Anglian manor and its tenants, and a play whose concluding "Doctor's" speech substitutes a moral lesson about enduring human grief for the theological typology of the doctors in the Chester version:

> And thys women that wepe so sorowfully
> Whan that hyr chyldryn dey them froo,
> As nater woll, and kynd;
> Yt ys but folly, I may wyll awooe . . .
> . . . groche not aʒens owre Lord God,
> In welthe or woo, wether that he ʒow send,
> Thow ʒe be neuer so hard bestad,
> For whan he wyll, he may yt amend.[125]

It was women and such maternal feelings for their children, charged the author of *Pierce the Ploughman's Crede,* that the mystery plays sought "to lyken" with their episodes of midwives and Mary's lullabies.[126] While it is true that the loving attention to the childhood of Mary in the N-Town cycle was a subject of lay devotional preoccupation for both men and women in the late Middle Ages, it is significant, I think, that at least one East Anglian play, the Purification sequence of the Digby "Killing of the Children" violates the English medieval custom of all-male performers, with a cast of Virgins "as many as a man wylle" who file by the altar with lighted candles in reenactment of the womanly rite of postpartum churching, as well as of parish Candlemas ritual. Indeed, the old priest Simeon in that play is all but overshadowed by his wife, "Anne Prophetissa," who speaks the final words of the play and who leads the Virgins in a concluding dance.[127] Although Anne Harling surely danced neither the role of Candlemas Virgin nor the women's dance in *Wisdom* that Donald Baker has called "a dancing brothel,"[128] she almost certainly did play a role in East Anglian theater as patroness of theater performed in her own parish of East Harling.

Figure 4.11 shows Anne Harling's church, the parish church of St. Peter

FIGURE 4.11. The parish church of St. Peter and St. Paul, East Harling, Norfolk (Photo by G. M. Gibson).

and St. Paul at East Harling, Norfolk. The perpendicular-style steeple was erected and much of the church rebuilt in 1449 through the patronage of Anne and her first husband, Sir William Chamberlain, probably as a thanks-offering for his safe return from the French wars.[129] Three years later, in 1452, the East Harling churchwarden's accounts list expenses paid for the "original of an Interlude, played at the Church gate."[130] There were four other payments for drama in East Harling in the 1450s and 1460s—expenses for bread and ale when Lopham game and Garblesham game came to town in 1457, and in 1463 and 1467, when expenses were listed for the players of Kenningale, for Kenningale game and for Garblesham game.[131] It seems highly likely that Anne Harling, as heiress of Harling Manor and patroness of East Harling Church in these years, would have seen the play at the church gate; it is also likely that she was a patroness of the interlude.

If we can only argue from probability for Anne Harling's connections with the East Harling plays, we do have documented evidence of her crucial role in directing other kinds of images in the devotional life of her parish.[132] For it was Anne Harling who presented East Harling church with the stained-glass windows whose twenty surviving panels are today considered among the greatest monuments of English fifteenth-century glass painting.[133] These windows, discovered in the eighteenth century in the attic of East Harling manor house,[134] closely resemble the east windows of St. Peter Mancroft in Norwich in style and iconography and like those windows were products of the Norwich glass workshops.[135] The subject of Anne Harling's windows is the Joys and Sorrows of the Virgin Mary. What is immediately noticeable about them is the inclusion of small domestic details that celebrate, as do Margery Kempe's disarming visions, the touching human joys of the Incarnation—especially those joys seemingly created for a womanly eye. In the scene of the Visitation, for example, the Virgin Mary and her cousin St. Elizabeth are sweet-faced, and visibly expectant, mothers; St. Elizabeth even loosens her cape to reveal one of the rare medieval representations of a maternity dress, loosely laced over her swollen womb (fig. 4.12). Two prayerful midwives solicitously attend Mary and the Christ Child in the Nativity and in the scene of the Adoration of the Shepherds, prominently in the left foreground the artist has provided a little porringer and spoon for the Christ Child's gruel (fig. 4.13).

Such affectionate lingering over the maternity of Mary renders all the more poignant Christ's mother's despairing swoon in the scene of the Crucifixion and in the sorrowful Deposition. Indeed, these glass paintings at Anne Harling's church are as self-consciously manipulative of emotional response as the Lydgate lyrics in John Clopton's chantry. The East Harling

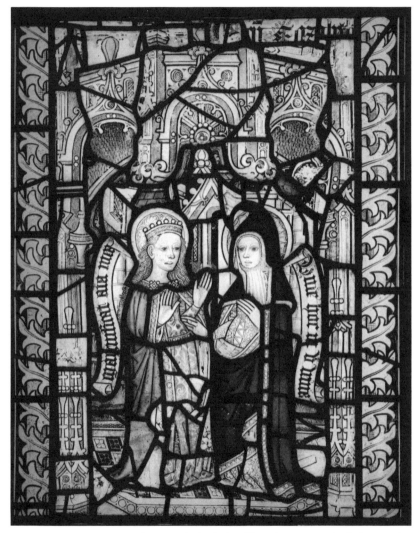

FIGURE 4.12. *The Visitation of Mary and Elizabeth,* a fifteenth-century stained-glass window in East Harling church (Royal Commission on the Historical Monuments of England).

images are touching monuments to the late medieval devotional piety that celebrated Christ's life by reminding viewers of their own; the Virgin's joys and her sorrows were those her suppliants, too, had known. And it is significant that these devotional Christian images are also talismanic images, pictures whose functions of blessing and safeguarding the human rites of conception and childbirth are part of their fullest meaning. Anne

In Search of East Anglian Devotional Theater

FIGURE 4.13. *Adoration of the Shepherds,* a fifteenth-century stained-glass window in East Harling church (Royal Commission on the Historical Monuments of England).

Harling's windows remind us again that we must not forget how difficult and dangerous—and also how essential—childbearing was to a fifteenth-century woman. And here we return to Anne Harling's will, for what Anne Harling's somewhat plaintive filial reminder to her nephew really underscores is that the raising of one of her second husband's nephews from the age of three was the closest Anne Harling ever approached motherhood. It is painful and clear that what this wealthy and powerful heiress,

FIGURE 4.14. A stained-glass portrait of Anne Harling's second husband, Sir Robert Wingfield, in East Harling church. A companion portrait of Anne Harling was reported by the
antiquary Francis Blomefield to be in East Harling church, in his *Essay towards a Topographical
History of the County of Norfolk* (1805–10), but is now lost or destroyed (Royal Commission
on the Historical Monuments of England).

this eminent lady who counted a king among her houseguests, viewed as both her dynastic and her personal tragedy was her childlessness. The simple fact that Anne Harling, heiress of the Gonvilles and the Harlings, had no child gives another and deeply intimate level of poignance to those wrenching images of the Joys and Sorrows of Mary that she commissioned for East Harling church. When we look at the stained-glass paintings of St. Elizabeth, miraculously fruitful in her old age, and of Mary's loving attentions to her newborn son—or when we read the play performed at some nearby N-Town of St. Anne, who prays that her old husband Joachim be spared the pain and humiliation of her barrenness—we should also hear the very real prayers of a woman like Anne Harling. And we should think of these visual and dramatic images as straddling a very narrow line between religious icon and reassuring talisman.

Anne Harling's first husband, Sir William Chamberlain, had died in 1462 after exploits in the French wars praised by Holinshed.[136] Anne was then thirty-six years old. It does not take much imagination to know the hopes, at her age, fading hopes, that attended her next marriage to Sir Robert Wingfield, controller of the household to Edward IV (fig. 4.14).[137] It was during this marriage to Robert Wingfield that Anne gave the Joys and Sorrows windows to East Harling church, in an act of largesse and piety, but also, I feel sure, of supplication. It was also about this same time, in the 1460s, that Anne Harling founded a chantry chapel of St. Anne, her patron saint and name saint, in the north aisle of East Harling church.[138] Anne Harling and her chantry priest would have spent hundreds of hours in that chapel praying to the old and barren saint who had miraculously conceived a child, and many of those prayers must have been for an heir. But there was no heir. Sir Robert Wingfield died in 1480, and at his death Anne endowed two chantry priests at Rushworth College to sing for the good of her soul and the souls of her parents and her two dead husbands.[139] In 1490, before Anne Harling had taken her third husband, the husband of her old age, Lord Scrope of Bolton, she gave another endowment to Rushworth College.

Anne Harling's own copy of the Rushworth charter endowment is today in the muniment room of Gonville College, Cambridge. That charter begins with a touching preamble in which Anne Harling describes herself as a widow, growing old, childless, and with no hope of children. It is impossible not to hear in this five-hundred-year-old document a human voice. She has not even, that voice explains, any living kinsmen "within three degrees." So it is, she says, that through her love for the college that her ancestors had founded (she is speaking here of Rushworth, not of Gonville) "the woman to whom God had denied the blessing of children will still leave children of her own who shall call her blessed."[140] She deeds the income from three of her estates for the establishment and maintenance of a free grammar school at Rushworth for thirteen children of the diocese of Norwich, five of whom, she says, are to be poor children who shall be fed and clothed and raised within the college itself. Those five little ones, she says, are to be known as "Dame Annys Childeryn."[141]

In 1501, after Anne Harling's death, her will executors gave a further bequest for the maintenance of two "honest priests" to teach the grammar school and increased the number of scholarships for poor children from five to seven.[142] Although they were overriding the significance of the original numerology (five was the number of the Virgin's Joys and of her Sorrows), those executors nonetheless reaffirmed the essential symbolic meaning of Anne Harling's earlier endowment: These poor children were to be maintained in the college until they were eighteen years of age, in perpetuity, and were to be called, the charter stipulates, "Dame Annys Childeryn."[143]

That the Reformation would make of this "in perpetuity" a little more than thirty years was the final irony of the life of Anne Harling. Yet it is that life and the lives of other men and women like her that we should know, if we would fully know the pageants that played by the streets and churchgates and marketplaces of English towns and parishes—played and, like the men and women who watched them, prayed for God's grace, and then passed on.

Chapter Five
Monastic Theater

It was in Benedictine monastery churches that Christian drama was born. Because those same Benedictine monasteries were also the main repositories of classical culture, it is difficult to know whether Benedictine monasteries were mother or midwife to the Latin liturgical drama; whether they self-consciously transformed the ideas of drama they found in play manuscripts of Plautus and Terence (the christianized Terence plays of Hroswitha are enough to make us wonder)[1]; or whether Christian drama reemerged from ritual as theater did in its most ancient Greek beginnings. What we do know is that the European monastic community created and spread Latin church drama and that a manuscript like the *Fleury Playbook* from St. Benoit-sur-Loire records a dramatic tradition of extraordinary scope and variety. The surviving play manuscripts themselves are nearly our only source of information about medieval Benedictinism and liturgical drama. We do not know if there was usually an audience or even frequently an audience. We cannot know if the "people" who were to join in the triumphant vernacular affirmation at the close of the twelfth-century *Visitatio Sepulchri* from St. Lambrecht were devout laymen from the village or special guests or perhaps parents of novices.[2] Certainly it is striking how closely the liturgical dramatic tradition seems to be tied to the child-monk, to the instruction of the young. There is the boy-bishop ceremony, the multiplicity of St. Nicholas plays celebrating the saint's genial patronage of clerks and school boys, the Beauvais *Danielis Ludus,* in which the insistent youth of Daniel is pitted against the aged and pagan incomprehension of King Belshazzar and his soothsayers.[3] Novices, pious spectators, fond parents—whoever chanted that chorus of lay affirmation at St. Lambrecht, it was probably a shout not unlike the revival meeting chant "Jesus, Jesus, Jesus" that a stage direction demands from the lay audience in the vernacular East Anglian play *Mary Magdalen.*[4]

It is one of those curious and unconsidered stereotypes of our patchwork history of early drama that we acknowledge that Christian drama began in monastic churches, assume that the service books of Benedictine churches spread dramatic elaborations of the liturgical ritual, and yet reject the notion of monastic involvement in medieval vernacular drama. To be sure, even among the medieval secular clergy there were objections to drama in the Middle Ages[5]; latent Puritanism existed in English culture long before it had a name. But there is also evidence that as lay and monastic piety increasingly overlapped in late medieval culture, the dividing lines between parish and monastic devotional spectacle grew ever more blurred.

The Benedictine abbey of Bury St. Edmunds, Suffolk (fig. 5.1), is a case in point. The monastery of Bury, housing the shrine of the ancient East Anglian king and martyr Edmund, was one of the great cultural centers of England for over five hundred years. The most prolific writer of the fifteenth century, the Bury monk John Lydgate, was virtual poet laureate for the Lancastrian dynasty; he wrote mummings for the London streets as well as devotional and Chaucerian verse for court and local East Anglian patrons. Other learned Benedictine monks copied manuscripts in Bury's famous scriptorium, wrote sermons and saints' lives, supervised their vast estates, quarreled with the grasping merchants and shopkeepers of their town, socialized with visiting prelates and princes, watched the pilgrims milling before the golden miracle-working tomb of St. Edmund (fig. 5.2), and also, I believe, helped create one of the most diverse and important English dramatic traditions of the fifteenth century, a tradition that now lies buried in a rubble of clues and riddles.

We might begin with the clues in the complete text of the morality play *Wisdom,* a fifteenth-century ecclesiastical masque in the East Anglian Macro plays manuscript, now in the Folger Library in Washington.[6] On folio 121 of that manuscript, at the end of *Wisdom,* there is a single Latin inscription: "O liber si quis cui constas forte queretur / hynghamque monacho dices super omnia consto" ("O book, if anyone shall perhaps ask to whom you belong, you will say, I belong above everything to Hyngham, a monk").[7] The surname "Hyngham" designates simply the monk's origin in the southwest Norfolk village of Hingham (cf. John Lydgate, from the village of Lidgate, Suffolk), a village whose gameplace just to the west of the parish church is even today named "The Fairland." If the gameplace topography of Hingham village is suggestive, even more so is the connection between the village and the Morley family, lords of Hingham manor. The *Paston Letters* provide evidence of the Morley family's patronage of drama in the fifteenth century[8] and the splendid red stone Easter sepulchre (fig. 5.3) built in Hingham church as monument to Thomas, Lord Morley (d. 1435), attests to the Morley interest in devotional spectacle.[9] Given the resonance of the name Hyngham, any of the half-dozen or so Monk Hynghams known to have lived in East Anglia in the second half of the fifteenth century might be a suitable candidate for the Hyngham of the

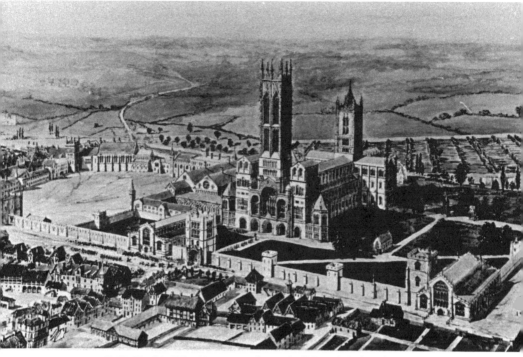

FIGURE 5.1. W. K. Hardy's "The Monastery of Bury St. Edmunds before the Dissolution, conjectural restoration, chiefly from existing remains" (1883) gives a useful sense of the immense scale of the now-destroyed abbey church and of the looming presence of the abbey in the borough of St. Edmund. The west door of the parish church of St. James juts out from the abbey wall adjacent to the main entrance to the great pilgrimage church of St. Edmund; the church of St. Mary of the Assumption is seen at the far right, at the southeast corner of the abbey precinct (Jarman Collection: with permission of O. G. Jarman and the St. Edmundsbury Borough Council).

FIGURE 5.2. A fifteenth-century illumination showing John Lydgate praying before the shrine of St. Edmund, from Lydgate's *Life of St. Edmund* (BL MS. Harley 2278, fol. 9) (By permission of the British Library).

FIGURE 5.3. The Morley Tomb and Easter sepulchre, the church of St. Andrew, Hingham, Norfolk (Royal Commission on the Historical Monuments of England).

Macro plays, but the likeliest is, as Donald Baker and John Murphy argued in 1967 in an important article in *Research Opportunities in Renaissance Drama,* Richard Hyngham, abbot of Bury St. Edmunds.[10]

What is very significant, however, is that the same monastic ownership inscription appears in the Macro manuscript at the end of the play *Mankind,* the implications of which have apparently been ignored by those who would have had us see *Mankind* as a "play [which] has apparently been carried on the road for one does not know how long by a low-class company of strolling players, players whose appeal was to the uneducated and the vulgar."[11] In fact, *Mankind* is a brilliant and daring comedy of man's ruefully human condition, filled with learned and latinate in-jokes[12] and with scatological language appropriate to its theme of Mercy cleansing what its companion morality play, *Wisdom,* calls the "ordure" of sin.[13] David Bevington's influential *From Mankind to Marlowe* has convinced many scholars to see the money-collecting speech in *Mankind* as the first evidence of English professional theater.[14] But I suspect the money-gathering of New Guise—"For a man wyth a hede þat ys of grett omnipotens"—is acknowledgment not of a professional traveling troupe, but of the real fundraising motive behind the play's performance—to raise money for Christ's church.[15] New Guise's solicitation speech is, in fact, a kind of sacral parody of Mercy's introductory speech to the audience:

> O ȝe souerens þat sytt and ȝe brothern þat stonde ryght uppe,
> Pryke not yowr felycytes in thyngys transytorye.
> Beholde not þe erth, but lyfte yowr ey wppe.
> Se how þe hede þe members dayly do magnyfye.
> Who ys þe hede forsoth I xall yow certyfe:
> I mene Owr Sauyowr, þat was lykynnde to a lambe;
> Ande hys sayntys be þe members þat dayly he doth satysfye
> Wyth þe precyose reuer þat runnyth from hys wombe.[16]

Mercy's use of the Pauline metaphor of Christ as the "head" and the members of his church as the "body"[17] is parodied not just in the money-gathering speech but throughout the play in the obscene language of the Vices, who substitute for Mercy's "head" (who is Christ) a "head" which is a penis, emblem of the unruly passions of postlapsarian man. Thus, for example, Nowadays, wounded in the genitals, parodies the cult of Christ's Five Wounds by wailing, "Remember my brokyn hede in þe worschyppe of þe fyve vowellys."[18]

There are general local references in *Mankind* to St. Etheldreda's shrine at Ely and to piping with a "Walsingham whistle," and the Vices are sent out to do harm at a cluster of villages near King's Lynn and Cambridge. But Nought walks on stage wearied from lovemaking with the "comyn tapster [barmaid] of Bury," and he asserts both her proximity and his intent by declaring "ȝyt xall I be þer ageyn to-morn."[19] The barmaid of Bury and the ownership inscription of a Bury monk would seem to argue for a direct link of some kind with the town of Bury—as well as to argue that "monastic" drama could range from the ritual theater of *Wisdom* to a play shattering as many stereotypes about Benedictine monastic theater as the audacious *Mankind*. The daunting facts are that Richard Beadle has recently presented detailed paleographical argument that "Hyngham himself, or someone who wrote very similarly" was the scribe as well as the collector of both *Wisdom* and *Mankind*[20] and that the marginal staging marks in the Macro manuscript show it to have been a working text for performance.[21]

There can be no doubt that the Macro manuscript itself has links with Bury St. Edmunds. There is the explicit evidence, first of all, of another inscription on folio 105; this is in a later, perhaps early sixteenth-century, hand, and begins "In the name of God amen I Rychard Cake of Bury."[22] The second manuscript link to Bury lies in the evidence or quite remarkable coincidence that the earliest recorded owners of the two medieval manuscripts that contain texts of *Wisdom* were both natives of Bury St. Edmunds. The full *Wisdom* text in the Macro plays first surfaced in the library of the Reverend Cox Macro, an eighteenth-century collector who was not only born in Bury St. Edmunds but whose family included some of Bury's most eminent citizens. Both Macro's grandfather and father had been aldermen of the town, and his father Thomas, a wealthy grocer, had built the elegant Cupola House that is still a Bury landmark.[23] Cox Macro is known to have owned a number of manuscripts that had come from the monastery of Bury St. Edmunds, including the great register of the abbey kept by Lydgate's abbot, William Curteys, in the 1430s and 1440s[24]; it seems very possible that the monastery was the provenance of "Monk Hyngham's" plays as well. A closely related but incomplete text of *Wisdom* appears in the Digby plays manuscript, now Bodleian MS. 133, an early sixteenth-century manuscript that belonged to an alchemist, physician, and book collector named Myles Blomefylde, who was born in 1525, also in Bury St. Edmunds, and who was probably related to William Blomfild, an alchemist and dissenting preacher who had been a monk at the abbey of St. Edmunds before the Dissolution.[25] It would appear, in other words, that in Monk Hyngham, in Richard Cake, in Myles Blomefylde, and in Cox Macro we have evidence for drama manuscripts containing the plays *Wisdom* and *Mankind* being at Bury St. Edmunds in the fifteenth, sixteenth, and eighteenth centuries.[26] Bound with Monk Hyngham's plays in the Macro manuscript is also the early fifteenth-century morality play *The Castle of Perseverance*. That play may too have come to Macro from a Bury collector, especially if the "John Adams" who inscribed his name in a sixteenth-century hand on folio 158 verso of the play is the same "Adames of Bury" who presented a Christmas "interlude" in 1572 at Hengrave Hall

FIGURE 5.4. Hengrave Hall, near Bury St. Edmunds, built in the early sixteenth century by Sir Thomas Kytson, a London merchant. A stunning series of stained-glass windows representing Creation, the Life of Christ, and the Last Judgment still remains in the chapel; the windows are quite Flemish in style although household accounts of the 1520s and 1530s record payments for the windows to a glazier named Robert Wryght from Bury St. Edmunds (Photo by G. M. Gibson).

(fig. 5.4), the home of the recusant Kytson family, three miles from Bury.[27]

The incestuous relationship between the Macro and Digby manuscripts even suggests that still other plays in those two important drama manuscripts may have had their provenance at Bury St. Edmunds. As Donald Baker has written:

> The fact that *The Killing of the Children* [from the *Digby Plays* manuscript] is largely in the hand of the scribe who wrote the Digby half of *Wisdom* would argue that, if the Digby *Wisdom* had its origin in Bury, then so probably had *The Killing of the Children*. Some strength is provided for this slender hypothesis by the nature of the Macro manuscript itself. At least two and probably three of the late fifteenth-century plays in it, very similar in language and style to the Digby plays, were at Bury— *Wisdom, Mankind,* and probably *The Castle of Perseverance*. Bury may well have been a centre of dramatic activity with which all the Digby plays could have been associated.[28]

The mounting evidence of Bury provenance for several important late medieval play texts raises, however, a number of thorny questions about the implications of a dramatic center that was also a monastic borough— and especially about the implications of that "Monk Hyngham." We know that manuscripts of the comedies of Plautus and Terence were in the library of the monastery of Bury by the twelfth century, but that does not prove they were performed there—or indeed that they were not. When the monastery school for the sons of the town burgesses became the Bury grammar school after the Dissolution, its statutes specified that all third-form students were to study "the chaster plays of Plautus and Terence" and that a play was to be performed by the school every year at the end of winter term.[29] If the schoolboy ciphers and inscriptions in the Macro plays manuscript are any indication, Bury school may well have inherited medieval play texts as well as a taste for Roman comedy from the old monastic school. But the evidence for actual dramatic performance at Bury St. Edmunds is as fragmented as the ruins of the great abbey itself. We do not even know if it was a play or a ball game or a wrestling match that ended in the famous Christmas Day brawl between the townspeople of Bury and the abbot's servants in 1197; the *Chronicle of Jocelin of Brakelond* tells us merely that Abbot Sampson responded by prohibiting any further "spectacula" in the monastery churchyard.[30] That the abbey continued to encourage "spectacula" somewhere, however, can be inferred from the Rickinghall Fragment, a fragmentary early fourteenth-century speech in Anglo-Norman, and the single stage direction "Tunc dicet nuncio," found on the back of a scrap of parchment that had been recycled to record manorial accounts from the abbey's Rickinghall estate.[31]

The first certain evidence of dramatic activity at Bury comes from a guild certificate return of 1389 that tersely lists among the functions of the Corpus Christi guild of St. James church of Bury that of providing an "interludium" of Corpus Christi.[32] By the fifteenth century there was a procession of Corpus Christi pageants at Bury, but we cannot know from the evidence whether the pageants were actual mystery plays or were elaborate visual spectacles. (Such a distinction, it is important to observe, is entirely a modern scholarly preoccupation and not a medieval one.) The Bury Weaver's guild ordinance of 1477 simply decrees that half of all fines for craft guild violations were to go to the sacristan of the abbey (who had titular control over all town trade) and that the other half was to go toward the expenses of the guild pageant of the Ascension and Pentecost "as yt hath be customed of olde tyme owte of minde yeerly to be had to the wurschepe of God, amongge other payenttes in the processione in the feste of Corpus Xte."[33] Unspecified "pageants" are listed in a Bury guild-hall inventory of 1558, the first year of Queen Elizabeth's reign, but we can only speculate as to whether these were the old carts from Corpus Christi processions.[34]

Perhaps the most tantalizing of all these trace records of dramatic activity at Bury is a single line in an unpublished early sixteenth-century Bury will. A Thomas Pykrell of Bury bequeathed "all my pleying garements to Seynt Edmunds pley in the Frayt[er]" (i.e., the refectory or monk's dining hall) in his will of 1509 and instructed that "Mast[er] Fornham have the keepyng of them."[35] Thomas Pykrell makes no guild bequests in his testament, but a very similar bequest in the will of a wealthy draper named John Benale in 1494 reveals that a lay confraternity of St. John the Baptist was associated with what the Benale will calls the St. Edmund's Night "revell." John Benale, in a will with an impressive list of prestigious executors, left a long black gown and a short gown of damask "to the gylde of Seynt John Baptyst in Bury and also for the revell on Seynt Edmund's nyght."[36] Like Thomas Pykrell, John Benale deemed these playing costumes important enough to designate a caretaker for them—another prominent draper named John Basse[37]—and even specified that "aft[er] the decease of the same John Basse [the costumes] were to remain to the use of [the] aboveseid." It appears from these bequests as though the Bury guild of St. John the Baptist participated in the performance of an annual "revell" on the eve of the abbey feast that commemorated the translation of King Edmund's relics to Bury. Whether "Seynt Edmunds pley" was a musical entertainment, a masque, or a play about the life of the abbey's patron saint, we cannot know. What we do know from the guild certificate returns of 1389 is that the guild of the Nativity of St. John the Baptist met regularly in the abbey church and was a guild of great antiquity; the guild certificates say that it had been founded in "time without memory by men of the town."[38]

Surely, the most important scrap of information provided by these will bequests is the fact that a lay guild's "Seynt Edmunds pley" was performed in the monastic refectory, presumably to spectators who would have included the monks of the abbey. We have no clues at all as to the extent of monastic involvement with the sponsorship or performance of the St. Edmund's night revels, nor can the ruins of Bury abbey provide any sense today as to what kind of theater the Bury "Frayt[er]" would have been. We know only that the refectory was a rectangular stone building just to the north of the abbey cloister and adjacent to the monk's dormitory (fig. 5.5). The antiquarian William of Worcester, who visited Bury St. Edmunds in 1479, recorded the dimensions of the refectory (which he too, called "le ffrayter") as being 90 paces long (about 171 feet) and 40 feet wide.[39] It was, we know, a hall quite big enough for drama of another sort—a special meeting of Parliament was held there in 1446 to try Humphrey, Duke of Gloucester, for treason (during the proceedings, the Duke died suddenly and suspiciously at St. Saviour's Hospital)—and expansive enough for

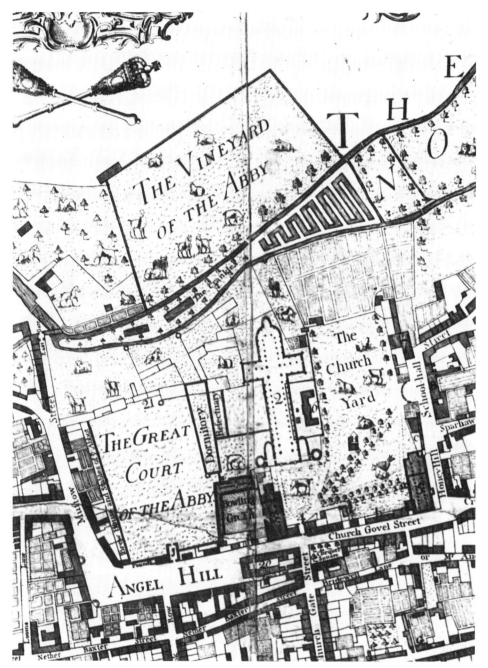

FIGURE 5.5. Detail from Thomas Warren's 1748 map of Bury St. Edmunds, Suffolk, showing the location of the refectory within the ruins of the Abbey of St. Edmund (from a map in the possession of Margaret Statham).

entertaining the monastic guests and their dependents who came to a bustling pilgrimage center, and sometimes, important secular guests as well.[40]

There is thus both manuscript evidence for Bury St. Edmunds as a dramatic center in the late Middle Ages and archival evidence that acknowledges that possibility—even if the scraps of evidence are far less instructive than the archival documentation that has left such a gratifying, if often still ambiguous, record of dramatic activity at York and Chester. In a monastic borough like St. Edmund, the absence of a chartered town government necessarily ruled out the possibility of civic archival documentation or indeed of a civic motive for dramatic celebration. Medieval theater at Bury St. Edmunds would have been the responsibility of religious guilds, and these, it is important to stress, were directly linked to the powerful Benedictine abbey that was temporal as well as spiritual lord of the borough. The parish church of St. James, for example, in which the Corpus Christi guild of the "interludium" worshipped, was not only under the rectorship of the abbey but was actually built within the monastery walls.

Indeed, in the monastic borough of St. Edmund, the abbot of Bury held a virtual monopoly over every conceivable activity within the legal limits of the *banleuca* of St. Edmund—the town and suburbs of the town for a mile in every direction. The abbey controlled the Bury marketplace and town tournaments; it was landlord of all property in the borough and immediate suburbs; it had its own court where it tried legal cases and probated and registered wills; it was responsible for the town jail; it minted coins; and it held the rights to everything from street manure, for the abbey's vast vineyards and fields, to the appointment of parish priests and chaplains to lead the spiritual life of every man, woman, and child in the town.[41] Since the monastery was directly or indirectly involved in every aspect of civic life in the borough, it should hardly be surprising that fifteenth-century life in the abbey of Bury seems to have been marked by interest and involvement in the court politics and cloth trade and harvests of the world outside its walls—or that Monk Hyngham's play *Wisdom* should show such a generous understanding of the seductions of the lay world.[42]

It is not Benedict's *Rule,* then, that should be in our minds as we envision the fifteenth-century abbey and borough of St. Edmund, but the households of great East Anglian magnates like the dukes of Norfolk. Because of his temporal authority within the Liberty of St. Edmund, the abbot of Bury sat in Parliament, bore the title of Lord, and like other provincial lords, maintained a London palace (at "Bevis Marks," originally "Bury Marks," beside Christ Church, Aldgate).[43] The rich and pious Bury cloth merchant John Baret, who as we have seen was a personal friend or patron of the poet John Lydgate, referred to himself in his will of 1463 as "a gentleman of my lord abbot's household" and left alms gifts to all the monks of the abbey as well as a series of personal remembrances to the chief officers of the abbey and to their yeomen, grooms, and pages. Baret's will also bequeathed a purse of silk and gold to "every gentylman of my lord abbotte which be comyng and goyng as officeres and menyal men longyng to the houshold of my felaschippe;" the bequest confirms that the Bury abbot's palace was much like the court of a great lord, a place bustling with civil servants, functionaries, and courtiers.[44] The abbot, prior, and sacrist were the chief officers of what was by the fifteenth century an immensely wealthy household corporation. The monastery walls enclosed forty acres, but the abbey, through a combination of royal grants and favors and pious bequests, had managed to amass by the end of the fifteenth century most of the estates and church tithes in southwest Suffolk.

Unlike other great lords, however, the abbot of Bury claimed a charter of privileges that made the abbey exempt from all other jurisdiction except that of the King and the Pope—a claim that frequently led to friction with the bishop of Norwich and even more frequently to friction in the town of Bury. Bury St. Edmunds was not just an ancient and rich Benedictine abbey, but a powerful political unit that jealously guarded its interests and its monopolies, both spiritual and temporal. Even by the end of the twelfth century the burgesses of Bury St. Edmunds had begun to chafe under the authority of the borough's absolute monastic lords and to petition, sue in court, and occasionally resort to riot to acquire powers of self-government. In the late Middle Ages, the town of Bury continued to depend upon the old privileges and advantages bestowed by the abbey, notably on the commerce and pilgrim trade that the shrine of St. Edmund brought to the town (even as late as 1520 men and women from the town were being paid to take charge of pilgrims' staves while the suppliants were at their devotions),[45] but the monastery's diligence in maintaining its authority over the town raised increasing resentment as the town of Bury grew and flourished. The conflict was, at its heart, an economic one. As M. D. Lobel has observed:

> The real issue between the town and the convent was an economic one. From the twelfth to the sixteenth century the town's main objective, though often disguised under the form of municipal liberties, such as the right to a common seal and a perpetual alderman, was to rid itself of the financial burdens imposed by the convent and all other restrictions which interfered with its chances of acquiring wealth and influence. These disputes also make the convent's attitude quite clear. It was anxious, if it could not make more money out of the borough, to

preserve at least the status quo. The ambitions of the growing community filled it with alarm and induced it in its own interests and the interests of the Saint, as it believed, to adopt a policy of repression.[46]

Most of what we know of the late medieval history of the town of Bury comes from the records of litigation between the borough, growing increasingly rich in the Suffolk wool-cloth trade and zealous to grow richer, and the abbey, resolutely enforcing its economic monopolies and tithes. The recorded history of Bury St. Edmunds is the story of a series of struggles ranging from the town's reluctance to allow the abbey its ancient right to claim street manure for the monastery's own fields[47] to the town's hostility at paying the so-called Abbot's Cope, the one-hundred marks tax demanded by the monastery at the installation of a new abbot. In the late fifteenth century, John (Jankyn) Smith of Bury was to ensure his reputation as town benefactor forever (his death-day is still commemorated in an annual civic ceremony) by bequeathing his considerable land holdings to be held in trust by the town to pay this hated financial obligation.[49]

There is no doubt that the monastery of St. Edmund and its borough were locked into economic conflict for several centuries, nor that the town wanted to enjoy the economic and social advantages of the monastery's presence without owing economic obligation to it. And there is no doubt that the antimonastic sentiments of the burgesses rose to the opportunities afforded by the Peasant's Revolt of 1381. That violent uprising, in which the monastery was looted and the prior murdered, is both well documented and memorable, but the heavy penalties levied by both the Crown and the abbey for the Bury riot seem to have resigned the town to more peaceable forms of protest. We have seen already the evidence in fifteenth-century will bequests that there were continuing close personal relationships between abbots and prominent Bury burgesses despite the continuing, uneasy economic issues. Even Jankyn Smith, who was so troublesome an advocate for town rights that the monastery refused to accept him as town alderman, left in his will his best gilt and silver cup to the prior of Bury: the bequest, as M. D. Lobel has observed, looks more like a token of friendship than an act of piety.[49] That wealthy draper, John Baret, "gentleman" of the abbot's own household, may stand as a useful emblem of that bridging of town and abbey that daily occurred, despite the frictions that history recorded. David Knowles' remarks on the fourteenth-century rebellions of English monastic boroughs, are absolutely to the point:

> It is clear that the inhabitants of the monastic towns exploited a rising in which they had no originating share in order to reiter-

ate their old demands without any definite or thorough-going programme. The organized forces of conservatism were everywhere victorious here, as in the contemporary struggle against Lollardry, and they were strong enough to preserve the *status quo* for more than a century. . . . [At] Bury and other monastic towns, the troubles were on a small scale and indecisive in their results, and it is noteworthy that most of these towns allowed a considerable period to elapse, even after the Dissolution had removed their masters, before obtaining royal charters of incorporation.[50]

Lobel describes the years immediately following the Dissolution of the monastery at Bury as a time of "public ignorance and apathy on the subject of municipal government."[51] In fact, it was nearly a hundred years, in 1606, until the town of Bury at last petitioned King James I for the charter which would give them the status, ostensibly so long sought, of an incorporated borough.[52]

The supposed antagonism between Bury townspeople and the monastery seems thus to have been a conflict of economic interests, neither more nor less important than any such conflict might be deemed during changing historical and social circumstances, and probably just as readily shelved as drawn out again whenever economic self-interest so indicated. It may not be irrelevant that East Anglian drama harps insistently on the matter of greed and covetousness; that the soldiers who guard the sepulchre in the N-Town Resurrection play are bribed to silence by a cynical Annas, who observes that "mede doth most in every qwest / and mede is mayster bothe est and west"[53]; that the dominant sin of *The Castle of Perseverance,* a sin given its own stage and scaffold, is the sin of Covetousness. And yet the wills of Thomas Pykrell and John Benale present irrefutable proof that a play honoring the abbey and its patron saint in the monks' own refectory was important enough to at least two prominent Bury merchants to be remembered even in their last testaments.

Nor should we in interpreting the history of Bury St. Edmunds assume that the ruins of the monastery are evidence that the burgesses so hated the abbey that they "destroyed it willingly in the Reformation."[54] The pillaging of monastic properties during the Dissolution is at Bury, as elsewhere, testimony more to human greed than to antimonastic fervor. It is important to realize that in East Anglia the abandoned monastic churches and abbey buildings were especially tempting prizes, for the quite simple reason that they offered an accessible source of stone and brick for a region which had no native stone of its own,[55] which had been forced to import heavy stone by sea to build its cathedrals and great abbey churches, and which had developed a distinctive local architectural style for its parish churches using chips of knapped flint set in mortar as a substitute for block stone. The monastery of Bury St. Edmunds became a quarry for the town because of that most urgent and natural of human reasons—need.

It was just this simple need that had bound the town and the abbey together in earlier, sometimes contentious, centuries. The town depended on the monastery to provide for the needs of the soul as well as for temporal needs—to clothe, feed, care for the sick and the poor, to provide pilgrims' trade for its merchants, to employ scores of artisans, household servants, and husbandmen. Ministering to the town's religious needs, from prayers to will probate, was a practical concern for the abbey, just as the town's physical needs were practical. Fifteenth-century records from the monastery of St. Edmund are sparse—the register of the abbey's history that had been carefully kept in the early Middle Ages was allowed to lapse.[56] The documents that do exist provide instructive evidence of the range of the abbey's involvement in the lay spirituality of the town parishes. A sacrist's account from 1418, for example, suggests something of the paradox at the heart of abbey-town relations in a borough where the very parish churches were placed within the monastic walls.[57] The sacrist's document notes that two of the brethren preached in the churchyard during Lent—an involvement in lay religious instruction of the most direct and obvious kind—and that the abbey paid twelve pence to the boy bishop at Christmas. The St. Nicholas tokens that have been found in Bury St. Edmunds, especially in the parish church of St. Mary where the boy-bishop ceremony was observed, bear inscriptions honoring the abbey's patron saint as well as "Dusse guild," the prestigious town guild of priests and prominent burgesses that sponsored the boy-bishop ceremonies.[58] These two activities, noted simply and without comment, indicate something of the crucial involvement of the abbey in the affairs of lay religion and ritual. And yet, that same sacrist's account, for the same year, 1418, also lists expenses incurred, in some unspecified way, in connection with a lawsuit with the town.[59]

It may be useful to consider briefly some contradictions of a like kind from Chester, a city about which we have not only documentary evidence of productions of late medieval drama but the five manuscripts that preserve the Chester cycle of mystery plays. Although the REED project is making increasingly clear that there is a complex pattern of regional variation in the ways that late medieval English theater was developed and produced, Chester and its Benedictine abbey of St. Werburgh may serve as an instructive lesson in the sheer difficulty of attempting to deduce from the chance survival of public records the likely facts of dramatic activity.

Chester, unlike Bury St. Edmunds, had a recognized civic government; the ambitious productions of the Chester plays almost certainly involved

the collaborative efforts of secular and monastic clergy and the city council. The mayor and council had ultimate responsibility and control of the
cycle performances, but all the local traditions concerning the origins of
the plays, no matter how doubtful their literal historical value, emphasize
a long-term relationship between ecclesiastical and civic authorities.[60] Perhaps most significant is the tradition recorded in a Chester document of
1532 that the Chester cycle was composed by a Benedictine monk of St.
Werburgh's abbey named Henry Francis. Unlike the later civic legend that
attempted to validate the cycle by associating it with the town's most eminent man of letters, the monk Ranulf Higden (as well as, in total defiance
of historical chronology, its very first mayor), there seems to be, as F. M.
Salter has plausibly argued, no apparent ulterior motive for attributing the
authorship of the plays to a man "whom Chester had forgotten."[61] Although we know no more about Henry Francis than that his name appears
in three lists of monks of St. Werburgh's, in 1377, 1379, and 1382,[62] the fact
that these dates correspond to the decade in which in other English towns
we encounter the earliest references to mystery plays lends, as Salter notes,
credence to the story of Francis' authorship.[63]

If the tradition that the abbey of St. Werburgh supplied the text of the
cycle seems plausible, indisputable is the evidence for the abbey's support
of the plays and its cooperation with the civic authorities that produced
them. By the sixteenth century, the first station on each day of the three-
day performances of the cycle was a movable stage before the gates of St.
Werburgh's abbey, where the symbolic backing of the monastery's religious authority was given visible image.[64] In 1499, in honor of a visit to
the town by Prince Arthur, a play of the Assumption of the Virgin Mary
was performed at the abbot's Midsummer Fair "at the abbey gates & high
Crosse," the two sites symbolic coordinates of the powers, monastic and
civic, that defined the identity of the town.[65] Even in the latter part of the
sixteenth century, the abbey of St. Werburgh, now Chester cathedral, continued to assert its relationship to the plays and its patronage of the players; the Chester archives reveal that in 1568 and 1572 St. Werburgh's cathedral generously bestowed upon the actors a barrel of beer to fortify them
for their performances.[66]

And yet if the Chester cycle were a homeless and problematic manuscript like Cotton Vespasian D. viii, we might well, I suggest, be doubtful
about naming Chester as the home for a cycle of mystery plays. During
the same years in which Henry Francis seems to have been writing a series
of religious plays for the people of Chester, records show that there was
an uprising of serfs from the abbot's manor; the legal documents of 1381
accuse these rioters of "damage and destruction of the said abbot and his
convent and the goods and chattels of his house and church."[67] This local

version of the Peasant's Revolt was hardly on the order of the violence at Bury, but it should give us pause that nineteen prominent Chester citizens were sufficiently sympathetic to this hostility against the abbey to pay the exhorbitant forty pounds bail needed to liberate all the accused men.[68] There is at Chester, as at Bury St. Edmunds, considerable evidence of litigious struggle between town and abbey in the fifteenth century over legal and economic sovereignty.[69] When, for example, the wife of one of the abbot's servants was arrested and jailed by the town constable for brawling in the street during the abbot's Midsummer Fair, the "exultant clerk" who recorded the case in the Mayor's Book wrote in the margins, "Make a triple note of this as affecting our freedom to imprison during the Fair contrary to the abbot's claim."[70] As a matter of fact, "discord and action at law" between the Ironmongers' and Carpenters' guilds over the production of the Crucifixion play give us our earliest irrefutable evidence of a Corpus Christi play at Chester. This was during the abbacy of Thomas Erdeley (1413–34), a man who was somehow elected abbot despite the fact that historical records show us Thomas Erdeley, three years before his election, accused of robbing a brother monk, rifling and stealing from the abbot's chamber, and abducting and raping one Alice Pykmere as she was on her way home from a pilgrimage to Walsingham.[71] The point is that though there is the certain evidence of the Chester plays themselves, the picture that documentary evidence paints for us makes Chester look like a rather unlikely setting for the elaborate collaborative effort necessary to produce an entire cycle of religious plays. In fact, the existence of the mystery cycle at Chester is no more contradictory than the abbacy of Thomas Erdeley himself. What the pattern of town-abbey conflict at Chester shows is simply that we should be wary of assuming that Bury could not have been a dramatic center merely because of the historical record of litigious relationships between the town and the abbey.

Let us accept, then, that there are drama texts linked with the monastery of St. Edmund, and let us accept that there was religious drama performed under its aegis at Bury St. Edmunds, Suffolk, and very probably also at other parishes within the abbey's far-flung Suffolk empire. Even though we know little more about that drama except that it existed, even though we know nothing at all about the extent of the involvement of the monks themselves in the production of this devotional theater and spectacle, and even if it is, as John Wasson called it in his edition of the Suffolk dramatic records, "an under-exposed picture," it is nevertheless a suggestive one[72]— suggestive all the more when we consider that it is by sheer chance that any records at all survive from the monastery at Bury. When the abbey of St. Edmund was confiscated by the Crown in 1539, the very lead was stripped from the roof of the magnificent church, the stones of the great complex of monastery buildings broken up and sold by the cartload for building stone, manuscripts dispersed, and most abbey records not of immediate utility to the new owners of abbey lands scattered, lost, or destroyed.[73] As we have already seen, only a handful of documents remain to hint at the entire last century of festival observance at the monastery of Bury. Yet even these documents—sacrist registers of 1418, of 1429–30, and of 1537, and two years of early sixteenth-century feretrar's (shrinekeeper's) accounts—can tell us something about the festival life of Suffolk's richest and greatest abbey.

These documents can tell us that the monastery of St. Edmund not only made annual payments to the boy-bishop festivities (sponsored jointly by the monastery school and the town confraternity named Dusse guild; these payments "in honorem sancti Nicholai" appear until 1537[74]), but paid for minstrels at Christmas and on the feast day of its patron, November 20, (noted in 1418 and 1429–30),[75] and for singers (noted in a feretrar's account roll of 1520) in the Chapel of St. Robert of Bury, a local child-saint said to have been martyred by the Jews.[76] In the fewer than ten years of relevant account records that survive from the fifteenth and early sixteenth centuries, there are also numerous references to the abbey's payments to other unspecified minstrels, "players," and mimes, as well as to minstrels and mimes of the king (these "regis mimis" were paid during the reigns of Henry VII and Henry VIII), and to the minstrels of the count of Oxford, the lord of Arundel, the earl of Darby, the duke of Norfolk, and the duke of Somerset.[77] It was the prior who ordered the entertainment in most cases, and there is a payment in 1506 to "ludentibus in aula et camera prioris" ("to players in the hall and chamber of the prior").[78] (The prior is also mentioned in one of the most intriguing of the payments listed in the 1520 feretrar's accounts: "To men who came with a camel, by the prior's order 1 d."[79])

None of these abbey account records are from the 1460s, the likely date of the N-Town cycle compilation and of the *Wisdom* play in the Macro manuscript (although we do have a record of players from Bury St. Edmunds performing a play [*ludus*] in King's Hall, Cambridge, at Twelfth Night, 1469).[80] None of these brief records of payments offer any elaboration about the kinds of dramatic and musical entertainments presented in the chapels and chambers of St. Edmund's abbey, or of plays performed in the streets of Bury and at neighboring parishes and colleges. We can therefore prove neither that one of the surviving East Anglian play texts was or was not performed at Bury. We can, though, conclude confidently that Bury St. Edmunds was the site of festival revels and entertainments and pageants; that dramatic manuscripts ranging from the Rickinghall fragment to the Macro plays have links with the abbey itself; and that both

the Digby plays and the N-Town cycle have some kind of family relationship to the Macro plays. I shall summarize as tactfully as possible by saying
simply that the monastic borough of St. Edmund is an entirely possible
setting and provenance for several East Anglian play manuscripts linked
in some cases even by shared scribal hands.

It is of course impossible to know the full range of motives, economic
and political as well as altruistic, that might have bound together the abbey overlords and the burgesses of Bury St. Edmunds in sponsoring productions of religious drama. However Benedictine sponsorship might
have been defined—direct involvement, financial support, or mere tacit
approval—the financial rewards to the monastery of St. Edmund from
increased attendance at Bury fairs featuring dramatic spectacles must be
included in any speculation about motives for monastic involvement in lay
vernacular drama.[81] As we have already seen, it was the abbey that controlled the Bury marketplace and that received tolls and rentals from all
trade conducted there. This revenue would have been of no little importance even to a monastery as wealthy as Bury, especially in the decades
following 1430, when the collapse of the great west tower of the abbey
church brought huge reconstruction costs to the monastery; in 1432 Lydgate's abbot, Abbot Curteys, had the remaining walls of the west tower
pulled down and obtained from Rome a free pardon for all those who
contributed to the cost of their reconstruction.[82] A Bury will of 1457 tells
us that a new steeple was still under construction at that date,[83] as indeed
it apparently still was in 1465, when a brazier left burning by builders
working on the church tower started a disastrous fire in the abbey church
that brought a tower and spire crashing down in flames into the choir.
The eyewitness account that survives in British Library MS. Cotton Claudius A. xii tells how the flames destroyed the Lady Chapel and raged
fiercely all around the famous shrine of St. Edmund, consuming the elaborate gilded canopy (although, according to the writer, the gold shrine
itself and the revered body of Edmund were left miraculously unharmed).
The narrative of the Bury fire ends with Latin verses imploring the faithful
to replace the lost ornaments of the church.[84]

It seems that for most of the fifteenth and early sixteenth centuries, then,
the monastery at Bury faced tremendous construction expenses—especially since the abbey was also supporting the rebuilding of the two splendid parish churches of St. James and St. Mary of the Assumption.[85] There
is evidence elsewhere in East Anglia of the performance of village plays to
raise money for parish church building funds; perhaps, as I have suggested
elsewhere,[86] the 1468 date that appears in the N-Town plays manuscript, a
manuscript with dialectal, dramaturgical, and stylistic connections to the
Bury Macro plays and Digby plays manuscripts, is significantly connected

with this Bury fire of only three years before. At the very least, we know that the abbey of Bury would have been beginning to rebuild the Lady Chapel in the 1460s; we know that the N-Town Mary plays have some striking thematic links with devotional verse written by the Bury poet-monk, John Lydgate;[87] and we can assume that the plays of Mary and her mother, St. Anne, that are at the heart of the N-Town cycle compilation would have had much in common with the liturgy, cultic observances, and visual imagery of a Lady Chapel named, as Bury's was, the Chapel of the Salutation of the Conception of the Blessed Virgin.[88]

Whatever the full repertoire of devotional theater at Bury St. Edmunds, I think it very likely that the religious guilds that linked the townspeople of Bury both to the abbey and to the parish churches under the abbey's rectorship produced plays, and not just in the monks' refectory but, for example, at the abbot's Bury Fair held at Angel Hill, a large, sloping open market square in front of the monastery gates and immediately adjacent to the parish church of St. James. One of the pieces of evidence that might argue for the Bury provenance of the N-Town plays is the congruence between the importance of St. Anne in those plays (more than thirty years ago Hardin Craig suggested that the N-Town cycle was not a Corpus Christi cycle but a St. Anne's Day cycle)[89] and the very dates of the summer Bury Fair, a three-day fair held at the feast of St. James, on July 24, 25, and 26.[90] The culminating day of the Bury Fair was thus July 26, St. Anne's Day. The Digby plays manuscript, which as we have seen, first showed up in the sixteenth century in the possession of a Bury St. Edmunds book collector, specifically indicates in the prologue to the late medieval mystery play "The Killing of the Children," a text with a remarkable family resemblance to the N-Town cycle compilation,[91] that the play was performed on St. Anne's Day. The Digby plays manuscript also twice ascribes "The Killing of the Children" to Jhon Parfe/Parfre—the name of one of Bury's most famous early sixteenth-century benefactors, a rich draper whose will left a bequest for paving the Bury road and whose grant of a meadow to endow the ringing of the St. Mary sanctus (and curfew) bell was celebrated by annual civic pageantry well into the seventeenth century[92] (and indeed is still memorialized today in the Bell Meadow Housing Estate, on the site of the former Parfre meadow, just north of Bury).

But finally the issue is not to prove conclusively where the plays in the notoriously problematic N-Town cycle compilation were performed (indeed, the fragmentary evidence probably makes that impossible[93]), but to recognize that the possibility of provenance in a monastic borough raises some crucial questions about the nature of the plays. Although Bury St.

Edmunds has the manuscript and circumstantial evidence on its side, whether they are from Bury or from nearby Thetford Priory or Castle Acre Priory in Norfolk or from some other East Anglian monastic center, it is very likely that the N-Town cycle plays are linked in some way to a major religious house.[94] At the very least, we will be misled if we expect the N-Town cycle to look like the civic cycle staged at York, the cycle that has nearly always served as the paradigm for our understanding of the form and function of the mystery play.[95] Indeed, it is essential to recognize that a strong monastic presence—or, more accurately, that hybrid blend of monastic and lay spirituality that is such a signature of fifteenth-century Suffolk and Norfolk culture—is a crucial context of the N-Town cycle and indeed of much of the religious drama of East Anglia, whatever the town of provenance. Although the abbey at Bury St. Edmunds was unique in terms of the far-flung nature of its influence and its wide range of temporal powers, the very high proportion of vicarages owned by monasteries was a fundamentally important fact of spiritual life in late medieval East Anglia. Over a land area amounting to about one-twentieth of the kingdom were concentrated nearly an eighth of the religious houses of late medieval England. "So extensive indeed were the temporal possessions of the religious institutions [of Suffolk and Norfolk]," wrote Richard Taylor in the preface to his *Index Monasticus,* "that there were few, or probably none of the parishes in this district, numerous as they are, which were not, in part, claimed by the regular orders, or in which the religious had not an interest."[96]

Again, it must be emphasized that this "monasticism" that pervades East Anglian drama—as it pervaded all other aspects of the social reality of fifteenth-century Suffolk and Norfolk—was as much if not more social and economic than it was spiritual. As David Knowles has pointed out, by the fifteenth century English monks were being allowed personal funds for purchasing clothes and spices, were being paid for chantry duty, and were in fact, living in monasteries so interwoven into the social pattern of the community that they remained only remotely like the cloisters envisioned by Benedict's *Rule.*[97] Likewise the fifteenth century, as we have seen, was an age that increasingly blurred the distinction between devotional acts and texts intended for monastic worshippers and those directed at the laity. The Middle English *Abbey of the Holy Ghost* directs the lay worshipper to a life of contemplation that is to take place not within a convent wall but in a spiritual monastery of the human heart.[98]

It might even be fair to say that in the incarnational aesthetic of the fifteenth-century world, the monastery had become a visible sign of an invisible contemplative ideal relevant to every Christian life. But if the cloister wall came less and less to stand for the physical reality of contemplative withdrawal in the busy world of a monastic center like Bury St. Edmunds, it still remained a cogent and powerful *symbol* of the mental aspiration toward heaven that defined the ideal spiritual life. That symbolic direction toward God continued to be signaled by the word *contemplacio* (contemplation). Even so uncloistered a Benedictine monk as the social-climbing poet laureate John Lydgate, lauds in his verse miracle *St. Austin at Compton* the priest who chooses after the saint's miraculous intervention to seek the life of an enclosed contemplative, rather than to continue the active life of holy preaching: "O brothir myn, this choys is for thy beste!/Contemplatiff, fulfilled of al plesaunce."[99] The priest of this miracle tale is Lydgate's "brother" because both have adopted the black habit that signals their symbolic leaving of the world for the *idea* (if not, in Lydgate's case, the reality) of prayerful contemplation.

It is interesting that the same resolutely platonic vision of *contemplacio* is affirmed by the East Anglian morality play *Wisdom* which, as we have seen, is connected with Lydgate's monastery at Bury. In the allegorical drama *Wisdom,* Anima is instructed in the levels of contemplation and then is tempted by Lucifer to adopt the "mixed life" of contemplative prayer and worldly activity. As Milla Riggio has observed, in the notes to her 1984 production of *Wisdom,* "Denying the validity of that concept is a somewhat radical assertion of contemplative values," especially since it was just such an extension of the contemplative ideal that actually characterized fifteenth-century lay piety. To make Lucifer argue for the value of the contemplative life lived in the lay world is, of course, to discredit it absolutely and to affirm the older monastic ideal as resonant symbol. It is also to prove, despite the evidence that *Wisdom* also speaks of London courts and politics and retinues (as did, presumably, the abbot's own worldly household), that the play is a monastic play in provenance and in spirit.[100]

It is likewise striking that the expositor figure in the East Anglian N-Town plays is named "Contemplacio." It is curious that no one has ever commented on the implications of the fact that the Contemplacio of the N-Town Mary plays seems to signal not an "expositour in doctorys wedes"[101] as a rubric describes the commentator in the N-Town Passion plays, but the personification of contemplation in the technical sense of monastic prayer and withdrawal.[102] The Mary plays begin and end with a blessing by Contemplacio upon "þis congregacion," a blessing that invokes God's presence as well as his aid. Indeed, Contemplacio's prologue is one of the most telling of the expositor speeches in medieval drama, making manifest that it is both Christ and his creatures who are being played for in these holy stories:

Cryst conserve þis congregacion
fro perellys past · present and future
and be personys here pleand · þat be pronunciacion
of here sentens to be seyd · mote be sad and sure
And þat non oblocucyon · make þis matere obscure
but it may profite and plese eche persone present
ffrom þe gynnynge to þe endynge so to endure
þat cryst and every creature · with þe conceyte be content.[103]

Contemplacio then very briefly proclaims the matter of "þe processe" to come. "Processe" is a word that frequently signals the play itself in East Anglian dramatic texts, but it may also mean more generally the procession of thought or image or idea (as it does, for example, in Lydgate's Marian lament *Quis dabit,* inscribed around the Clopton chantry walls in Long Melford church.[104]) These are the plays that Contemplacio announces to his spectators: a play of Anne's Conception of Mary, a play of Mary's Presentation in the Temple, the Wedding of Mary and Joseph, the Annunciation, and the Visitation. In fact, this group of plays also includes two additional plays that have apparently been interpolated into the Contemplacio group. One of these inserted plays is "Joseph's Doubt," very likely the same play mentioned in the N-Town banns, and which, as we shall see in chapter 6, is linked by its imagery not to the other Contemplacio plays but to the cycle plays of the Fall, Christ's Nativity, the Adoration of the Shepherds, and the Adoration of the Magi elsewhere in the manuscript. The second interpolated play, "The Trial of Joseph and Mary," is a play of unique structure, introduced by its own comic parody of an expositor, the Summoner.[105]

This first proclamation of Contemplacio ends by calling for attention and silence. Similar is the prologue spoken by Contemplacio at the beginning of the Presentation play. Mary, Mother of Mercy, is here invoked in the prayer, but the prologue otherwise is a practical one, summarizing the preceding action and outlining what is to come. "As a childe of iii ȝere age · she xal appere," Contemplacio explains. This particular speech could have been spoken by nearly any set figure, most appropriately perhaps by the kind of stage manager who appears as Poeta in the Digby plays.[106] Much more preacherly is the final Contemplacio speech from the conclusion to the Visitation play, a speech that was clearly intended as epilogue and that makes no reference to "The Trial of Joseph and Mary," which follows in the manuscript—nor indeed to the following cycle of plays of Christ's birth, ministry, death, and resurrection. Contemplacio in this epilogue to the Mary group performs a function much like the preaching Moses at the end of the N-Town Moses play. His didactic purpose is to teach the *Ave Maria* (much as Moses' final sermon is to instruct in the Ten Commandments) and to promise that whoever "seyth oure ladyes sawter dayly ffor A ʒer þus / he hath pardon ten thousand And eyte hundyd ʒer."[107] Contemplacio narrates the conclusion of the Mary story as far as the birth of John the Baptist, then thanks the audience for its patience and "good supportacion." He asks "good deliveracion" of any inconvenient thing said or done in these plays and brings the Mary group and the role of Contemplacio to a close.

A totally expanded conception of Contemplacio's role, however, emerges in the prologue to the Parliament of Heaven and Salutation play. Stephen Spector has made the likely suggestion that this prologue was a later revision, added perhaps even as the plays were being transcribed in the manuscript, for he notes that the speeches of Contemplacio here are written in a different form from the long-lined octaves of the earlier speeches.[108] At whatever stage of the complicated composition history of the N-Town cycle the role was written, this Contemplacio functions as the most extraordinary expositor figure in medieval drama. He also certainly represents the old ideal of monastic contemplation, so fiercely does he exemplify not only devotion to heaven but the mysterious mediation of the monk's own prayer and sacred learning on behalf of the Christian community. Here, Contemplacio invokes the prophets Isaiah and Jeremiah, and like a prophet himself calls out to God for mercy. Contemplacio, mysteriously and inexplicably as the monk's *opus dei* performs its sacramental function, becomes not only a part of the play, but as he calls out three times to God to "come downe," he becomes the impassioned and efficient cause of the Parliament of Heaven and the Incarnation. The scribe who inserted the N-Town Passion plays into the N-Town compilation once calls that expositor "Contemplacio," too, and specifies his dress as "doctor's wedes," but I think it is very likely that the independent Contemplacio character of the Mary group would not have been garbed as learned "doctor" but as religious contemplative, as a monk.

An expositor's role would have been, of course, the most likely part for a monk to play in a religious dramatic performance (especially if he was, like Chester's Henry Francis, also the Poeta of the play), but we should not rule out the possibility that other authoritative roles—of prophets, of God himself—customarily reserved for clerics might have been performed by monks in the English religious drama.[109] Evidence is maddeningly sparse about clerical participation in medieval English theater; what are we to make, for example, of the brief notation in the register of the Cluniac priory of St. Mary at Thetford that in nearly every year between 1519 and 1534, players performed there "cum auxilio conventus" ("with the help of the convent").[110] As Richard Beadle observes, it is impossible to know precisely what "with the help" of the monastery signified, but I concur with his belief that it "would not be surprising to find that monks or lay members of the religious community took an active part in the staging or acting of plays"[111]; at a monastery like Bury with a large monastic school, novitiates would have been an especially likely source of performers for religious drama.

Whatever the precise nature of monastic involvement in the N-Town cycle, whatever the extent to which monastic contemplation is lauded in the plays as the type and highest ideal of devotional response, there has never been any doubt that the cycle shows evidence of uncommon learning and what Hardin Craig termed "theological culture."[112] The most frequently cited illustration of the theological sophistication of the N-Town cycle is the N-Town play "Christ and the Doctors." The plays of the child Christ in the Temple in other cycles generally show neither convincing displays of erudition by the twelve-year-old Christ nor originality. As Rosemary Woolf has observed, "The curious feature of the five surviving plays of the doctors is that four of them are closely related, Towneley, Chester, and Coventry all being variants of the play first recorded in the *York Cycle*."[113] Woolf admits to bewilderment as to why "this dull and infelicitous version should have had such a diffusion,"[114] but the answer seems to be simply that it was very difficult for the writers of the civic cycles, despite the resources of considerable energy, talent, and funds, to invent out of the context of popular urban piety a convincing script in which a Christ Child dazzles with his erudition. In the York cycle, the twelve-year-old Jesus astonishes the learned "doctors" of the Temple by merely listing the Ten Commandments; indeed the play directs little time or attention to the theme of contemplative wisdom at all. What dramatic energy the play contains is focused upon the parental anxiety of Mary and Joseph and the vexed, human search for a lost child that frames the Temple encounter. The York Doctors play and its variants in Towneley, Chester, and Coventry are not about divine wisdom, but about the anxiety of a worried mother and a timid father, awed by great men dressed in the finery of their priesthood.

The poignantly human focus of Incarnation that is so characteristic of the late medieval religious drama is not neglected by the N-Town "Christ and the Doctors"; indeed the playwright intensifies it by a skillful use of simultaneous action made possible by the scaffold staging. Considerable dramatic irony is created by the speeches of the anxious parents in lines 201–32, speeches that intrude into the play just as the young Jesus is concluding an explanation to the priests of his "dobyl byrth and dobyl lenage"[115] and of the necessity of his kinship to a human mother married to an aged and all-too-human Joseph. This exposition highlights the domestic plot situation, but also culminates the incarnational focus of the questions posed by the Temple priests. And those are genuine and thorny questions, ranging over the mysteries of Creation, Last Judgment, Incarnation, and Atonement, and precociously answered by the Child Jesus in the language of theology, not by simple credal response as in all the other plays. The doubleness of this scene is underscored by the playwright's near-macaronic use of vernacular and Latin language. The posturing wise men of the Temple signal their learning and their churchly authority by beginning their speeches with lines of untranslated Latin, but the authority established by the "otherness" of Latin language is immediately undercut by the first—Latin—words of the young Jesus, who utters "Omnis scientia a domino deo est," ("All learning is from God").[116] These words function as a simple shorthand for the learning and authority of the twelve-year-old Jesus since he, too, speaks the erudite Latin of the church, and they serve to deflate the pretensions of the learned priests. Those Latin lines also, of course, function for the spectators of the play, at least those who themselves have the learning to translate them, with considerable dramatic irony, since, as that audience knows, Jesus is one with the God who has bestowed all wisdom. But perhaps most interesting is the way that the simple Latin line "Omnis scientia a domino deo est" functions as both dismissal of the pride of erudition in the spectator and as humility *topos* for the playwright of the play. This is a play that has manifested learning, but only to insist that the "Temple" of learning is properly not a place of honor and pride, but a celebration of that Wisdom who is Christ. Such is, in fact, a functional definition of the study that is part of the monastic *opus dei* (as well as the significance of the title character of the Macro play *Wisdom*). As Kathleen M. Ashley has astutely pointed out:

> The rather vague perception of N-town's "learned tone" is in
> fact rooted in specific features of this cycle's characterization
> and theme, and . . . these features give the cycle a coherence
> and unity which has been sensed but never satisfactorily ex-
> plained. A recurring concern in this cycle is learning itself.
> Above all, Christ is the personification of Wisdom in this cycle,
> and all human knowledge must be measured against that divine
> standard.[117]

The Temple of Jerusalem in "Christ and the Doctors" is a type of the Christian church and of Christian learning, as it is ubiquitously in the typological and symbolic architecture of the Middle Ages, but it is even more immediately a type of the monastery. The "Temple" that functions as crucial setting in the interpolated N-Town Passion plays is likewise not just a place of ritual and worship but of monastic withdrawal. In a curiously gratuitous scene immediately following the N-Town Crucifixion play, John the Evangelist comforts Mary and takes her for solace to "where þat it plesyth ȝow best"—to "goddys temple"[118] where Christ's mother vows to lead her life:

> Here in þiˢ temple my lyff I lede
> And serue my lord god with hertyly drede
> now xal wepynge me fode and fede
> Som comforte tyll god sende[.][119]

The comfort that Mary awaits will be the Resurrection appearance of her Son; following the *Meditationes vitae Christi* (which freely invented the tender filial scene unaccountably missing in the gospel texts), Christ's very first appearance in the N-Town cycle will be to his grieving mother. But unlike the *Meditationes,* the risen Christ will appear to her not in her own house, but as the play's introductory " 'Proclamation" instructs, "in temple þer she lyse."[120] Mary is not only a type of the cloistered medieval nun, but in the purposeful anachronism of the N-Town cycle compilation, the "Temple" becomes an important thematic and iconographic part of the spectacle of the Passion drama.

Like the narrator named Contemplacio, the importance of the Temple and of Mary's enclosure there in the Passion play seems to suggest an ecclesiastical context for the N-Town cycle rather different from the parish piety of the other civic cycles. But nowhere in the N-Town cycle, I think, are the monastic preoccupations of the compilation made more explicit than in the play "Mary in the Temple," the play that dramatizes the story from the apocryphal gospels of Mary's dedication from a child of three to a life as a Temple Virgin. The N-Town "Mary in the Temple" is the only extant or recorded English play on the theme of Mary's Presentation, and its style and purpose are much different from the only surviving French play of the Presentation, Philippe de Mezières' fourteenth-century church drama, with its brawling, comic contest between Synagoga and Ecclesia.[121] The N-Town "Mary in the Temple" rivals the "Assumption of the Virgin" as the play in which the cycle's devotional focus on the mother of Jesus ascends to fervent liturgical celebration. But it is liturgical celebration not only of the virginity and purity of Mary, but of her ascent to the "Temple" of Jerusalem, the dwelling place of God for which the medieval monastery was both image and preparation.

The play's outlines are furnished by the apocryphal accounts in the *Protevangelium* and *Pseudo-Matthew* of the child Mary's enclosure in the Temple following her miraculous birth to the aged, barren Anna[122] (accounts that had themselves borrowed heavily from the Old Testament story in 1 Samuel of the dedication of Samuel to the Temple after his birth to his barren mother, Hannah). The child Mary is brought to the Temple, dressed "al in whyte as a childe of iii ȝere age"[123] by her parents, Joachim and Anne, who are fulfilling their vows to dedicate their "ffayr ffrute" to the Temple to be God's bride.[124] The N-Town play, however, freely embroiders the narrative supplied by the apocryphal tradition with its customary emotional and incarnational piety. The child Mary humbly protests her unworthiness to be God's spouse, and, like Margery Kempe seeking that paradoxical exaltation by humility, begs only to be handmaiden to the handmaid, to "ley my handys · vyndr hire fayr fete."[125] Mary is blessed in the name of the Trinity by her doting parents and then she kisses them goodbye in a wrenching scene in which the three-year-old child begs forgiveness for any childish misdeeds, "yf evyr I made ȝow wrothe."[126] St. Anne is even made to linger uneasily at the Temple after these tearful goodbyes have been said until she is satisfied that Mary has safely climbed the steps, for "I wold not for al erthe se here fal."[127] But then, the familial concerns of the play pass to ritual action as the toddling Mary is transformed to spiritual instructress and her "miraculous" ascent of the fifteen steps rises to liturgical celebration of the fifteen gradual psalms, those fifteen degrees "which a holy man has erected in his heart."[128]

Episcopus explicates Mary's journey up the Temple steps as the allegorical journey from "babylony to hevynly jhersalem"[129] and the psalms as instruction to "every man þat thynk his lyff to Amende."[130] It is significant, however, that many of the steps named by Mary in her cataloging of the psalter's scale of virtues—desire to dwell with God, obedience, humility, avoidance of carnal temptation, and brotherly concord and unity—are precisely those virtues demanded by the monastic life that her own enclosure in the Temple prefigures.[131] Indeed, in the characteristic double perspective of the N-Town cycle, Mary's exegesis of the psalms is both sermon to the listening laity and exposition on the life of the enclosed contemplative. For example, the precept of the second step, "Leuaui oculos meos in montes: vnde ueniat auxilium mihi" ("I will lift up my eyes to the hills from whence comes my help"), is curiously glossed in the play not as imploring God's aid but as the virtue of contemplative study:

> The secunde is stody · with meke inquysissyon veryly
> How I xal haue knowynge of godys wylle
> To þe mownteynes of hefne I haue lyfte myn ey
> Ffom qwens xal comun helpe me tylle.[132]

There is perhaps no better definition of the highest goal of mystical *contemplatio* anywhere in late medieval literature than Mary's fervent prayer before the Temple, "O my god. devocion depe in me dryve/ þat myn hert may wake in þe · thow my body slepe."[133] That this contempla-tive ideal involves not only intense emotion but also studious devotion to learning may perhaps be best demonstrated by the scene in which the angels who come to feed Mary in the Temple promise also to instruct her in "þe lyberary of oure lordys lawe."[134] That waiting "library" of spiritual knowledge taught in the cloistered walls of the Temple is as assuredly rel-evant to the monastic mythology of this play as the popular late medieval iconography elsewhere of St. Anne teaching the Virgin to read is domestic and lay in its meaning.[135]

When the child Mary finally attains the top step of the Temple of God she humbly asks Episcopus how she should be ruled in God's house. Her question leads to a sermon on the love of Trinity and love of neighbor; the Hebrew "bishop," like St. Benedict himself, further tells her to serve her God by prayer (the *opus dei*) and by bodily labor, and he entrusts her to five allegorical maidens who will be her fellowship. Mary kneels to be received into this holy community of contrition, compassion, cleanness, and spiritual "fruyssyon" (fruitfulness), and then is further entrusted to seven priests who will be her chaplains—"dyscressyon · devocion · dylex-cion · and deliveracion . . . With declaracion determynacion · dyvyna-cion."[136] This whole scene is a striking example of the hybrid quality of the N-Town text as well as its double reference. What began as a play of devotional emotion not unlike the lay piety in the nativity plays of a civic cycle like York, has by now veered into liturgical allegory—and into an aureate style in which latinate language is the real focus of the play. The journey to purity of soul taken by the child Mary with unfaltering steps in the *N-Town* Presentation play is an ideal type of that allegorical progress found in another East Anglian drama, the morality play *Wisdom,* whose Anima makes a stumbling and painful journey into sin and despair before finally attaining her own spouse and crown at the top of the Temple steps.

Mary in her childlike humility and in her simple "dedys of mercy" per-forms as a recognizable and emulatable model for lay piety, and the N-Town playwright's scene of Mary's separation from her aged and tearful parents willfully tugs on the heartstrings of a popular audience.[137] But the play at the same time bridges, as the East Anglian towns did themselves, the lay and the monastic worlds. For the play of Mary's ascent to the Temple of her holy *contemplatio* is at its heart a contemplative play about that same ladder, "[c]alled in the reule grees of humylite," that the Bury poet-monk John Lydgate celebrated in his autobiographical poem *Testa-ment* as the true pilgrimage of the monastic life.[138]

Chapter Six
Mary's Dower: East Anglian Drama and the Cult of the Virgin

No account of the devotional theater of late medieval Suffolk and Norfolk could fail to acknowledge the extraordinary importance in that time and place of the cult of Mary, the Mother of Jesus. Although framed by plays of Old Testament heroes and by plays of Christ's Incarnation, Passion, and Resurrection, the heart of the East Anglian N-Town compilation is a play cycle, unique in extant medieval English drama, of the conception, birth, and life of Mary.[1] At the heart of fifteenth-century devotion, too, was Mary, the Virgin Mother of God, Queen of the Saints. The kind of divine radiation through which the saints normally transferred their powers of intercession, healing, and grace was emitted in her case not from treasured bones (for Church tradition taught that Mary's greatest honor was the honor of bodily Assumption), but from holy images that made visible the mysterious union of divine and human. The incarnational preoccupation of the late Middle Ages tended to make the Virgin Mary—perhaps even more than Christ himself—the very emblem of Christian mystery. Mary of Nazareth had been chosen God's bride and God's mother; her body had enclosed divinity, had given Godhead a human form and likeness, had finally been transported to heaven, where Mary, ever Virgin, reigned not only as Queen of Heaven, but as Gabriel extols her in the N-Town "Salutation and Conception," even as "empres of helle."[2] The Virgin Mary was for late medieval Christendom a mother goddess of powers conceivable and inconceivable, a saint raised uniquely among the whole company of saints to the highest pantheon with the sacred Trinity.

In England, fervent devotion to the Virgin Mary, already begun in the Anglo-Saxon period, had by the thirteenth century so penetrated English culture and spirituality that it is nearly as difficult to trace the outlines of the cult of the Virgin as to describe the meaning of Jesus of Nazareth for the medieval Christian Church. Indeed, for the fifteenth century, it is probably *more* difficult, so complex and omnipresent had Marian devotion grown in the life of the Church. Marian hymns and poetry, the soaring Lady Chapels being built by armies of stone masons for parish churches and for great cathedrals, the new lay devotional liturgies and Books of

Hours, the images in pigment and stone of Mary and her holy Child placed on house walls and bridges and city gates as well as on altars—all these things sang of the worship of the Virgin. Christ might be approached and invoked as the babe in Mary's arms or as the suffering, bleeding Lord upon the cross, but it was Mary who had contained the whole awe of his godhead in the tabernacle of her womb, Mary who had been God's bride and his mother, Mary whose image figured that union sought by all Christian souls and whose body hallowed by Christ's presence was both type and model for the Church itself and for its holy sanctuaries.

The Marian fervor that we associate today with Italy or Spain—or link with the Gothic cathedrals of Our Lady that glorified the plains and the Capetian politics of medieval France—was in the Middle Ages of English renown. It was not Italy or Spain but medieval England that was known by the popular epithet "the dower of the Virgin,"[3] England whose intensity of Marian devotion would be eradicated finally, not by the fanatical zeal of Puritan iconoclasts (although every medieval English church bears terrible, mute witness of it), but by a shrewdly calculated transference of the cult of the Virgin to the political cult of the Virgin Queen Elizabeth in the Renaissance.[4] In the Middle Ages, it was not primarily continental theologians but English ones who were so eager to proclaim Mary's powers and her saving grace, her freedom from original sin; not French exegetes but English Benedictines like Anselm of Canterbury, Eadmer, William of Newburghe, and the Cistercian abbot Aelred of Rievaulx, who were in the twelfth century arguing passionately for the doctrine of Mary's Immaculate Conception by St. Anne's and St. Joachim's chaste kiss before the golden gate of Jerusalem. English theologians were those who were insisting upon a kind of quaternity of heaven, writing emotional prose that amounted to a feminization of divinity. "Sometimes salvation is quicker," wrote Anselm's disciple, the Saxon Eadmer (d. 1124), if we remember Mary's name than if we invoke the name of the Lord Jesus. Why should this be so? I can only say what I feel."[5]

In fact, the development of the medieval cult of the Virgin, in both her English dower and in France, which produced fewer but highly influential theologian-troubadours like St. Bernard of Clairvaux and his disciples, depended hardly at all on logic, on scholasticism, or indeed on theological *argument* of any kind. In the first five centuries of Christianity, Mary had been decreed the perpetually virgin mother of Christ to settle raging *christological* controversy. As Mary had carried Jesus of Nazareth in her womb for nine months and suckled him at her breast, he was truly man; as she had conceived him as inviolate virgin and brought him forth "as sunlight passes through glass," he was truly God. When in the twelfth century, Mary became herself the focus of intense popular devotion, creative energy in the arts, and furious doctrinal controversy, her cult developed by the power of metaphor rather than metaphysic. In both the Latinate, learned tradition and in popular vernacular texts, Mary's authority is asserted through linguistic pun (the "Ave" of the angel that reverses the curse of Eva, the Virgo from the Virga of Jesse), by typological metaphor seized from exegetical readings of scripture (Mary as the fleece of Gideon, the burning bush of Moses), and especially, after the twelfth century, by ecstatic love language from the Song of Solomon, in search of a coherent object of affection. Much like the love songs of troubadour lyric, the cult of the Virgin is about the meaning—and the sensuously evocative power—of words and images. Divinity comes to rest in Mary, who is image and sign of the Word-bearer; her attribute of maternity asserts the principle, both incarnational and linguistic, of saving fecundity. The sensuous language praising the throat of the beloved in Song of Solomon 7:4—"Thy neck is as a tower of ivory"—substitutes for any needful logical argument or Pauline authority to make Mary understood as the "neck of the Church . . . the mediatress between God and men."[6] The paradox of human and spiritual *amor* becomes in these texts of the Mary tradition a self-conscious hankering after verbal riddle as well as pun, an erotic and sublimated game of language in which, as for example in a poem from the thirteenth-century *Carmina Burana* manuscript, the poet is torn on a wheel of desire that will only gradually be revealed to be passionate love-longing for the virginal mother of God.[7] When Middle English Marian lyrics are not catalogues of metaphors and epithets, they are often riddles, slyly singing of a maiden whose real identity is as often obscured as it is revealed by the language.[8]

Riddling, punning, singing a love song of religious signification, the cult of Mary in medieval devotion was a meditation on the Word made Flesh. In late medieval England, images of the Virgin Mary were rarely out of sight or mind; this was especially true in East Anglia, where to the very eve of the English Reformation, the roads and streets and bridges of Suffolk and Norfolk thronged with men and women who were not only Mary's worshippers, but her pilgrims. These pilgrims journeyed to "England's Nazareth," the holy shrine at the village named Little Walsingham in the northwest corner of Norfolk, that had become by the fifteenth century not only the most important pilgrimage site in England but an international center of pilgrimage whose importance was probably rivaled only by Santiago de Compostela in Spain and by Rome itself. In this Norfolk village in the early twelfth century, a wealthy widow named Richelde de

Faverches had claimed visions showing her the Nazareth dwelling in which Mary had received the angel's Annunciation of the birth of Christ. Specifying the building dimensions and the dry ground, in a meadow otherwise wet with dew, where the house was to be built (cf. Judges 6:36–40), the Virgin had commanded Richelde to build a wooden replica of the sacred house and, according to the Walsingham legend, had even sent angels in the night to move the house two hundred feet from the site where workmen had first labored in vain to erect it. A stone chapel built to enclose the Virgin's little house in Walsingham meadow became the site of miraculous healings, especially after returning crusaders presented to the shrine a phial said to contain drops of milk from the Virgin's breasts. Mary's actual dwelling place, lost to the infidels who had seized the Holy Land, had seemingly transferred its spiritual powers to Walsingham, and the intercessory presence of the Virgin was, as the miracles of the Walsingham house manifested, now available on this Christian, English ground.

In about 1153, a Geoffrey Fervaques, probably Richelde's son, gave lands and tithes to establish a monastery of Augustinian monks at Walsingham to serve as custodians of what had already become a local pilgrimage shrine. The royal patronage of King Henry III, a frequent pilgrim to Walsingham in the early thirteenth century, and of his son, Edward I, helped spread the fame of the Holy House much wider,[9] and by the reign of Edward III in the fourteenth century Walsingham was an important and wealthy priory, whose Gothic church and convent buildings towered over the little chapel of the shrine.[10] Royal patronage of Walsingham continued, and indeed the Holy House of Walsingham seems to have come to represent a kind of divine blessing upon the "house" of the royal dynasty itself, recalling the Davidic prophecy of 2 Samuel 7:13: "He shall build a house to my name, and I will establish the throne of his kingdom for ever." What seems clear at any rate is that the dynastic struggles of the War of the Roses made English kings even more eager for the Walsingham benediction. Kings Henry VI and Edward IV made impressive state pilgrimages to Walsingham, and Henry VII, after military victory at Stoke sent his banner to Our Lady of Walsingham "where before he made his vows."[11] No late medieval king, however, seemed more devoted to Our Lady of Walsingham than Henry VIII, who installed his own chantry priest at Walsingham and who made several pilgrimages there early in his reign, once walking two miles barefoot to the shrine to pray to Our Lady of Walsingham for an heir. When Erasmus visited Walsingham in 1511, the priory was in the middle of a major building campaign to erect a more impressive stone chapel to enclose the Holy House, and we know that

East Anglian Drama and the Cult of the Virgin

King Henry VIII generously contributed in 1511 and in 1512 to the cost of glazing the new windows of the Walsingham Lady Chapel. Even in 1538, only months before the famous cult statue of Our Lady of Walsingham was burned with much fanfare in the streets of Chelsea, annual payments were still being made by Henry VIII on the feast of the Annunciation to maintain "the King's candle" that burned perpetually before the altar of Our Lady of Walsingham.[12] Thus, to the very eve of the Dissolution, the tradition of royal favor helped ensure that Walsingham was still a major national as well as local shrine, even when the fortunes of other English pilgrimage sites had declined sharply. Although the annual total of pilgrims' offerings to St. Thomas' shrine at Canterbury had plummeted to thirty six pounds a year by 1535, Our Lady of Walsingham was still receiving 260 pounds in that year from pilgrims, and Walsingham Priory was still the second-richest monastic foundation in all Norfolk (second only to the cathedral priory at Norwich).[13]

The proliferation of other, lesser East Anglian Marian shrines in the late Middle Ages—at Ipswich, Thetford, Woolpit, and Long Melford, for example—was both explained and validated by proximity to Walsingham.[14] For Walsingham attracted pilgrims like a magnet. In the chapel built around the wooden house of the Annunciation, Our Lady of Walsingham heard prayers and supplications, pardoned sinners, and healed the sick. Margaret Paston promised in 1443 to go on pilgrimage to Our Lady of Walsingham to ensure her husband's recovery from an illness, and a wax image bearing the same weight as the sick man's was sent as gift and supplication to the Walsingham shrine.[15] Robert Reynes of Acle, Norfolk, left a description in his fifteenth-century commonplace book of the altarpiece of the Walsingham Chapel and of the famous, miracle-working statue of Our Lady of Walsingham attended by golden images of saints: "Gabriel gretyng Our Lady; in the myddes of the tabyll at the avter stante Our Lady, on eche syde of her stante an angell, Seynt Edward, Seynt Kateryne on the ryght hande, Seynt Edmond, Seynte Margarete on the left hand; alle clene gold."[16]

Late medieval wills offer abundant evidence that popular piety often bore the image and likeness of this most renowned of English cult statues; it was not the image of Mary but of Our Lady of Walsingham, specified Mabel Maloysel, that adorned the gold-and-diamond ring that she bequeathed in a Norwich will of 1383.[17] Hundreds of pious testators gave precious jewelry *to* the statue, as did, for example, John Baret's niece Anne, who bequeathed to the statue of Our Lady of Walsingham in 1504 both her coral rosary and her wedding ring, with "all thyngys hangyng thereon."[18] Other testators bestowed fine garments on Our Lady of Wal-

singham, or gave devotional images to her shrine, like the "Image of oure
lady with a glasse to-fore hit" mentioned in the 1439 will of Isabella, countess of Warwick.[19]

The miraculous statue was not the only destination of the pilgrims.
Within the gates of Walsingham priory were two ancient wells that healed
the sick and granted wishes; hopeful pilgrims might carry away drops of
the holy water in small hollow flasks marked with a crowned *W*.[20] In return
for a suitable offering, pilgrims to Walsingham were also shown the crystal
phial said to contain drops of Mary's milk, displayed in a silver reliquary
on the high altar of the priory church. But the center of Walsingham piety
and the very reason for the existence of cult statue, shrine, and pilgrimage
was a simple wooden house, a replica as simple as a child's drawing if the
pilgrim badges show it rightly (fig. 6.1). Erasmus, though a mocking observer in his visit to Walsingham in 1512, describes in his satiric *Colloquy on
Pilgrimages* the steady procession of pilgrims who passed through the narrow wooden house at Walsingham.[21] Deemed too sacred to be demolished
and reconstructed, by the late Middle Ages the much-patched house that
Richelde's village workmen built had become a canonical image of the
sacred house that had enclosed the Virgin—in whom God himself had
been enclosed. Although claims were never made for the Walsingham
shrine, as they were for its chief fifteenth-century rival, the Holy House of
Loreto, that it was the *actual* house of the Virgin's Annunciation,[22] its
sacramental and symbolic power was none the less real for being a mimetic
representation of the indwelling of God. Indeed, no better example exists
of the image theology of the late Middle Ages than the Walsingham
shrine, a replica or stage setting that pilgrims saw as proof of the Virgin's
accessibility, the place where Mary—particularized, localized, in bodily
likeness—had made her home, and had heard the angel's message. That
"lytyl praty [pretty] hous"[23] in which the Joseph of the N-Town "Betrothal" places his new bride could not have been neutral playing space for
any East Anglian audience, so conditioned were they to call to mind's eye
the familiar and particular image of the Holy House of Walsingham.

The general rule that the cultic importance of any sanctuary or shrine
or image in late medieval art is in inverse relationship to the physical evidence the Reformation allowed to survive is well proved by Walsingham.
After the cult statue of Our Lady of Walsingham was burned publicly in
the streets of Chelsea, the priory and shrine were so obliterated that today
controversy rages as to whether the modern brick sanctuary that com-
memorates the old Walsingham pilgrimage is even on the correct site of
the old shrine. So it is difficult to remember that in the fifteenth century,
in the Holy House of Walsingham, the Virgin Mary listened with a human, merciful ear. It is difficult to remember that for East Anglian audi-

East Anglian Drama and the Cult of the Virgin

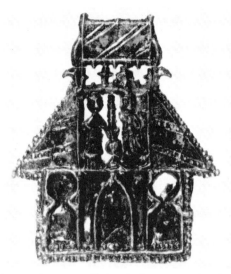

FIGURE 6.1. Late fourteenth-century pilgrim's badge representing the Holy House of Walsingham and the Annunciation to Mary. Found at Swan Wharf, London Bridge in 1976
(Reproduced by permission of the Museum of London).

ences a wooden house on Norfolk soil—in the sacramental mystery of
incarnate image if not in empirical fact—was the place of the angelic Salutation. The fullest importance of the Walsingham shrine lay not only in
its miracles and healing power, but in the profound implications of its
connection with the Incarnation event itself, since it was a commonplace
of medieval thought that it was not at the Nativity, but at the Annunciation to Mary when the Incarnation began.

Nothing in the brief account in the gospel text of Luke 1:26–38 (in
which Gabriel merely promises that at some future time "The Holy Ghost
shall come upon thee, and the power of the most High shall overshadow
thee") prepares us for the commentaries of medieval Christendom, that by
the fourth century were confidently teaching that Mary through the power
of her faith had conceived God's Son at the very instant she had heard and
believed the angel's message. A vernacular sermon by Aelfric from the
beginning of the eleventh century repeats the same doctrinal commonplace ("and she believed the angel's message, and thus with faith conceived
God in her body")[24] that Lydgate extols in his fifteenth-century rendering
of the Latin hymn *Gaude virgo mater Christi:*

> Gaude virgo mater christi
> Be gladde, mayde moder of Cryst Ihesu
> Whiche conceyvedist oonly by hering.[25]

Incarnation thus began with a word—and with God's overshadowing presence. Luke's Gospel had used language carefully chosen to echo Old Testament texts like Exodus 40:34, in which the cloud in which Jahweh dwells "overshadows" the Ark of the Covenant and fills it with his glory. The typological fulfillment is clear; Mary by her acceptance of the angel's words becomes the new Ark of the Covenant, bearing within her sides not the tablets of the Law, but the Holy of Holies of the new order—the incarnate body of God's Son. In the mystery plays, whose very subject and theoretical justification was the Word made Flesh, Mary's Conception of Christ was a crucial act in the salvation drama. But nowhere is Christ's Conception and the centrality of Mary's crucial role in God's plan given more emphasis than in the "Salutation and Conception" play in the East Anglian N-Town cycle. The N-Town dramatist, as David Mills has so astutely observed, even "risks stillness and silence to enforce his point," daringly staging Mary's deliberation as she agrees to conceive God's son.[26] Gabriel "makyth a lytyl restynge and mary be-holdyth hym," while in the charged and expectant silence, the actors on heaven's scaffold and the prophets and patriarchs in Hellmouth join the uneasy audience in waiting for the word.[27]

And when Mary has freely chosen to become the tabernacle for God's son, the N-Town dramaturgy shifts from silence to dazzling visual spectacle. Not content with the descending dove of the Holy Spirit found in other Annunciation plays,[28] the N-Town dramatist stages the miraculous Conception of Christ with triune images of the Incarnation descending to Mary in gilded splendor:

> here þe holy gost discendit with iii bemys to our lady · the Sone of þe godhed nest with iii bemys · to þe holy gost · the fadyr godly with iii bemys to þe sone · And so entre All thre to here bosom.[29]

Although "þe holy gost" may have been a representation of the traditional dove, the N-Town rubric seems to say that incarnate images of both God the Father and the Son descend to become visible signs of miracle on Mary's body—as they were, for example, in late medieval devotional images of Mary like the "Vierges ouvrantes," cult statues that opened on hinges to reveal images of the Trinity carved or painted within the tabernacle of Mary's womb (fig. 6.2).[30] Indeed, Mary, as Gabriel extols, is the "throne of þe trinyte,"[31] an epithet that will be echoed by Mary's cousin, Elizabeth, in the N-Town Visitation play when she clasps the pregnant Mary in her arms: "All hefne and herthe wurcheppe ȝow now/ Þat are trone and tabernakyl of þe hyȝ trinite."[32]

Given both the evidence of the astonishing N-Town rubric and the tre-

FIGURE 6.2. "Vierge ouvrante" (opened), a German fifteenth-century devotional statue of painted and gilded wood in the collection of the Musée de Cluny in Paris (Marburg/ Art Resource, New York).

mendous local importance of Mary's Annunciation and its shrine in East
Anglia, it seems clear that, however bewildering to reconstruct, this gilded
Incarnation descent in the N-Town "Salutation and Conception" was intended to be ambitiously and impressively staged. Archival stage evidence
provides us with little more than speculation—M. D. Anderson's, for example, that dolls on gilded wires were somehow rigged to descend to
Mary to signify the moment of Incarnation. (She noticed that there is such
a doll [an "enfant futif"] listed in the properties inventory of the fifteenth-
century stage-director's book known as the *Livre du Regisseur*.[33]) But visual art provides many analogies to the N-Town Conception rubric and
testimony to the iconographic authority for such spectacle. Although they
sometimes incurred the displeasure of theologians, representations of the
actual "descent" of the Christ Child to his mother's body are not uncommon in fifteenth-century art, especially in the art of Flanders and Germany,
with which East Anglia was closely linked by trade, geography, and religious ideology.[34] In the most famous of such Annunciation paintings, the
central panel of the Merode Altarpiece by the Master of Flemalle, a tiny
homunculus Christ bearing the Cross on his shoulder dives down to Mary
in an explicit imaging of the Conception mystery (fig. 6.3). The bedchamber in which the Virgin of the Merode Altarpiece sits reading scriptural
prophecies of the Incarnation is both setting and symbol of the Virgin's
womb; the closed glass window and the beam of light on which the infant
Christ enters the room (fig. 6.4) concretely images the same familiar
medieval analogy for the mystery of virginal Conception that the young
Christ expounds upon in the N-Town play "Christ and the Doctors":

> Lyke as þe sunne doth perysch þe glas
> þe glas not hurte of his nature
> ryght so þe godhed entryd has
> þe virgynes wombe and sche mayd pure . . . [35]

That images of Christ descending to his Incarnation existed in East Anglian churches we know from the order of 1561 by Bishop Parkhurst of
Norwich commanding that all representations of the Annunciation containing the "second person of the Trinity" were to be defaced and destroyed.[36] Remarkably, one such painting still survives, in a fifteenth-
century stained-glass window in St. Peter Mancroft church, Norwich (fig.
6.5), in which above the head of the angel Gabriel there descends to Mary
on golden beams of light both a nimbed dove and a diminutive Christ
Child shouldering the Cross of his preordained Passion.[37] How this window in the most prominent parish church in Bishop Parkhurst's diocese
managed to survive the edict we can only surmise; wherever its original
position, the offending image must have been so very high and small in

the soaring space of the nave (it takes a pair of binoculars to see the Christ Child clearly in the present position of the glass in the great east window) that it was either deemed no danger to the reformed faith or simply over-looked.[38]

The St. Peter Mancroft window offers both proof that the Annunciation with Christ Child iconography existed in East Anglia and a striking par-allel to the N-Town rubric, but little specific help in reconstructing the stage technology by which the spectacular Conception in the N-Town cycle could have been achieved. And compared to what the N-Town rubric demands, even the most theatrically-staged Annunciation and Conception images that I know about look mechanical and unconvincing—for ex-ample, the Annunciation in a stained-glass window of about 1430 from Tamsweg, Austria, in which the Christ Child and a dove are lowered down on a heavy chain wrapped around God's waist,[39] and the Annunciation tympanum from the north door of the Frauenkirche in Wurzburg (fig. 6.6), in which an homunculus Christ slides down from the mouth of God to Mary's ear by means of a long tube that looks suspiciously, and even comically, like a stage property.[40] The N-Town Conception rubric, how-ever, seems to insist upon more dazzling visual effects than pulleys or chains or gilded wires can easily explain. Indeed, since the astonished Jo-seph of the N-Town play "Joseph's Return" finds the face of Mary so shining with light after her Annunciation and Conception that he cannot even look at her,[41] the pyrotechnics of staging the N-Town "Salutation and Conception" may well have been far closer to the explosive scene of flame and God-bearing shadow described in Bonaventure's mystical trea-tise *Lignum vitae:*

> After she consented to his word, the Holy Spirit descended
> upon her in the form of a divine fire that inflamed her soul and
> sanctified her body in perfect purity, and the power of the Most
> High overshadowed her, to enable her to bear such fire. In-
> stantly, by the operation of that power, a body was formed, a
> soul created, and both were united to the Godhead in the Per-
> son of the Son; so that this same Person was God and Man,
> with the properties of each nature unimpaired.[42]

Mary, radiant after Conception, is like, says the N-Town Joseph, "þe sonne with his bemys."[43] Medieval choirs chanted the same wonder in the Grad-ual of the Advent Mass: "In sole posuit tabernaculum suum" ("He made the sun to be his tabernacle").[44] Evidence from continental liturgical plays tells us that elaborate and blazing light effects could be achieved in medie-val theater and especially for the blazing into incarnate form of the Word. For a Florentine Annunciation play, Brunelleschi himself devised a

FIGURE 6.3. *The Annunciation to Mary,* the central panel of the Merode Altarpiece, a Flemish triptych painted by Robert Campin, the Master of Flemalle (d. 1444) (All rights reserved, The Metropolitan Museum of Art, The Cloisters Collection, 1956 [56.70]).

FIGURE 6.4. Detail from the Merode Altarpiece *Annunciation,* showing the Christ Child descending to his Incarnation (All rights reserved, The Metropolitan Museum of Art, The Cloisters Collection, 1956 [56.70]).

FIGURE 6.5. *Annunciation with Descending Christ Child*, a fifteenth-century stained-glass panel from a series of windows representing the Life of Christ in the parish church of St. Peter Mancroft in Norwich. The St. Peter Mancroft windows are very close in style and iconography to the East Harling windows of the Joys and Sorrows of the Virgin—which were also made in the Norwich workshops (Royal Commission on the Historical Monuments of England).

FIGURE 6.6. *Annunciation with Christ Child Descending to Mary's Ear*, a fifteenth-century tympanum over the north-door entrance to the Frauenkirche, Wurzburg, Germany (Marburg/ Art Resource, New York).

Heaven full of living and moving figures, and a quantity of lights which "flashed in and out," elaborate garlands of flame in lanterns that "looked like stars from the ground."[45]

What is at least certain from the extraordinary N-Town Conception rubric is how very concretely the late medieval audiences of mystery plays were likely to have "witnessed" the very instant that Incarnation began in the body of Mary. As the N-Town Mary exclaims:

A now I ffele in my body be
parfyte god and parfyte man
having Al schappe · of chyldly carnalyte
Evyn Al at onys · þus god began.
Nott takynge ffurst o membyr and sythe A-nother
but parfyte childhood ʒe haue Anon.[46]

Some medieval theologians like St. Antonius of Florence had been nearly as disapproving as Bishop Parkhurst of images of the Christ Child of the Annunciation (because of their heretical suggestion that the flesh of Jesus was not assumed *within* the Virgin's womb),[47] but in fact the function of such representations seems to have been merely to insist upon the visible reality of Incarnation—even as the image of the house of the miraculous Annunciation was visible to the bodily eyes of the pilgrims and suppliants who flocked to Walsingham.

Even given the evidence of the dazzling and elaborate Conception rubric in the N-Town cycle, it is of course not possible to argue that East Anglian audiences were more preoccupied with the Conception of Christ than mystery play audiences elsewhere in fifteenth-century England—the psalter of about 1420 once owned by John Bolton, chamberlain and sheriff of York, contains an illumination of the Christ Child descending to his Conception, too[48]—but it would be surprising, I think, if the proximity to Walsingham did not affect in some important ways devotional focus on the Annunciation feast, or the sense of the local accessibility of the Virgin, or the fervor of East Anglian Marian piety. It is probably significant, for example, that Abbot Curteys of Bury St. Edmunds ordered the emblems atop his pastoral staff include the Annunciation to the Virgin as well as the abbey's patron saint, Edmund,[49] and that two East Anglian parish churches—at Long Stratton, Norfolk, and Yaxley, Suffolk—provide us with the only two known examples of medieval English "Sexton's wheels," revolving devices marked with Mary's fleur-de-lys emblem, used for determining the calendar days for penitential fasting in honor of the Virgin's Annunciation (fig. 6.7).[50]

What I think is demonstrably true is that the East Anglian N-Town cycle makes the Incarnation mystery enclosed within the Holy House and the holy body of Mary part of the iconic spectacle of the cycle in important and meaningful ways. The scene of Joseph's discovery of Mary's pregnancy, for example, presented in the other English mystery plays as the mere farcical comedy of disordered human understanding,[51] is shaped by the N-Town dramatist into a compressed parodic enactment of the Incarnation mystery itself:

FIGURE 6.7. Sexton's wheel, a late-medieval mechanical device for determining (or absolving) by spin the day of the week in which the worshipper should observe a fast in honor of the Virgin Mary. Long Stratton, Norfolk (Royal Commission on the Historical Monuments of England).

Joseph: How dame how · vndo ȝoure dore vn-do
            Are ȝe at home why speke ȝe notht
Susanna: Who is ther why cry ȝe so
            telle us ȝour herand wul ȝe ought.
Joseph: Vn-do ȝour dore I sey ȝow to
            Ffor to com in is all my thought.
Maria: it is my spowse þat spekyth us to
            On-do þe dore his wyl were wrought.
            well-come hom myn husbond dere
            how haue ȝe ferd in fer countre.
Joseph: To gete oure levynge with-owtyn dwere
            I haue sore laboryd ffor þe and me.
Maria: Husbond ryght gracyously now come be þe
            it solacyth me sore · sothly to se ȝow in syth.
Joseph: Me merveylyth wyff surely · ȝour face I can not se
            but as þe sonne with his bemys · quan he is most bryth.[52]

The scene opens with Joseph returning from his long labors in a far country to the house where Mary is cloistered and enclosed. Finding the door locked, old Joseph, with rising irritation, asks twice that the locked door of the Virgin's house be opened to him, and it is only the third time, when Mary herself orders "on-do þe dore," that her handmaidens unbolt the locked door of that very house imaged and celebrated by the Walsingham shrine. Joseph's ill-tempered impatience before the locked door does establish his character as "stubborn, boorish, irascible,"[53] but it is also a remarkably inventive translation into dramatic action of the medieval exegetical commonplace of Mary's virginity as the *porta clausa*, the locked door in Ezekiel's vision of the new Temple (Ezekiel 44:1–2).[54]

St. Jerome had bequeathed to medieval Christendom a reading of the porta clausa of Ezekiel not only as Old Testament prefiguration of the Virgin Birth but as proof of the doctrine of Mary's *perpetual* virginity. The door of the Temple, wrote St. Jerome in his commentary *In Hiezechielem*, "signifies the Virgin Mary, who during and before and after childbirth remained virgin."[55] Jerome's influential exegetical proof ensured that the porta clausa would become one of the most familiar images of Mary's virginity and one of the most commonly invoked epithets of praise in Marian hymns and devotional lyrics.[56] In theological commentary, in literature, and in the visual arts, the porta clausa was so omnipresent a symbol for the Virgin Mary's miraculously inviolate participation in the Incarnation that a medieval audience would scarcely have needed the reminder of Ezekiel in the N-Town "Prophets" play[57] to recognize the locked door of Mary's holy house as both literal detail confirming the cloistered life of the Virgin and as a visual sign of the fulfillment of Ezekiel's prophecy that a Virgin, a door ever closed, would be the spouse of God.

Like the three images descending on beams of light in the Conception scene, the thrice-repeated commandment to open the porta clausa has Trinitarian significance in the N-Town cycle; its function in the play of Joseph's Return is, however, parodic rather than iconic, since Joseph, the human husband, is not the Virgin's true Bridegroom. Hapless Joseph, of course, does not understand that Mary is mother of the Messiah; he knows neither the sign and significance of the locked door of her house nor the meaning of the miraculous fecundity of her virginal womb. Rueful Joseph is only a human being, like the spectators themselves, whose complaints and hard toil at his labors "To gete oure levynge" reveal him to be marked with Adam's sin. Dazzled, but blind to the meaning of the supernatural light on Mary's face, Joseph will have to be instructed by an angel for that blindness and doubt to be transformed by affirmation of the Incarnation mystery.[58] What is instructive is that the play assumes that the audience will recognize through the human comedy that Joseph has unwittingly reenacted before the porta clausa the entrance of the true, the divine, Bridegroom.

The devotional importance of the Incarnation within Mary's virginal womb is given further elaboration in the plays of the N-Town cycle compilation through an iconographic sign that is bound, not unexpectedly, with the community identity of East Anglia itself, with its spinners and fullers and weavers and with the woolen-cloth looms that dominated the culture and the economy of East Anglian towns and villages. Let us return to that bewildered Joseph, the dazzled and then incredulous and then furious old man of the N-Town cycle, who has not witnessed as the audience has those triune images of Godhead descending to Mary's body on beams of light, who sees only his young bride huge with child. In all the extant English mystery plays, Joseph's formal doubting of the Incarnation mystery—and the resolution of that doubt—are part of the plot and strategy of telling salvation history. The Chester cycle plays it simplest; Joseph doubts and Mary does not explain or even speak until an angel has revealed the miracle to Joseph. In the more extended confrontations in the Wakefield, York, and True Coventry cycles—and at first in the N-Town cycle—Mary answers the accusations of Joseph by speaking a riddle that laconically sums up the Incarnation mystery: the child, she says, is both God's and Joseph's. Mary's enigma only infuriates Joseph, so ruefully

comic and human in his assumptions of Mary's adultery and guilt that it
will take an angel to still his doubts. But before that final revelation, Mary
speaks to Joseph thus:

> It is no man but swete jhesus
> he wyll be clad in flesch and blood
> and of ȝour wyff be born.[59]

Mary's assurance to Joseph that the child in her womb is Jesus who will
be "clad" in the garment of human flesh and blood invokes an analogy for
the mystery-play audience that was as much a commonplace of Christian
poetry and sermon as the sunlight-through-glass analogy for the miraculous Conception. Christ came from heaven, St. Augustine wrote in *De
civitate dei,* "to be clothed with a body of earthly mortality, in order that
He might clothe it with heavenly immortality."[60] So familiar was the garment
or robe as a figure for the Incarnation mystery in Christian exegesis and
sermon that William Durandus in his famous liturgical treatise of 1295,
Rationale divinorum officiorum, could say that the sacristy (the room where
the priest put on his celebrant's robes) was a symbol of "the womb of the
Blessed Mary in which Christ dressed himself in his robes of humanity."
"The priest," Durandus continued, "having robed himself comes forth
into the public view, because Christ, having come from the womb of the
Virgin proceeded forth into the world."[61] Those visible images of the
Trinity who descended to Mary's body in the N-Town "Annunciation"
were to be clothed there in the vestments of Incarnation; in Mary's womb,
says Gabriel in Lydgate's *Lyf of our Lady,* "all the vertu of the trynyte shall
yshrouded be."[62]

Lydgate's word "yshrouded," however, bears a double edge, for the
cloth of Christ's incarnate birth is also figure and premonition of his
shroud. Even at the instant of Conception, the Christ Child of the St.
Peter Mancroft window, we remember, already shoulders his Cross. The
mother who clothes the Christ in flesh, therefore, knits, as inexorably as
the Fates who held the threads of earthly destiny, the agony and death of
Calvary. As Mary laments in the Wakefield "Crucifixion" play:

> To deth my dere is dryffen
> his robe is all to-ryffen
> That of me was hym gyffen
> And shapen with my sydys.[63]

Although the "robe" shaped by Mary's sides is here the garment of flesh
that is the incarnate body of Christ himself, the garment metaphor elsewhere sometimes tangles with the concretizing imagination of the late
Middle Ages to produce the curious legend that Mary herself had sewn

East Anglian Drama and the Cult of the Virgin

for the Christ Child the seamless tunic for which the Roman soldiers cast lots on Calvary. That tunic was so wonderfully made, said a thirteenth-century Latin poem from Germany called the *Vita Beatae Mariae Rhythmica,* that it had neither blemish nor seam, never became old or dirty, and was never outgrown as Christ grew to manhood.[64] Garment of flesh and magical tunic are ominously joined, as they are in a fifteenth-century German panel painting from the Master Bertram workshop (fig. 6.8) in which Mary sits calmly knitting the seamless tunic, while the Christ Child playing at her feet is interrupted by two angels who stand bearing the instruments of the preordained Crucifixion—a lance, a crown of thorns, nails, and the Cross.

To answer Joseph's comic doubt with the garment of the incarnate Christ's flesh and blood is, then, to invoke profoundly serious associations for the audience of the play, associations that define the very meaning of *corpus Christi*—the gift of Christ's incarnate body that is also the bread of the Eucharist. It is hardly surprising that a medieval text, especially a mystery play, should invoke the garment of Incarnation—we have already seen Mary's lament at the Cross in the Wakefield cycle—or that an East Anglian text should be thinking of the making of cloth. But what I think is significant is that Mary's revelation to Joseph that Christ will be clothed in flesh is at the center of an important iconographic theme that echoes in the N-Town cycle compilation from Fall to Redemption, and, interesting enough, in those pageants that the evidence of paleography and prosody argue are those of the original Corpus Christi cycle into which the St. Anne (or Contemplatio) plays and the two-day Passion play have been interpolated.[65] It might be useful to look at the theme of Mary's "clothing" of Christ in these pageants in some detail.

Mary's answer to Joseph's doubt is echoed in the N-Town cycle by another doubter. Salome, the apocryphal midwife of "The Birth of Christ" doubts the virginity of Mary, probes her womb, and then affirms the miracle, proving, just as doubting Thomas will prove the Resurrection, a mystery of the faith. For Salome's human incredulity, as in the apocryphal gospels, her hand is withered, until Mary urges her to "towch his clothis be my cowncelle."[66] As an N-Town rubric emphasizes ("hic salomee tangit fimbriam Christ"),[67] Salome touches the infant Christ's swaddling cloth to be healed and is not only made whole but is transformed into a joyful witness of the miracle:

> In every place I xal trelle þis
> Of a clene mayd þat god is born
> And in oure lyknes god now clad is[68]

FIGURE 6.8. *The Virgin Mary Making the Seamless Tunic and Angels Announcing the Passion,* by a follower of Master Bertram. Panel from the Buxtehude Altarpiece (c. 1410) in the Kunsthalle in Hamburg (Marburg/ Art Resource, New York).

Recognition and epiphanal celebration of the gift of Incarnation also occur in the N-Town cycle in the two Adoration plays. The second shepherd in the "Adoration of the Shepherds" hails the infant Prince of Paradise who is "clad in oure kende,"[69] and the third shepherd likewise marvels that "Cryst in oure kend is clad."[70] In the "Adoration of the Magi," it is Jasper, the third king, who brings the gift of bitter myrrh and with it the prophecy that the Child shall suffer upon a bitter tree who "in a maydonys flesch is clad."[71] The king's lament for the poor rent "clothing" of Christ's human suffering is skillfully and ironically juxtaposed in the play with the vainglorious self-admiration of Herod on another stage who boasts his rich rings and "robys of array . . . In kyrtyl of cammaka kynge am I claddė."[72] All of these signs and showings of the incarnate body of God's Son culminate in the testimonial of John the Baptist in the play that will begin the public ministry and purpose of Christ's life:

> In place where I passe · wyttnes I bere
> the trewth xal I telle where-so-evyr I go
> þat cryst þe sone of god is be-come oure fere
> clad in oure clothynge to sofer for us wo.[73]

Mary's clothing of Christ in her womb is thus celebrated in the N-Town cycle in a regular verbal pattern of public affirmation and recognition. But it is important to realize that the cycle would not have depended only upon repeated words like "clad," "cloth," and "clothing" to establish the theme. The resonant implication of the Christ's garment of Incarnation is also revealed visually and iconographically in the N-Town pageants, beginning with "The Fall of Man." Fallen and sorrowfully cast out from Eden, Adam and Eve must face the hardships of a new hostile world by obeying God's commandment to labor and toil for their sustenance (Genesis 3:17–19). The labors the N-Town dramatist assigns them are the traditional ones ascribed to them in the visual arts by centuries of iconographical tradition (fig. 6.9): "ʒe must delve and I xal spynne/ in care to leydn oure lyff" says the N-Town Eve to her woeful spouse. Adam must delve in the cursed and unyielding earth and Eve must spin because humankind has discovered its own frailty and must struggle in the world to feed and clothe itself. Spade and distaff were thus articulate symbols of the Fall, and the mimed stage actions, in their very familiarity to the daily chores of medieval audiences, reminders of the sorrowful inheritance of original sin—but also of God's continuing care and solace.[74] Such is precisely the thematic function of the two ostensibly farcical actions in the plot of *Mankind*, in the East Anglian Macro manuscript. Mankind delves in that play, as Steven May has pointed out, not because it is some kind of rural peasant's play, but because the labor of Adam designates him as "rep-

Comment vn aungel de vn espee. Gardoit la porte ela vere. Ke adam
ne enteist. por la defencdeu q̄ il baiseit. E dut adam va fuer tere.
Car ici ne alez iames a fere. Adam vne beche prist. Sicū le aungel li a
noit dist. E le moist ble ⁊ fruit tere. E eue filoit por vesture fere. Adam
uuoit ✝ alees des aunz. E engendrat deus enfaunz. Cayin le esne ⁊ li
autre Abel. Li primer faus ⁊ le derrner tel.

FIGURE 6.9. *The Labors of Adam and Eve*, from the *Holkam Bible* (BL Add. MS. 47682, fol. 4v), a fourteenth-century picture Bible with Anglo-Norman commentary from East Anglia or southern England (By permission of the British Library).

resentative of Fallen Man in general."[75] But what Steven May has not seen is that the board that the devils place under Mankind's God-given spade to thwart his labors is exactly parallel to New Guise's undermining in the play of that other sign of the Fall and God's consolation for it. New-Guise promises Mankind a "fresch jakett, after þe new gyse"[76]—which turns out to be a coat cut so ridiculously short it is no longer a sheltering defense against the cold of the postlapsarian world. In perverse parody of the gifts of spade and garment brought to Adam by God's angelic messenger (the fourteenth-century English manuscript known as *Queen Mary's Psalter* shows clearly the iconographic convention that is being inverted in the play of *Mankind* [fig. 6.10]), the comic Vices of the play strip away *Mankind's* postlapsarian solaces even as they tempt him to abandon Mercy.

In the N-Town compilation, Adam, more prescient than Mankind, foresees and explicitly links Eve's labor of the distaff with the "comfort of God's messenger" who will bring news of the Atonement:

And wyff to spynne now must þou ffonde
oure nakyd bodyes in cloth to wynde
tyll sum comforth of godys sonde
with grace releve oure careful mynde.[77]

The second Eve, the woman who will bring forth the Child who will atone for the children of Adam and Eve, is, of course, Mary, and Adam's prophecy will be confirmed in the N-Town cycle by the familiar medieval pun spoken by the angel Gabriel as he hails God's bride and handmaiden:

fful of grace god is with the
Amonge All women blyssyd art thu
here þis name Eva · is turnyd Aue
þat is to say with-owte sorwe are 3e now.[78]

The spinning Eve thus both prefigures and is perfected by the "clothing" of Christ in Mary's womb. The typological connection was visually reenforced in Christian art of the fourth to the eleventh century by the convention of showing Mary, as the apocryphal gospels of *Protevangelium* and *Pseudo-Matthew* described her, spinning purple wool for the temple veil when surprised by Gabriel's announcement.[79] The old attributes of spindle, distaff, and wool basket had become rare in Annunciation paintings by the thirteenth century, when the new emphases on lay piety and affective devotion brought a Bible or prayer book to the Annunciation scene.[80] The Virgin Mary, transformed from spinner to contemplative, now was interrupted by the angel as she sat reading prophecies of Christ's Incarnation and Passion.[81] The old spinning attributes were occasionally reintroduced in late medieval Annunciation paintings (Mary holds a

FIGURE 6.10. *Adam and Eve Cast out of Paradise and the Gift of a Spade and a Garment*, from *Queen Mary's Psalter* (BL MS. Roy 2, B.VII, fol. 4), a manuscript produced in London about 1310 or 1320 (By permission of the British Library).

FIGURE 6.11. *Joseph's Doubt,* a panel painting of about 1420 from the Strasbourg region. Strasbourg, Musée de la Ville de Strausbourg (Marburg/ Art Resource, New York).

spindle, for example, in the Annunciation painting of about 1400 by Melchior Broederlam),[82] but the motif of the Virgin's cloth-making tended to be transferred in the fourteenth and fifteenth centuries to depictions of her girlhood life in the Temple[83]—and especially to the newly popular subject in late medieval art and vernacular literature of Joseph's doubting of Mary's miraculous pregnancy.[84] As perplexed old Joseph wonders about Mary's pregnancy in this Strasbourg painting of about 1420, Mary serenely works at her sewing basket (fig. 6.11), a model of wifely industry (cf. Proverbs 31:13–22), but her room is a symbolic interior landscape lighted by a trinity of windows and furnished with emblems of her chaste womb—the white cloth, the basin of water[85]—and what she sews, as the apocryphal gospel makes clear, is the veil for the Temple that will be rent with Christ's death.[86] The cloth-making for the temple veil which is Mary's occupation during her cloistered pregnancy is, like her later cloth-making for the Child's seamless tunic, both foreshadowing of the Passion and symbol of the Messiah's own garment of flesh. So John Lydgate explains the meaning of the purple wool that Mary spins before Christ's birth for the veil of the Temple:

> And of this purpill, that I of spake to forne
> I fynde playnely, how that Marye wrought
> Thilke vayle that was in tweyn torne
> The same houre whan he so dere vs bought
> Loo howe þat godd in his eternall thought
> Provydede hathe, by Iust purvyaunce
> The purpull silke, vnto his moders chaunce.[87]

In a fifteenth-century Joseph's Doubt painting that is a paradigm of late medieval incarnational sensibility, the mysterious and providential workings of God's plan for atonement that Lydgate proclaims as God's "purvyaunce" is envisioned as explicitly as the most palpable holy vision of Margery Kempe (fig. 6.12). That bewildered Everyman, Joseph, peers out from behind the great throne on which Mary, radiantly nimbed, sits spinning. And as the Virgin Mary spins, drawing the thread from her distaff down across her body to the spindle in her right hand, the symbolic thread of Incarnation passes over a tiny naked figure of the Christ Child, painted in an aureole of light over her womb. In visual and verbal pun as providential as medieval Christendom found the Eva-Ave reversal, the Virgin Mary spins both *filum* (thread) and *filium* (son), crafting the garment of flesh and of human mortality for the still embryonic Word.[88]

No rubric explains Mary's stage actions in the analogous N-Town "Joseph's Return" in which Joseph confronts the miracle of the virginal Conception, but both iconographic tradition and the fact that Mary is accompanied in that play by companions named Susanna and Sephora (the names of two of the virgins assigned along with Mary to spin thread for the Temple veil)[89] argue that in the staging of the N-Town play, too, Joseph's profusely ranting doubts were answered for the spectators by a spindle and distaff that were no less visible and no less charged with significance than Eve's. The simple and familiar cloth-working tools of every East Anglian household were thereby made incarnations of that theological mystery that defied Joseph's human understanding, tangible icons as

FIGURE 6.12. *Joseph's Doubt,* a panel painting of about 1400 from the Upper Rhine. Berlin, Staatliche Museen, Gemaldegalerie (Marburg/ Art Resource, New York).

resplendent with meaning as the spectacular descending images of the triune Conception. Eve's sorrowful cloth-making, whose inheritance of guilt and postlapsarian solace was the very signature of the cloth wealth of East Anglian towns, is in this cycle invoked and redeemed by the pure womb that would "clad in flesch and blood" the long-awaited Messiah. And that spiritual cloth-making is recreated and incarnated in the physical signs of stage attributes, actions, costumes. Although it is clear from the handful of wardrobe and production accounts that survive from other plays (and from the N-Town rubric for staging the Conception) that we should not underestimate the sophistication and financial resources at the service of the staging of both civic and parish plays, a fifteenth-century panel (fig. 6.13) from a small Annunciation diptych in the Abtei Nonnberg in Salzburg offers useful suggestion about the kind of iconic statement that could have been achieved simply by a distaff and a painted costume in the N-Town "Joseph's Return." In the Salzburg diptych, the Annunciation to Mary is paired with an image of Joseph confronting Mary with a finger pointed accusingly at the womb which "to hyʒe doth stonde."[90] But Joseph's doubt is wordlessly answered for the spectator by the thread from Mary's distaff that passes over the front of Mary's gown—and over the painted cross of Christ's preordained Atonement that marks her pregnant womb.

As to contemplate Mary's maternal joys is to contemplate too her sorrows, as the Holy House at Walsingham is the shrine of the inexorable passage to Calvary as well as the celebration of Conception, so the N-Town cycle's devotional focus on the pure womb of Mary (and that of her own mother, Anne), like all late medieval bodily feasts of Mary is also meditation on the gift, both joyful and sorrowful, of *corpus Christi*. The influential thesis formulated by Charles Phythian-Adams that we should understand late medieval piety to have been structured according to the "ritual half" of the year, Advent to Corpus Christi, and not by midsummer to Advent, the "secular half," is refuted by the evidence of the Marian preoccupations of the fifteenth century.[91] Although it is manifestly true that the central events of Christ's life take place in the Christmas to Easter liturgical calendar, most of the Marian feasts of the late Middle Ages sanctified the other, extra-biblical, half of the year. All but two of the so-called Lady Days in honor of the Virgin Mary were actually high feasts of what Phythian-Adams has called the "secular half" of the year; the midsummer to Advent calendar included the Visitation to Elizabeth (July 2), the Nativity of Mary (September 8), St. Anne's Conception of the Virgin Mary (December 8), and especially the Assumption of the Virgin (August 15). The feast of the Assumption of the Virgin seems in many ways, in fact,

East Anglian Drama and the Cult of the Virgin

FIGURE 6.13. *Joseph's Doubt*, a fifteenth-century panel from a small devotional diptych in the collection of the Abtei Nonnberg in Salzburg (© Abtei Nonnberg).

the single most important liturgical event in late medieval Christian piety, an event linked with a "secular" calendar only in the sense that the Assumption of the Virgin—her ascent in soul and in body to heaven and her triumphant coronation—is the apotheosis of the incarnational preoccupations of the culture. The fact that the doctrine of the Assumption of the Virgin was not formalized until 1950 confirms rather than refutes the significance of this feast in late medieval England;[92] the very centrality of bodily feasts of the Virgin in popular piety was both the most insistent and most debated element of conflict between medieval and Reformation sensibilities. It could even be argued that the history of dramatic censorship in Reformation England is to an important degree a history of furious debate over plays of the Virgin's bodily feasts, a debate manifested by the missing initial page of the "Last Judgment" in the Wakefield cycle—evidently lost when a censored Assumption play was removed from the play register; by the York Purification play that was hastily inserted at the end of the manuscript, out of proper sequence; by the missing play of Mary's Assumption performed by the town wives of Chester;[93] and probably by the Assumption play written on different paper and by a different hand that was added to the N-Town cycle manuscript.

Incarnation has no higher celebration than in the Assumption plays, plays that daringly stage the annihilation of distance between body and spirit, in which the carnal mother who is Mary—more approachable and less problematic a human image than the Son of God—receives her glorious triumph and coronation in exchange for what is, no matter how transcendently purified, an act of human creation. In the N-Town cycle compilation, more so than in any other extant English mystery cycle, the play called Corpus Christi is also the play of salvation history heralded by the body of Mary. In the N-Town "Assumption of the Virgin," the elaborate music and the liturgical pageantry frame a drama that self-consciously recapitulates Christian history in the life of Mary. An Annunciation angel brings once more a message of Mary's union with her heavenly Spouse; the apostles (apparently by awesome stage machinery) are whisked to Mary's bedside to rehearse the New Testament history that has once more been compressed to a locked room and an inviolate womb[94]; Christ's death and its foil, the Resurrection, are replayed complete with comic tricks upon nonbelievers at a holy tomb; and with music of organs and of singing angels the final apocalypse of Mary's soul and (in second thought) her body as well is played out. Christ calls Mary to him in a liturgy of holy espousal and coronation that is the final and ecstatic triumph of her creating womb.[95] "[T]abernacle of Joye · vessel of lyf," Dominus calls his mother and his spouse in the N-Town "Assumption of the Virgin" as he returns to earth for her fleshly body.[95]

If we cannot know with certainty in what East Anglian church this spectacle of singing angels and music of organs was played out, the fifteenth-century church of St. Mary of the Assumption in Bury St. Edmunds (fig. 6.14) is a church whose devotional and iconographic setting provides not only a congruent stage for the play and documentary evidence of "pleyers at ye orgenys" there by 1463,[97] but even a stunning series of roof sculptures

FIGURE 6.14. View of the parish church of St. Mary, Bury St. Edmunds, from the northwest. All but the street entrance to St. Mary's was built within the monastery precinct at the extreme southwest corner of the abbey of St. Edmund. The monks of St. Edmund's Abbey (who appointed priests and guild chaplains to serve the congregation) had their own entrance. Remains of the old monastery wall can still be seen immediately adjacent to the church tower (Royal Commission on the Historical Monuments of England).

FIGURE 6.15. The nave roof of Bury St. Mary's, looking east (Photo © Hallam Ashley: with the permission of Mrs. Dorothy Ashley).

that image the profound meaning of the Marian feast of Assumption in the devotional life of late medieval East Anglia.

The hammerbeam roof of Bury St. Mary, built about 1445, is justly one of the most famous of the splendid East Anglian timber roofs (fig. 6.15). It stretches 140 feet down the length of the nave, spans the nave's 28-feet width, and is divided on each side by eleven great timber beams into ten bays; each of the bays supports a full-length, exquisitely-carved wooden angel. The two angels at the far eastern end held scrolls (now missing) and were painted and gilded as a canopy of honor to the rood, the devotional image of the Crucifixion that until the Reformation would have loomed just beneath them, mounted on the rood screen separating the congregation from the high mysteries of the chancel and the altar.[98] Inscribed on the arching supports beneath the eastern pair of angels are the words "God me gyde" and "Grace me governe," the mottoes used by Bury St. Mary's wealthy patron, John Baret. In his will Baret referred to "alle the werk of the aungellys on lofte wiche I haue do maad for a rememberaunce of me and my frendys" in St. Mary's Church,[99] and at the very least, we can be sure the painting and gilding of the canopy-of-honor angels bearing his motto was due to his patronage. "Alle the werk," however, seems to mean just what it says, that Baret was the patron who gave St. Mary's its spectacular angels. Although the present visitor's guide to the church of St. Mary is cautious about attributing the entire series to Baret,[100] the striking similarity of the Bury angel-roof to the now-mutilated angel-roof at the nearby Suffolk parish of Rougham St. Mary, with which Baret was also directly connected (Baret left a generous will bequest to Rougham church, the parish church of his in-laws, the Drurys), argues that Baret can probably be linked with the entire sculpture group.[101] Perhaps the likeliest reason, however, for believing John Baret was responsible for the angel-roof of Bury St. Mary is the complexity of its iconographic program. As we have already seen in chapter 4, both John Baret's didactic tomb and his profusely detailed will proclaim him to have been not only rich and pious, but learned, knowledgeable, and nearly obsessively interested in the architectural and iconographic details of his chantry and church.

Baret's "werk of the aungellys' processing to the rood celebrates not only his memory but glorifies the church of Bury St. Mary, the high feast of the Assumption of the Virgin to which Baret's parish church was dedicated, and even the mystical meaning of Holy Church itself.[102] The procession of angels, all garbed in liturgical vestments and bearing the emblems of a solemn High Mass, includes, from east to west, incense bearers, thurifers, taperers with candlesticks, gospelbook bearers (perhaps subdeacons?), chalice bearers (fig. 6.16), priests (deacons?), and choirmasters.

East Anglian Drama and the Cult of the Virgin

FIGURE 6.16. Angel bearing the chalice to the Eternal Mass, wooden sculpture from the nave roof, church of St. Mary, Bury St. Edmunds (Photo © Hallam Ashley: with the permission of Mrs. Dorothy Ashley).

The Bury angels vested as priests have previously been identified as the angelic celebrants of the Mass,[103] but since the pair of angel priests lack the stole worn ritually on the shoulders of the celebrant, it is, in fact, likely that here as elsewhere in late medieval depictions of angels in liturgical vestments, those angels were intended to represent attendants for a mystic mass in which it is Christ, garbed in the stole and vestments of his incarnate flesh, who will be both the sacrifice and the celebrant.[104]

It is when we understand that the holy procession to the altar proclaims that Christ himself is the rightful High Priest that the significance of the final three pairs of roof sculptures—a long-standing iconographic puzzle—becomes clear.[105] Following the procession of angel priests and choirmasters come feathered and crowned archangels bearing scrolls and scepters like angels of Annunciation—and then on each side of the nave a mysterious female figure, her waist cinctured by the narrow girdle that emblemized virginity,[106] who bears her crown in her hands (fig. 6.17). The female figure was interpreted by J. B. L. Tolhurst as Queen Margaret of Anjou. He believed the final figure in the ceremonial procession—a crowned king bearing (on the north) scepter and book (fig. 6.18) and (on

FIGURE 6.17. The Virgin Mary as Ecclesia processing to her Coronation and Mystic Marriage, sculpture on the nave roof of the church of St. Mary, Bury St. Edmunds (Photo © Hallam Ashley: with the permission of Mrs. Dorothy Ashley).

FIGURE 6.18. Christ processing to the Mystic Marriage, sculpture on the nave roof of the church of St. Mary, Bury St. Edmunds (Photo © Hallam Ashley: with the permission of Mrs. Dorothy Ashley).

the south) an object that looks like a flaming orb or a heart—to be her husband, King Henry VI.[107] Given John Baret's close Lancastrian connections (the silver collar of *SS* that figures on his tomb and in his will was bestowed by Henry VI in recognition of extraordinary personal service[108]), the long-standing alliance between the abbey of St. Edmund and the Lancastrian dynasty,[109] and the tradition of messianic iconography in the political propaganda of Henry VI,[110] typological allusion and compliment to the kingship of England is in fact highly likely to have been intended. King Henry VI was a close personal friend of Abbot Curteys and a lay brother of the Abbey. Indeed, Henry had made several well-publicized visits to Bury St. Edmunds in the very years that the angel-roof was being carved, and the abbey had been directly involved with the plans for Margaret's coronation of 1445.[111] Much as the Capetian dynasty is invoked in the religious iconography of many twelfth-century French cathedral sculptures,[112] the Bury sculptures of a crowned king and his queen must have been intended to invoke Henry and Margaret as the contemporary incarnation of the messianic and just rule of wisdom and peace.[113]

But the primary meaning of the royal figures is not earthly kingship but the glorification of the eternal kingship of Christ, and the angelic procession to the High Mass and the mystery of *corpus Christi* is also a procession to the coronation of the Virgin. In this Suffolk church whose dedication was to the Assumption of the Virgin Mary, the virginal queen is both image of Mary and the personification of Ecclesia—Holy Church—which Mary, who is Spouse as well as Mother, traditionally figured.[114] The holy house of Mary's womb and the Holy House of Walsingham's maternal mysteries were also mystically the bridal chamber "where God was united to man's nature as a bridegroom to a bride."[115]

High above the heads of worshippers at their whispered prayers and devotions—high above the chanting spectacle of priests in their own splendid vestments—processed silently not only the Virgin Mary to her mystic wedding with Christ and to the coronation that was the final glory of her bodily Assumption, but *in figura* the Bury church of Mary of the Assumption, Queen Margaret as contemporary English embodiment of holy queenship, and the universal Christian Church to its glorious triumph. All these signs and significations merge in the perspective of eternity as the Bride bears her crown toward the sanctifying altar of the Mystic Marriage and the Eternal Mass, making the Word flesh in the visible signs that speak of the invisible grace. The shifting and multileveled resonance in this carved roof of sacred queenship and triumphant marriage is reminiscent of the royal entry for Margaret of Anjou to her coronation and wedding of 1445, a series of elaborate pageants in which the blessing of Mary, that heavenly Queen "Assumpt above the hevenly Ierarchie," was asked for the new queen, not only in her coming reign, but

Chapter Six

ever after "in blisse eterne."[116] The Bury angel-roof recalls, too, the bridal triumph of Anima and Wisdom lovingly joined in the conclusion of the Macro morality play *Wisdom;* but especially it images the play of the risen Christ transformed and glorified as Sapientia in the N-Town "Assumption of the Virgin," as he is moved by his mother's prayer of love-longing to send forth angels to bring his beloved to his side:

Sapientia: My suete moderis preyere on to me doth assende
         here holy herte and here love · is only on me
         Wherfore aungyl to here thou schalt now dyssende
         seying here sche shal comyn to myn eternyte.[117]

But in this roof-high allegory of eternal union, the reminder of the physical body of that mother "þat is carnall" also resounds.[118] Just below the eastern angels who honor rood and altar of St. Mary's church are carved on the wall posts the angel Gabriel (on the north) proclaiming the message of Annunciation to the Virgin Mary (on the south wall) who is carved already huge in expectation of the childbearing that is her attribute and the reason for her coronation and her triumph (fig. 6.19). Mary's Assumption is the fulfillment of her miraculous maternity; it is, as well, the final blessing of the human body that has borne and incarnated holy mysteries, has transformed matter even as the priest before the altar transforms it. The Bury sculpture of the Virgin in her pregnancy, like Piero della Francesca's famous painting of the pregnant Madonna honored by angels as she stands beneath the ciborium of a high altar (fig. 6.20), frames and glosses the meaning of the Mass and reveals Mary's mother-flesh to be both mystical tabernacle for the Messiah and *tabernaculum*—holy receptacle for the Eucharist that joins the body of the Church to the body and blood of incarnate God.

Like Mary, the mother of Jesus, the priest standing before the bread and wine of the altar created his own Creator. The images of sculpture, painted glass, altarpiece, the actors in the theaters of public or private devotion likewise *in imitatio Mariae* created their own Creator, invoked Christ's birth and redemptive suffering from the salvation drama of the Incarnation. And with Mary's Assumption, "grettest solemnyte / Of al hir festys," comes the apotheosis of late medieval incarnational sensibility.[119] The Assumption of Christ's mother is the end of the Incarnation play until time be played out in Doomsday, and in that Assumption, the human body is glorified to eternity. The Assumption is God's highest benediction upon the human carnal kind made in his own image (fig. 6.21). As the Archangel Michael of the N-Town "Assumption of the Virgin" extols, "god throw mary is mad mannys frend."[120] God through Mary is made Man's friend; the Church through Mary is made Christ's triumphant bride. The incar-

FIGURE 6.19. Our Lady of Expectation, wooden carving at the extreme southeast end of the nave wall, just below the sculptures of the angelic procession to the altar. The companion figure at the northeast end of the nave represents the angel of the Annunciation (Photo © Hallam Ashley: with the permission of Mrs. Dorothy Ashley).

national devotion and theater of fifteenth-century parishes and cloth towns is this: a play called *corpus Christi*, but a play that is also body and tabernacle of Mary, a play of politics and of angels—priests, crowned King, and Virgin Mother aloft with rustling wings, mediating the dizzy distance from heaven to earth.

FIGURE 6.20. *The Madonna del Parto,* attributed to Piero della Francesca, a fresco of about 1440–50 from the cemetery chapel of Monterchi, outside Borgo San Sepolcro (Alinari/ Art Resource, New York).

FIGURE 6.21. *The Assumption of the Virgin Mary,* a fifteenth-century stained-glass window from the parish church of St. Peter and St. Paul, East Harling, Norfolk (Royal Commission on the Historical Monuments of England).

Notes

Chapter One

1. Arthur Brown, "The Study of English Medieval Drama," in *Franciplegius: Medieval and Linguistic Studies in Honor of Francis Peabody Magoun, Jr.* (New York: New York University Press, 1965), 269–70. Peter W. Travis' *Dramatic Design in the Chester Cycle* (Chicago: University of Chicago Press, 1982) and Clifford Davidson's *From Creation to Doom: The York Cycle of Mystery Plays* (New York: AMS Press, 1984), which considers the York cycle's iconographical relationships to the surviving imagery of York churches, are really the first book-length attempts since F. M. Salter's lectures, printed as *Medieval Drama in Chester* (Toronto: Toronto University Press, 1955), to study the medieval drama in its specific local setting and context, in spite of the ever-growing evidence for the need for such focused regional study. Donald C. Baker has stated the issue succinctly in "The Drama: Learning and Unlearning," in *Fifteenth-Century Studies: Recent Essays,* ed. Robert F. Yeager (Hamden, Conn.: Shoe String Press, 1984), 192:

> That the spirit that informed the religious drama was a single spirit we have really no reason to doubt; that the methods for selecting subjects, writing the plays, and ordering and performing them were similar from town to town, and that they were performed under similar conditions by similar people or groups of people, we now have every reason to doubt.

2. The announced goal of the Records of Early English Drama (REED) project is to "locate, transcribe and publish systematically all surviving external evidence of dramatic, ceremonial, and minstrel activity in Great Britain before 1642." See *Records of Early English Drama: York,* ed. Alexandra F. Johnston and Margaret Rogerson (Toronto: University of Toronto Press, 1979), 1:v.

3. Lawrence M. Clopper, "The History and Development of the Chester Cycle," *Modern Philology* 75(1978):219–46.

4. Donald Hall, *English Mediaeval Pilgrimages* (London: Routledge and Kegan Paul, 1965), 117.

5. H. S. Bennett, *Chaucer and the Fifteenth Century* (Oxford: Clarendon Press, 1947), 103.

6. Dom David Knowles, *The Religious Orders in England, vol. 2, The End of the Middle Ages.* Revised edition. (Cambridge: Cambridge University Press, 1979), 222–23.

7. Thomas W. Ross, "Five Fifteenth-Century 'Emblem' Verses from British Museum Additional MS. 37049," *Speculum* 32(1957):275.

8. Hope Emily Allen in *The Book of Margery Kempe,* ed. Sanford Brown Meech

and Hope Emily Allen, Early English Text Society, o.s., 212 (London: Oxford University Press, 1940; reprint, 1961), Notes section, 257.

9. Carleton Brown, ed., *Religious Lyrics of the XVth Century* (Oxford: Clarendon Press, 1939; reprint, 1967), xxxi.

10. See O. B. Hardison, *Christian Rite and Christian Drama in the Middle Ages* (Baltimore: Johns Hopkins University Press, 1965), 1–34.

11. Cf. Percival Hunt, *Fifteenth Century England* (Pittsburgh: University of Pittsburgh Press, 1962), 10, on "the confusion and contradictions of the century." Two interesting studies of Huizinga and his influence on fifteenth-century scholarship are E. F. Jacob, "Huizinga and the Autumn of the Middle Ages," in *Essays in Later Medieval History* (New York: Barnes and Noble; Manchester: Manchester University Press, 1968), 141–53, and Margaret Aston, "Huizinga's Harvest: England and the *Waning of the Middle Ages*," in *Medievalia et Humanistica*, n.s., 9(1979):1–24.

12. J[ohan] Huizinga, *The Waning of the Middle Ages* (London: Edward Arnold, 1927), 18: "So violent and motley was life, that it bore the mixed smell of blood and of roses. The men of that time always oscillate between the fear of hell and the most naive joy, between cruelty and tenderness, between harsh asceticism and insane attachment to the delights of this world, between hatred and goodness, always running to extremes."

13. Erwin Panofsky, *Early Netherlandish Painting* (New York: Harper and Row, 1971), 1:67.

14. C. G. Coulton, "The Plain Man's Religion in the Middle Ages," *The Hibbert Journal* 14(1915–16):596.

15. Meyer Schapiro, "The Image of the Disappearing Christ: The Ascension in English Art Around the Year 1000," *Gazette des Beaux Arts*, 6th ser., 23 (1943): 152.

16. Schapiro, p. 152.

17. Jonathan Sumption, *Pilgrimage: An Image of Mediaeval Religion* (Totowa, New Jersey: Rowman and Littlefield, 1975), 48.

18. See Sixten Ringbom, "Devotional Images and Imaginative Devotions: Notes on the Place of Art in Late Medieval Private Piety," *Gazette des Beaux Arts*, 6th ser., 73(1969):164.

19. For a study of the iconography of the Christ Child of the Annunciation, see David M. Robb, "The Iconography of the Annunciation in the Fourteenth and Fifteenth Centuries," *Art Bulletin* 18(1936):523–26.

20. *Book of Margery Kempe*, p. 8.

21. Cf. H. Munro Cautley, *Suffolk Churches and their Treasures*, 4th ed. (Ipswich: Boydell Press, 1975), 193.

22. Helen Rosenau, "A Study in the Iconography of the Incarnation," *Burlington Magazine* 85(1944):179.

23. John Fleming, *An Introduction to the Franciscan Literature of the Middle Ages* (Chicago: Franciscan Herald Press, 1977), 251.

24. See the edition by Lawrence Powell of *The Mirrour of the Blessed Lyf of Jesus Christ*, trans. Nicholas Love (Oxford: Clarendon Press, 1908).

25. Cf. *Ludus Coventriae; or, The Plaie Called Corpus Christi*, ed. K. S. Block,

Early English Text Society, e.s., 120 (London: Oxford University Press, 1922; reprint, 1960), lviii-lx.

26. *Meditations on the Life of Christ,* trans. Isa Ragusa, ed. Isa Ragusa and Rosalie B. Green (Princeton: Princeton University Press, 1961), 301.

27. *Meditations on the Life of Christ,* p. 5.

28. Cf. Rosemary Woolf, *The English Religious Lyric in the Middle Ages* (Oxford: Clarendon Press, 1968), 5: "There is, however, a distinction between naturally anonymous and accidentally anonymous poetry, and most medieval lyrics can be called genuinely anonymous, for they were written by self-effacing poets, who did not obtrude peculiarities of style and thought between the subject-matter and the audience."

29. For an interesting discussion of fifteenth-century artists' contracts, see Michael Baxandall, *Painting and Experience in Fifteenth Century Italy* (London: Oxford University Press, 1974), 3–24.

30. Walter F. Schirmer, *John Lydgate: A Study in the Culture of the XVth Century,* trans. Ann E. Keep (London: Methuen and Company, 1961), 194.

31. Frederick J. Furnivall, ed., *The Fifty Earliest English Wills in the Court of Probate, London,* Early English Text Society, o.s., 78 (London: Trübner and Company, 1882), 116.

32. Furnivall, pp. 116–17.

33. W. Dyde, *The History and Antiquities of Tewkesbury,* 2d ed. (Tewkesbury: W. Dyde, 1798), 58.

34. Madeline Harrison Caviness, *The Early Stained Glass of Canterbury Cathedral, circa 1175–1220* (Princeton: Princeton University Press, 1977), 102.

35. Caviness, p. 102.

36. See John Phillips, *The Reformation of Images: Destruction of Art in England, 1535–1660* (Berkeley: University of California Press, 1973), 14–15. Even the "archheretic" John Wycliffe accepted religious images on the grounds that the biblical injunction against graven images had been given to the Jews when "the Incarnation had not yet sanctified human form." See W. R. Jones, "Lollards and Images: The Defense of Religious Art in Later Medieval England," *Journal of the History of Ideas* 34(1973):27–50.

37. See the facsimile edition of Vatican MS Reg. lat. 124 edited by Hans-Georg Muller. Hrabanus Maurus, *De laudibus sancta crucis: Studien zur Uberlieferung und Geistesgeschichte mit dem Faksimile-Textabdruck aus Codex Reg. Lat. 124 der vatikanischen Bibliothek,* Miltellateinischen Jahrbuch 11 (Ratingen: A. Henn Verlag, 1973).

38. E[rnest] T[heodore] DeWald, ed., *The Illustrations of the Utrecht Psalter* (Princeton: Princeton University Press, n.d.), pl. 40.

39. See Otto Pächt, *The Rise of Pictorial Narrative in Twelfth-Century England* (Oxford: Clarendon Press, 1962), esp. pp. 2–4.

40. Cited in Ringbom, p. 166.

41. *Dives and Pauper,* vol. 1, pt. 1, ed. Priscilla Heath Barnum, Early English Text Society, o.s., 275 (London: Oxford University Press, 1976), pt. 1, p. 82.

42. *Dives and Pauper,* pt. 1, p. 82.

43. *Dives and Pauper,* pt. 1, p. 82.

44. *Book of Margery Kempe,* p. 14.

45. G. H. Cook, *Letters to Cromwell and Others on the Suppression of the Monasteries* (London: John Barker, 1965), p. 144.

46. Phillips, p. 73.

47. Julian Jaynes, *The Origin of Consciousness in the Breakdown of the Bicameral Mind* (Boston: Houghton Mifflin, 1976), p. 56.

48. See Sumption, p. 56.

49. See, for example, the 1504 will of William at Wood published in *Testamenta Cantiana: East Kent,* ed. Arthur Hussey (London: Mitchell Hughes and Clarke, 1907), 348.

50. Sumption, p. 270.

51. *Glossa Ordinaria,* "Evangelium secundum Joannem 20:19–24," in J. P. Migne, ed., *Patrologiae cursus completus, series latina* (Paris: J. P. Migne, 1844–66), (hereafter referred to as *PL*), 114:424.

52. Woodburn O. Ross, ed., *Middle English Sermons,* EETS, o.s., 209 (London: Oxford University Press, 1940), 134.

53. Cf. Gertrud Schiller, *Ikonographie der christlichen Kunst* (Gütersloh: Gütersloher Verlagshaus G. Mohn, 1971), 3:446–52. Compare early medieval representations of the doubting Thomas in plates 361 (p. 453), 363–66 (p. 454), to the late medieval images of plates 367, 369 (p. 455), in which Christ himself thrusts Thomas' hand in the wounds.

54. *The Chester Mystery Cycle, vol. 1,* ed. R. M. Lumiansky and David Mills, EETS, s.s., 3 (Oxford: Oxford University Press, 1974), 367 (l. 246).

55. *Ludus Coventriae,* pp. 348–49 (ll. 377–84).

Chapter Two

1. W. K. Jordan, *The Charities of Rural England, 1480–1660* (New York: Russell Sage Foundation, 1962), 91.

2. Jordan, p. 196.

3. See Alan R. H. Baker, "Changes in the Later Middle Ages," in *A New Historical Geography of England,* ed. H. C. Darby (Cambridge: Cambridge University Press, 1973), 242–43, and W. C. Hoskins, *The Age of Plunder: King Henry's England, 1500–1547* (London and New York: Longmans, 1976), 152.

4. Cf. Jordan, p. 18: "Norwich was the capital city of the county quite as truly as London was the capital city of the realm, exercising a powerful and forward-looking influence on the life and institutions of the entire shire and serving as the centre of its administrative, financial, and economic activities."

5. Norman P. Tanner, *The Church in Late Medieval Norwich, 1370–1532,* Pontifical Institute Studies and Texts, no. 66 (Toronto: Pontifical Institute of Mediaeval Studies, 1984), 109.

6. See Tanner, p. 143.

7. See Tanner, pp. 10–15.

8. *Book of Margery Kempe,* p. xxxii.

9. See Joel T. Rosenthal, *The Purchase of Paradise: Gift Giving and the Aristocracy, 1307–1485* (London: Routledge and Kegan Paul; Toronto: University of Toronto

Press, 1972), 120, for evidence that the London Charterhouse attracted noble patrons from other provincial areas as well.

10. Tanner, p. 124. On the Carthusians in fifteenth-century England, see Knowles, *Religious Orders,* 2:129–38.

11. See the discussion of John Baret's will in Chapter 4.

12. C. A. J. Armstrong, "The Piety of Cicely, Duchess of York: A Study in Late Medieval Culture," in *For Hilaire Belloc: Essays in Honor of his 71st Birthday,* ed. Douglas Woodruff (New York: Sheed and Ward, 1942), 85.

13. See Knowles, *Religious Orders,* 2:223.

14. Margaret Deanesly, "Vernacular Books in England in the Fourteenth and Fifteenth Centuries," *Modern Language Review* 15(1920):354.

15. On the East Anglian monasteries, see Richard Taylor, *Index Monasticus; or, the Abbeys and Other Monasteries, Alien Priories, Friaries, Colleges, Collegiate Churches, and Hospitals with their Dependencies formerly established in the Diocese of Norwich and the Ancient Kingdom of East Anglia* (London: Richard and Arthur Taylor, 1821), and Claude J. W. Messent, *The Monastic Remains of Norfolk and Suffolk* (Norwich: H. W. Hunt, 1934).

16. H. Munro Cautley, *Norfolk Churches* (Ipswich: Boydell Press, 1949; reprint, 1979), 1.

17. Sir William Parker, *The History of Long Melford* (London: Wyman and Sons, 1873), 70–74.

18. Jordan, p. 172.

19. Jordan, p. 172.

20. Cf. T. H. Swales, "Opposition to the Suppression of the Norfolk Monasteries; Expressions of Discontent, The Walsingham Conspiracy," *Norfolk Archaeology* 33(1962):264: "Prosperity, trade, and commercial links with Flanders tended to make East Anglia accept religious change more readily than the more conservative north and west. Protestant sectarianism and puritanism were to flourish in East Anglia."

21. See Tanner, p. 170.

22. Tanner, pp. 64–66.

23. On the Stour River cloth villages, see Barbara McClenaghan, *The Springs of Lavenham and the Suffolk Cloth Trade in the XV and XVI Centuries* (Ipswich: W. E. Harrison, 1924).

24. Tanner, p. 167.

25. See Christopher Woodforde, *The Norwich School of Glass-Painting in the Fifteenth Century* (London: Oxford University Press, 1950).

26. For a discussion of Suffolk church roofs see Cautley, *Suffolk Churches,* pp. 88–89. Cautley remarks with awe that "It is amazing to find no trace of iron bolts, straps, or nails" anchoring these spectacular roofs. "The most elaborate structures rely on framing alone, the various parts being merely morticed and tenoned together and fixed with wooden pins."

27. Samuel Tymms, ed., *Wills and Inventories from the Registers of the Commissary of Bury St. Edmund's and the Archdeacon of Sudbury,* Camden Society, ser. 1, no. 49 (London: J. B. Nichols and Son, 1850; reprint, New York: AMS Press, 1968), 39.

28. *The Journal of William Dowsing of Stratford, Parliamentary Visitor, Appointed Under a Warrant from the Earl of Manchester for Demolishing the Superstitious Pictures and Ornaments of Churches, Within the Country of Suffolk, in the Years 1643–1644,* ed. Rev. C. H. Evelyn White (Ipswich: Pawsey and Hayes, 1885), 29. On the Ufford font cover, which Munro Cautley called "the most beautiful cover in the world," see Cautley, *Suffolk Churches,* p. 86.

29. Hoskins, p. 161.

30. Tanner, p. 4.

31. Nikolaus Pevsner, *Suffolk,* 2d ed., rev. Enid Radcliffe, Buildings of England Series (Harmondsworth, England and New York: Penguin Books, 1974), 344.

32. See John Harvey, *English Medieval Architects: A Biographical Dictionary Down to 1550* (London: B. T. Batsford, 1954), 60–66.

33. Marginal notes saying "Worlych," "Vade worlych," and "nota worlych" appear several times in the text of the play of "The Appearance to Cleophas and Luke," just before Petrus makes his first speech; they are "presumably stage directions." See *The N-Town Plays: A Facsimile of British Library MS Cotton Vespasian D VIII,* ed. Peter Meredith and Stanley J. Kahrl Leeds Texts and Monographs, Medieval Drama Facsimiles, no. 4 (Ilkey, England: Scholar Press, 1977), xxv. Did Bury's famous master mason play the role of the apostle who was the rock upon whom Christ built his church? We can only guess. Worliche, or Worlych, was a fairly common name in fifteenth-century East Anglia, especially in the Bury St. Edmunds and Thetford area. See Harvey, p. 304, and M. A. Farrow, ed., *Index to Wills Proved in the Consistory Court of Norwich, 1370–1550,* British Record Society, no. 69 (London: British Record Society, 1945), 400, 405. A John Wurlych was master of the Harling family's Rushworth College near Thetford in 1443–44. See [Edward Kedington] Bennet, "Notes on the Original Statutes of the College of St. John Evangelist of Rushworth, Co. Norfolk, Founded by Edmund Gonville, A.D. 1342," *Norfolk Archaeology* 10 (1888):362–63.

34. Harvey, pp. 157–58, 303–4.

35. Edwin Smith, Graham Hutton, and Olive Cook, *English Parish Churches* (London: Thames and Hudson, 1976), 122.

36. See Norman Cohn, *The Pursuit of the Millennium,* rev. ed. (New York: Oxford University Press, 1970). However, as John A. F. Thomson notes in *The Later Lollards, 1414–1520,* 2d ed. (London: Oxford University Press, 1967), 240, "Millenarianism was not common in late medieval England, and there was no movements there comparable with those which can be seen on the continent."

37. Tanner, p. 70.

38. Tanner, p. 106.

39. Tymms, *Wills and Inventories,* p. 41.

40. Henry Harrod, "Extracts from Early Wills in the Norwich Registries," *Norfolk Archaeology* 4(1855):331.

41. On the fortunes of the Spring family, see McClenaghan.

42. Henry C. Malden, "Lavenham Church Tower," *Proceedings of the Suffolk Institute of Archaeology and History.* 9(1897):371.

43. John Clopton's will is printed in *The Visitation of Suffolke made by William*

Hervey, Clarenceux King of Arms, 1561, with Additions from Family Documents, Original Wills, Jermyn, Davy and Other MSS., ed. Joseph Jackson Howard (Lowestoft and London: Samuel Tymms and Whittaker and Company, 1866), 1:34–40. K. B. McFarlane, in *Lancastrian Kings and Lollard Knights* (Oxford: Clarendon Press, 1972), 210–11, has shown that injunctions against funeral pomp were a common characteristic of Lollard wills.

44. Cf. Michael R. Kelley, *Flamboyant Drama: A Study of "The Castle of Perseverance," "Mankind," and "Wisdom"* (Carbondale and Edwardsville, Illinois: Southern Illinois University Press, 1979), esp. pp. 1–28.

45. See Donald Weinstein, "Critical Issues in the Study of Civil Religion in Renaissance Florence," in *The Pursuit of Holiness in Late Medieval and Renaissance Religion,* ed. Charles Trinkaus and Heiko A. Oberman, Studies in Medieval and Reformation Thought, no. 10 (Leiden: E. J. Brill, 1974), 269.

46. *Visitation of Suffolke,* 1:38.

47. Margaret Deanesly emphasized that English Bibles were permitted only to nuns and "exalted lay people" by special license and by special exception. See Margaret Deanesly, *The Lollard Bible and Other Medieval Biblical Versions* (Cambridge: Cambridge University Press, 1920), 326. For possession of vernacular scripture as evidence in fifteenth-century heresy trials see Thomson, *Later Lollards,* pp. 242–43.

48. Tanner, p. 163.

49. Thomson, *Later Lollards,* p. 237.

50. Thomson, *Later Lollards,* pp. 120–31.

51. See Swales.

52. Swales, p. 261.

53. For a discussion of Lollard doctrines and beliefs, see Thomson, *Later Lollards,* pp. 239–50, and for the characteristic views of East Anglian Lollards, pp. 125–30. Thomson (p. 127) observes that "It is highly probable that the ideas of those [East Anglian Lollards] who abjured were less clear in their own minds than they were after they had been reduced to order by the episcopal authorities."

54. See *Book of Margery Kempe,* p. 147, and Tanner, pp. 231–32. Years before Caister's death, Margery Kempe had traveled to Norwich to give him a message she had received from Jesus: "I byd þe gon to þe Vykary of Seynt Stefenys and sey þat I gret hym wel & þat he is an hey chossyn sowle of myn, & telle hym he plesyth me mech wyth hys prechyng & schew hym thy preuytes & myn cownselys swech as I schewe þe" (*Book of Margery Kempe,* p. 38).

55. Tanner, p. 166.

56. Albert E. Hartung, ed., *A Manual of the Writings in Middle English, 1050–1500,* vol. 5, (New Haven: Connecticut Academy of Arts and Sciences, 1975), 1374–75.

57. Theodore De Welles, "The Lollard Controversy and the N-Town Passion" (Paper delivered at the Seventeenth Medieval Studies Congress, Western Michigan University, Kalamazoo, Michigan, May, 1982).

58. *Ludus Coventriae,* p. 230 (ll. 3–8).

59. De Welles.

60. *Book of Margery Kempe,* pp. 111–12.

61. See chapter 5.

62. Edwin Welch, "Some Suffolk Lollards," *Proceedings of the Suffolk Institute of Archaeology and History* 29(1963):160–61.

63. Thomson, *Later Lollards*, pp. 120–21.

64. Thomson, *Later Lollards*, p. 120.

65. *The Minor Poems of John Lydgate,* part 1, *Lydgate Canon and Religious Poems,* ed. Henry Noble MacCracken, EETS, e.s., 107 (London: Kegan Paul, 1911); part 2, *Secular Poems,* ed. Henry Noble MacCracken and Merriam Sherwood, EETS, o.s., 192 (London: Oxford University Press, 1934; reprint, 1961), 1:171 (ll. 313–24).

66. Thomson, *Later Lollards*, p. 235.

67. Thomson, *Later Lollards*, p. 234.

68. See *Non-Cycle Plays and Fragments,* ed. Norman Davis, EETS, s.s., 1 (London: Oxford University Press, 1970) lxxii, 59 (l. 58).

69. See *Non-Cycle Plays,* p. 77, ll. 620–21. The staggering list of the possessions of the abbey of St. Edmund returned to the Court of Augmentations at the time of the royal seizure of monastic property mentions "a certain messuage called le Tolcotte near the town of Burye" as well as the meadow called "le Hospitall Medowe near Babwell mill." See Lilian J. Redstone, "First Ministers' Account of the Possessions of the Abbey of St. Edmund," *Proceedings of the Suffolk Institute of Archaeology and Natural History* 13 (1909):313, 320.

70. David Bevington, *Medieval Drama* (Boston: Houghton Mifflin, 1975), 756.

71. *Non-Cycle Plays,* p. 89 ("IX may play yt at ease").
R.C.

72. John Wasson, personal letter to author, November 19, 1981.

73. *Non-Cycle Plays,* p. 85.

74. Norman Scarfe, *The Suffolk Landscape* (London: Hodder and Stoughton, 1972), 188.

75. Tymms, *Wills and Inventories,* p. 129.

76. Corpus Christi is a movable feast, celebrated on the Thursday after Trinity Sunday (i.e., between late May and late June). On the feast of Corpus Christi and the mystery plays see V. A. Kolve, *The Play Called Corpus Christi* (Stanford: Stanford University Press, 1966), 33–56, and Alan H. Nelson, *The Medieval English Stage: Corpus Christi Pageants and Plays* (Chicago: University of Chicago Press., 1974), 1–14.

77. *Non-Cycle Plays,* p. 65 (ll. 199–204).

78. Cecilia Cutts, "The Croxton Play: An Anti-Lollard Piece," *Modern Language Quarterly* 5(1944):p. 55.

79. The account of the Bury abbey fire of 1464/65 survives in British Library MS Cotton Claudius A.XII and has been printed by Montague Rhodes James in *On the Abbey of S. Edmund at Bury,* Cambridge Antiquarian Society, Octavo Publications, no. 28 (Cambridge: Cambridge Antiquarian Society, 1895), 204–12.

80. On the cult of the Five Wounds of Christ see R. W. Pfaff, *New Liturgical Feasts in Later Medieval England* (Oxford: Clarendon Press, 1970), pp. 84–91. Badges bearing the emblem of the Five Wounds are illustrated in the London Museum's *Medieval Catalogue* (London:n.d.), pp. 262–263, pl. 70. Robert Cooke,

vicar of Haughley, specified in his will that after his death he wanted "v messys songe of the v wond[s] of ow$_r$ Lorde." The five-dot emblem of the Five Wounds can still be seen, incidentally, marked upon eighteenth-century fire buckets preserved at Robert Cooke's church at Haughley, Suffolk. (See Cautley, *Suffolk Churches*, p. 292 and pl. 264).

81. A thought-provoking analysis of narrative irony in Mark appears in Werner H. Kelber, *Mark's Story of Jesus* (Philadelphia: Fortress Press, 1979).

82. *Non-Cycle Plays*, p. 77 (ll. 620–21).

83. David Bevington's, edition of the play in *Medieval Drama*, p. 756, mistakenly glosses "colkote" (i.e., Tolkote) as "coal-shed."

84. Cf. Cutts, p. 99 n. 88, who was also struck by the absence of anti-Jewish feeling in this play, in which "Jews" are merely signs and symbols for Lollard unbelievers.

85. See Robert S. Gottfried, *Bury St. Edmunds and the Urban Crisis, 1290– 1539* (Princeton: Princeton University Press, 1982), pp. 200–2, and Joy Rowe, "The Medieval Hospitals of Bury St. Edmunds," *Medical History* 2, no. 4 (1958): 253–63.

86. *Non-Cycle Plays*, p. 82 (l. 765).

87. See Cutts, p. 49, and Thomas Hoccleve, "The Remonstrance Against Oldcastle," in *Selections from Hoccleve*, ed. M. C. Seymour (Oxford: Clarendon Press, 1981), 64. (ll. 121–28):

Vnto seint Petir and his successours
And so foorth doun God hath His powers lent.
Go to the preest, correcte thyn errours,
With herte contryt vnto God ybent.
Despute no more of the sacrament.
As holy chirche biddith, folwe it.
And hennesforward, as by myn assent,
Presume nat so mochil of thy wit.

88. *Non-Cycle Plays*, p. 83.

89. *Non-Cycle Plays*, p. 84 (l. 837).

90. See V. B. Redstone, "Chapels, Chantries and Gilds in Suffolk," *Proceedings of the Suffolk Institute of Archaeology* 12(1904):24–27, and Karl Young, "An Interludium for a Gild of Corpus Christi," *Modern Language Notes* 48 (1933):85– 86.

91. The College of Jesus was endowed in 1480 by John Smyth, a prominent burgess who had many times served as alderman of Bury. The college obtained royal license in 1481 for a guild and perpetual chantry of "the Holy or Sweet Name of Jesus." The Bernewell Street College consisted of a warden and six priests who were to pray daily for the souls of John Smyth and his family, for the king and queen, and for the brothers and sisters of the guild of the Holy Name of Jesus. See *The Victoria History of the County of Suffolk*, ed. William Page (London: Archibald Constable and Co., 1906; reprint, William Dawson and Sons, 1975), 2:141; and Gottfried, pp. 189–90 (who suggests there was some connection between the guild of the Holy Name and Corpus Christi.) John Perfay, draper of Bury, who made his will in 1509, appointed "the gylde off the holy name of Ihu[s] in Sent Jamys Cyrche" as supervisor of the almshouse he endowed in his will. See Tymms,

Wills and Inventories, p. 111. This guild, too, included both "brothern and systern," and the Perfay will is probably evidence that the College guild of the Holy Name was also affiliated with St. James church. In Norwich, a much larger city than Bury, there were, however, several guilds of the Name of Jesus, many of them established to perform chantry services of the new fifteenth-century Mass of the Holy Name of Jesus. See Tanner, p. 349, and Pfaff, pp. 62–83. Adding to the difficulty of reconstructing the histories of town guilds which shared the same name is the fact that religious confraternities, unlike craft guilds or the religious guilds which were also town governing councils (like Holy Trinity guild in Lynn and Candlemas guild in Bury St. Edmunds), tended to be short-lived. Norman Tanner has emphasized (p. 74) that only four of the forty-four known religious confraternities of Norwich during the period 1370–1532 had a continuous existence for as long as a century.

92. *Non-Cycle Plays,* p. 89 (ll. 1004–7).

93. Cf. Richard R. Wright, "Community Theatre in Late Medieval East Anglia," *Theatre Notebook* 28(1974):24–39.

94. Clifford Flanigan, "The Medieval English Mystery Cycles and the Liturgy" (Paper delivered at the seventeenth Medieval Studies Congress, Western Michigan University, Kalamazoo, Michigan, May, 1982).

95. See Charles Phythian-Adams, "Ceremony and the Citizen: The Communal Year at Coventry, 1450–1550," in *Crisis and Order in English Towns, 1500–1700: Essays in Urban History* (Toronto: University of Toronto Press, 1972), 57–85.

96. See Swales, pp. 254–57, 260–61.

97. For a useful corrective to the usual studies of "folk" ritual and drama, see Thomas Pettitt, "Approaches to the Medieval Folk Drama," *Early Drama, Art, and Music Newsletter* 7(1985):23–27.

98. Keith Thomas, *Religion and the Decline of Magic* (London: Weidenfeld and Nicolson, 1971), 76.

99. Weinstein, "Critical Issues," in *Pursuit of Holiness,* ed. Trinkaus and Oberman, p. 267.

100. Donald C. Baker, John L. Murphy, and Louis B. Hall, Jr., eds., *The Late Medieval Religious Plays of Bodleian Mss. Digby 133 and E. Museo 160,* EETS, o.s., 283 (Oxford: Oxford University Press, 1982), 106 (ll. 309–12). (This edition is hereafter referred to as *Digby Plays.*)

101. Baker, Murphy, and Hall, *Digby Plays,* pp. 107–8.

102. Cf. Hartung, *Manual of the Writings in Middle English,* 5:1354: "At times the piece degenerates into low farce, as in the comic intrusion of the would-be Knight Watkyn who is bullied by Herod and capitulates to the women's distaffs in the massacre scene." But see the excellent essay by David Mills, "Religious Drama and Civic Ceremonial," in A. C. Cawley et. al., *The Revels History of Drama in English,* vol. 1, *Medieval Drama* (London: Methuen, 1983), 152–206, which is far more sympathetic to the comic function of the Watkyn episode: "'The Killing of the Children' is a play of *solas* in two senses—the 'consolation' of the operation of divine justice in the escape of Christ and the death of Herod; and the 'entertainment' arising from the absurd pretensions of Watkin" (p. 164).

103. A. R. Wright, *British Calendar Customs: England* (London: William Glaisher, 1938), 2:91.

104. *The Poetical Works of Robert Herrick*, ed. L. C. Martin (London: Clarendon Press, 1956), 315.

105. *Records of Early English Drama: York*, 1:362.

106. A similar play may have influenced the fifteenth or early sixteenth-century glass-painting of the Massacre of the Innocents in the parish church of St. Peter Mancroft, Norwich. In the St. Peter Mancroft window one of the mothers is shown attacking the knight who has skewered her baby on his sword; another woman and a man who is not in knight's armor but in ordinary fifteenth-century dress—and who wears what looks like a purse or a messenger's pouch buckled round his waist—are shown prominently in the foreground. Christopher Woodforde in his study of the St. Peter Mancroft windows found this male figure a "puzzling" addition to the scene, although "a close examination of the glass, as well as the expressions and postures of the man and woman, show that the panel is in its original form." (Woodforde, *Norwich School of Glass Painting*, p. 27 and pl. 3.) Although there are no distaffs in evidence in the scene and although the postures of the foreground figures are difficult to interpret (Woodforde refers to them as "standing" but the man's bent right leg and outstretched arm show he is either walking or running away from the female figure), I think it possible that the unusual iconography here may refer to an invented stage character like the Watkyn of the Digby plays. The canopied throne of Herod in the upper left-hand corner of the Massacre scene is also strongly suggestive of dramatic influence, as are many details from other windows in the St. Peter Mancroft series. (See Woodforde, pp. 25, 28, 31.)

107. Bede, *A History of the English Church and English People*, trans. Leo Sherley-Price, rev. R. E. Latham (Harmondsworth, England: Penguin Books, 1955; reprint, 1979), 86–87.

108. On the green children of Woolpit see Kevin Crossley-Holland, *The Green Children* (London, 1966), and on the Lady Well at Woolpit, see Edmund Waterton, *Pietas Mariana Britannica* (London: St. Joseph's Catholic Library, 1879), 2:249–50.

109. Cf. A. N. Galpern, "The Legacy of Late Medieval Religion in Sixteenth Century Champagne," in *Pursuit of Holiness*, ed. Trinkaus and Oberman, p. 161.

110. British Library MS Harl. 308, fol. 9v; PROE 327/252, 1533, printed in T. Madox, *Formulare Anglicanum* (London, 1702), 151 (no. 252); Sir William Dugdale, *Monasticon Anglicanum*, rev. ed., ed. and trans. John Caley et al. (London: James Bohn, 1846), 3:133; and Edmund Gillingwater, *An Historical and Descriptive Account of St. Edmund's Bury, in the County of Suffolk* (Bury St. Edmunds: J. Rackham, 1804), 141–49.

111. See Rodney M. Thomson, *The Archives of the Abbey of Bury St. Edmunds*, Suffolk Records Society, no. 21 (Bury St. Edmunds: St. Edmundsbury Press, 1980), 11, 166.

112. Gillingwater, pp. 147–49. On the white-bull procession of Bury see also R.

Hedger Wallace, "White Cattle in British Folktales and Customs," *Folk-Lore* 10(1899):352–57, esp. pp. 355–56.

Chapter Three

1. Despite several recent and very sympathetic studies by such scholars as Clarissa Atkinson, Susan Dickman, Deborah Ellis, and Karma Lochrie, of Margery Kempe's piety and its relationship to late medieval social history and the continental "feminist movement" (e.g., Susan Dickman, "Margery Kempe and the English Devotional Tradition," in *The Medieval Mystical Tradition in England: Papers Read at the Exeter Symposium, July 1980,* ed. Marion Glasscoe [Exeter: University of Exeter Press, 1980], 151) and despite the quite remarkable fact that selections from *The Book of Margery Kempe* were included in the new fifth edition of that arbiter of the literary canon, *The Norton Anthology of English Literature,* most scholars, especially male scholars, remain curtly dismissive. Cf. Derek Brewer, *English Gothic Literature* (New York: Schocken Books, 1983), p. 253. "Religion was to Margery what sex was to Chaucer's Wife of Bath."

2. *Book of Margery Kempe,* p. 47.
3. See appendix 3 in *Book of Margery Kempe,* pp. 358–59.
4. *Book of Margery Kempe,* p. 131.
5. *Book of Margery Kempe,* p. 156.
6. *Book of Margery Kempe,* p. 156.
7. On the "recurrence of divine pattern" in hagiographic texts see David L. Jeffrey, "English Saints' Plays," in *Medieval Drama,* ed. Neville Denny, Stratford-upon-Avon Studies, no. 16 (London: Edward Arnold, 1973), esp. pp. 72–73, and James W. Earl, "Typology and Iconographic Style in Early Medieval Hagiography," *Studies in the Literary Imagination* 8(1975):15–46.
8. *Book of Margery Kempe,* pp. 105–7.
9. Cf. Wolfgang Riehle, *The Middle English Mystics* (London: Routledge and Kegan Paul, 1981), 11: "The excessive emotional piety of this wife of a citizen of Lynn shows pathologically neurotic traits. Nevertheless some of the mystical passages in her autobiography are of some value. The very fact that Julian [of Norwich, another East Anglian mystic], who had a conversation with her, considered her piety to be genuine, forces us to include Margery in our study."
10. *Meditations on the Life of Christ,* p. 360.
11. *Book of Margery Kempe,* p. 18.
12. *Book of Margery Kempe,* p. 18.
13. See the discussion of the N-town play of Mary's Presentation in the Temple in chapter 5.
14. *Book of Margery Kempe,* p. 18.
15. *Book of Margery Kempe,* pp. 194–95.
16. *Meditations on the Life of Christ,* p. 347. Deborah S. Ellis in her otherwise perceptive article, "Margery Kempe and the Virgin's Hot Caudle," *Essays in Arts and Sciences* 14(1985):1–11, does not appear to realize the textual authority for Margery's vision of the Virgin's sickbed. Cf. Ellis, p. 7, "When presented with a formal occasion for piety—a Good Friday sermon or a Corpus Christi procession, for

instance—Margery reduces the public vision into a private domestic scene: 'Than þe creatur thowt . . . sche mad for owr Lady a good cawdel & browt it hir to comfortyn hir. . . .'"

17. See *Book of Margery Kempe*, p. xliv.

18. As Caroline Walker Bynum observes in her fascinating study, *Holy Feast and Holy Fast: The Religious Significance of Food to Medieval Women* (Berkeley: University of California Press, 1987), 294–95, the late medieval world was one "whose central ritual was the coming of God into food as macerated flesh, and it was compatible with, not contradictory to, new philosophical notions that located the nature of things not in their abstract definitions but in their individuating matter or particularity." In this sense the restoring caudle given to the grieving Virgin Mary is both a homily about Margery's affective participation and handmaidenship—and a foreshadowing symbol of the restoring food and drink of the Eucharist.

19. *Book of Margery Kempe*, p. 209.

20. *Book of Margery Kempe*, p. 19.

21. *Book of Margery Kempe*, p. 79.

22. Francis Newton, *St. Francis and His Basilica Assisi* (Assisi, 1926), 136, and *Book of Margery Kempe*, p. 298n.

23. *Meditations on the Life of Christ*, p. 32.

24. *Meditations on the Life of Christ*, p. 33.

25. Translated by Henrik Cornell in *The Iconography of the Nativity of Christ*, Uppsala Universitets Arsskrift (Uppsala: A. B. Lundequistska Bokhandeln, 1924), 12.

26. *Meditations on the Life of Christ*, p. 333.

27. Mary's girding Christ at Calvary with the veil from her head is also reported in another popular thirteenth-century meditation on the Passion, the so-called *Dialogus Beatae Mariae et Anselmi de Passione Domini*, a text attributed to St. Anselm (c. 1033–1109) in the Middle Ages, but which is probably contemporary with the Pseudo-Bonaventure's *Meditationes*. In this supposed dialogue between the Virgin Mary and St. Anselm, Mary reveals how "when they had arrived at that most ignominious of places, Calvary, where dead dogs and carrion were thrown, they stripped my only son of all his clothes; and I, made faint by it, nevertheless took my headcloth and bound it around his loins." See Pseudo-Anselm, *Dialogus Beatae Mariae et Anselmi de Passione Domini* 10 (*PL* 159:282): "Cum venissent ad locum, Calvariae ignominiossimum, ubi canes et alia morticina projiciebantur, nudaverunt Jesum unicum filium meum totaliter vestibus suis, et ego exanimis facta fui, tamen velamen capitis mei accipiens circumligavi lumbis suis."

28. Simon Metaphrastes, a Byzantine theologian of the tenth century, for example, wrote of the Virgin's lament at the Cross in the form of an imagined monologue in which Mary contrasts the joys of Bethlehem with the sorrows of Calvary. One of the images in this monologue is the cloth of swaddling garment and of shroud, though it is not here specifically identified with any garment of the Virgin's. In the Simon Metaphrastes text, the cloth which wraps Christ was simply one of a number of affective details whose purposes were to arouse the reader to

compassion and sympathetic participation in the joys and sorrows of the Virgin: "Formerly I zealously wrapped the infant's swaddling bands around you, and now I prepare your shroud. . . . As a child you often slept against my breast, and now you sleep there in death." See Simon Metaphrastes, *Oratio in Lugubrem Lamentationem Sanctissimae Deiparae Pretiosum Corpus Domini Nostri Jesus Christi Amplexantis,* in J. P. Migne, ed., *Patrologiae cursus completus: series graeca* (Paris: J. P. Migne, 1857–66), hereafter referred to as *PG*), 114:215.

29. Carleton Brown, ed., *Religious Lyrics of the XIVth Century* (Oxford: Oxford University Press, 1924), 91 (ll. 13–18). The lullaby is from Advocates Library MS 18.7.21, a commonplace book of 1372 which belonged to the English Franciscan preacher John Grimestone.

30. In Mirk's *Festial* (c. 1400), the "Homily on Lent" describes how "Cristis cloþys wern drawn of hym and don all naked, saue hur lady, his modyr, wonde hyr kerchef about hym to hyll his membrys." *Mirk's Festial: A Collection of Homilies,* Part 1, ed. Theodore Erbe, EETS, o.s., 96 (London: Oxford University Press, 1905), 247.

31. Dorothy C. Shorr, *The Christ Child in Devotional Images in Italy during the XIV Century* (New York: George Wittenborn, 1954), 116–17.

32. See *The Holkam Bible Picture Book,* ed. W. O. Hassall (London: Dropmore Press, 1954).

33. Herbert Friedmann, *The Symbolic Goldfinch: Its History and Significance in European Art* (Washington, D.C.: Pantheon, 1946), 7–10. Cf. Shorr, p. 172.

34. *Book of Margery Kempe,* pp. 237, 346n.

35. See *Das Hessische Weihnachtspiel,* in Richard Froning, ed., *Das Drama des Mittelalters* (Darmstadt: Wissenschaftliche Buchgesellschaft, 1964), 392–93 (ll. 582–97). And see F. G. Jenney, "The Comic in German-Folk-Christmas Plays," *Poet Lore* 27(1916):p. 686, for a nineteenth-century German folk Christmas play in which the Christ Child is wrapped in Joseph's "trousers."

36. Kolve, p. 247.

37. Kolve, pp. 151–74.

38. Joseph de Coo, "In Josephs Hosen Jhesus Ghewonden Wert: Ein Weihnachtsmotiv in Literatur und Kunst," *Aachener Kunstblatter* 30(1965):144–84.

39. Ross, *Middle English Sermons,* p. 223. Cf. *A Critical Edition of John Lydgate's Life of Our Lady,* ed. Joseph A. Lauritis et al., Duquesne Philological Series, no. 2 (Pittsburgh: Duquesne University Press, 1961), 367 (ll. 799–805).

40. Gertrud Schiller, *Iconography of Christian Art,* trans. Janet Seligman (Greenwich, Conn.: New York Graphic Society, 1971), 1:80. For other examples of the Nativity with the *Josefshosen* in German, Austrian, and Netherlandish paintings—and in the English *Holkam Bible*—see de Coo, pp. 144–45 (pl. 1–2) and pp. 163–75 (pl. 24–38).

41. Thomas Rogers, *The Catholic Doctrine of the Church of England: An Exposition of the Thirty-Nine Articles,* 1586, ed. J. J. S. Perowne, Parker Society, no. 40 (Cambridge: Cambridge University Press, 1854), 225.

42. Natalie Zemon Davis, "Some Tasks and Themes in the Study of Popular Religion," in *The Pursuit of Holiness* ed. Trinkaus and Oberman, pp. 307–36.

43. Davis, "Tasks and Themes," p. 312.

44. Thomas, p. 668.

45. *Pierce the Ploughman's Crede,* ed. Walter W. Skeat, EETS, o.s., 30 (London: N. Trübner, 1873), 4 (ll. 77–79).

46. See Carolly Erickson, *The Medieval Vision: Essays in History and Perception* (New York: Oxford University Press, 1976), 196–97.

47. *Visitation of Suffolke,* 1:48.

48. *Paston Letters and Papers of the Fifteenth Century,* Parts 1 and 2, ed. Norman Davis (Oxford: Clarendon Press, 1971 and 1976), 1:211.

49. On the Long Melford alabaster and other English fourteenth-century Nativity alabasters of similar iconography, see Francis Cheetham, *English Medieval Alabasters* (Oxford: Phaidon and Christie's Limited, 1984), 18–19.

50. On John Clopton, see chapter 4.

51. Parker, *History of Long Melford,* pp. 92–93.

52. *Book of Margery Kempe,* p. 77.

53. Christiane Klapisch-Zuber, "Holy Dolls: Play and Piety in Florence in the Quattrocento," in *Women, Family, and Ritual in Renaissance Italy,* trans. Lydia Cochrane (Chicago: University of Chicago Press, 1985), 310–29. Klapisch-Zuber also suggests (pp. 326–27) that mothering devotional play with the Christ Child effigies performed an important psychological function for late medieval nuns and laywomen:

> These play activities permitted young women, shut up from childhood or in a convent or subjected to a distant husband and separated from their own newborn children at birth, to identify with the mother of Christ and transmute their frustrations and tensions. . . . In fact, the infant Jesus allowed the recluse her primary social function—the maternal function—and put her desire and frustrations within limits that her male confessors recognized and could accept.

54. Erwin Panofsky, 1:101.

55. See Sumption, p. 49, and Waterton, 1:43, 91.

56. Waterton, 1:43.

57. Marina Warner, *Alone of All Her Sex: The Myth and the Cult of the Virgin Mary* (New York: Alfred A. Knopf, 1976), 280.

58. Waterton, 1:91.

59. See Panofsky, 1:203, and 2:fig. 247.

60. *Book of Margery Kempe,* p. 155.

61. *Book of Margery Kempe,* pp. 324n, 359, and Henry J. Hillen, *History of the Borough of King's Lynn* (Norwich: East of England Newspaper Company, 1907) 2:741–45, 814–15.

62. *Book of Margery Kempe,* p. 177.

63. *Book of Margery Kempe,* p. 178.

64. *Book of Margery Kempe,* p. 178.

65. *Book of Margery Kempe,* p. 7. On Margery Kempe's postpartum hysteria, see also Ellis, pp. 6–7, who focuses on the domestic rather than hagiographical implications of Margery's victory over the terrors of childbirth:

> Her regaining control of all aspects of her house, taking her place as housewife in the literal sense, is, then, equated with a return from the exile of insanity. And

her exile had been profounder because her Book continuously suggests that to be mad is to have no sense of place. Her recovery depends on her sense of integrity that also supports her religious identity, a self-esteem rooted first of all in her power to control her home.

Chapter Four

1. While John C. Coldewey has recently voiced caution about the ambiguity of medieval terms for games, sports, musical entertainments, and plays, and quite rightly has urged more scholarly scepticism about the uncritical penchant "for making games into play," the blurring of such distinctions was nonetheless a fundamental fact of the context of medieval theater. John C. Coldewey, "Plays and Play in Early English Drama," *Research Opportunities in Renaissance Drama* 28 (1985):181–88. The very difficulty of separating visual spectacles and ritual activities like St. Nicholas and boy-bishop ceremonies raises, as Ian Lancashire has pointed out, "questions about the adequacy of our present understanding of medieval play." Ian Lancashire, *Dramatic Texts and Records of Britain: A Chronological Topography to 1558*, Studies in Early English Drama, no. 1 (Toronto: University of Toronto Press, 1984), xxxv. See also Abigail Ann Young, "Plays and Players: The Latin Terms for Performance," *REED Newsletter* 9, no. 2 (1984):56–62; 10, no. 1 (1985):9–16.

2. C. L. Kingsford, *Prejudice and Promise in XVth Century England* (Oxford: Clarendon Press, 1925), 24–25.

3. *Testamenta Eboracensia, A Selection of Wills from the Register at York*, vol. 4, ed. James Raine, Surtees Society, no. 53 (Durham: Andrew and Company, 1869), 153.

4. Furnivall, p. xi.

5. Furnivall, p. xii.

6. Darlington, *London Consistory Court Wills*, p. xv.

7. Cf. the will of John Dalton (1487) in *Testamenta Eboracensia*, vol. 4, p. 25: "And in witnes hereof I have written this my testament and last will with my awne handes and setto my seale."

8. W. B. Stephens, *Sources for English Local History* (Manchester: Manchester University Press, 1973), pp. 36–37.

9. See Eber Carle Perrow, "The Last Will and Testament as a Form of Literature," *Transactions of the Wisconsin Academy of Sciences, Arts, and Letters*, 17, no. 1(1914):688–89.

10. *Testamenta Eboracensia*, vol. 4, p. 22n.

11. *Testamenta Eboracensia*, vol. 4, pp. 21–23.

12. Darlington, *London Consistory Court Wills*, pp. xxii, 67–68.

13. Tymms, *Wills and Inventories*, p. 131.

14. Tymms, *Wills and Inventories*, p. 138.

15. *Testamenta Eboracensia*, vol. 4, p. 200.

16. Cf. Rosenthal, p. 81: "A man of great wealth and large family is never as free of external obligations as when he makes his last will and testament."

17. *Testamenta Eboracensia*, vol. 4, p. 200n.

18. Tymms, *Wills and Inventories,* p. 233.

19. Tymms, *Wills and Inventories,* pp. 16, 20.

20. Tymms, *Wills and Inventories,* p. 15.

21. See Gail McMurray Gibson, "East Anglian Drama and the Dance of Death: Some Second Thoughts on the "'Dance of Paul's,'" *Early Drama, Art, and Music Newsletter* 5(1982):1–9.

22. For the full text of the tomb inscription see Tymms, *Wills and Inventories,* p. 234, and Kathleen Cohen, *Metamorphosis of a Death Symbol: The Transi Tomb in the Late Middle Ages and the Renaissance* (Berkeley and Los Angeles: University of California Press, 1973), 91. Such effigy tombs are unusual for fifteenth-century Englishmen who were not prominent members of the clergy, but not unprecedented. Kathleen Cohen (p. 192) lists eight such fifteenth-century English layman's tombs besides Baret's—one of them the tomb of Chaucer's granddaughter, Alice, duchess of Suffolk (d. 1475) at Ewelme. Not listed in Cohen's catalogue are the tomb effigies of an early Tudor couple just a few miles away from Bury in the Suffolk church of Denston. The figures, sculpted in decay and in funeral shrouds, are unidentified by inscription but are prominently placed to the north side of the chancel. They are thought to represent Katherine Denston, who was John Baret's niece by marriage, and her husband John. *Visitor's Guide to Denston Church* (n.p., n.d.).

23. Tymms, *Wills and Inventories,* p. 19.

24. Cf. Lydgate, *The Daunce of Death,* in *The Dance of Death,* ed. Florence Warren and Beatrice White, EETS, o.s., 181 (London: Oxford University Press, 1931), 2–4.

25. See John Stow, *A Survey of London,* ed. Charles Lethbridge Kingsford (Oxford: Clarendon Press, 1908; reprint, 1971), 1:327, and Schirmer, p. 128.

26. Tymms, *Wills and Inventories,* p. 19.

27. See Derek Pearsall, *John Lydgate* (Charlottesville: University Press of Virginia, 1970), 151. An elaborately illuminated East Anglian manuscript containing *The Siege of Thebes* is illustrated in P. Lasko and N. J. Morgan, eds., *Medieval Art in East Anglia, 1300–1520* (Norwich: Jarrold and Sons, 1973), 47–48.

28. For transcriptions of the pension documents see *Lydgate and Burgh's Secrees of Old Philisoffres,* ed. Robert Steele, EETS, e.s., 66 (London: Kegan Paul, Trench, Trübner and Co., 1894), xxvi-xxx.

29. See *A Critical Edition of John Lydgate's Life of Our Lady,* ed. Joseph A. Lauritis, Ralph A. Klinefelter, and Vernon T. Gallagher, Duquesne Philological Series, no. 2 (Pittsburgh: Duquesne University Press, 1961).

30. Tymms, *Wills and Inventories,* p. 17.

31. Tymms, *Wills and Inventories,* p. 17.

32. Tymms, *Wills and Inventories,* p. 21.

33. Tymms, *Wills and Inventories,* pp. 29–30.

34. Tymms, *Wills and Inventories,* pp. 27–28.

35. Tymms, *Wills and Inventories,* p. 38.

36. Tymms, *Wills and Inventories,* p. 41.

37. Tymms, *Wills and Inventories,* p. 39. The Adoration of the Magi and the

ancestry of Christ imaged as the Tree of Jesse are traditional and expected scenes in a chapel dedicated to the Virgin. Rather more ambiguous (to us, and not to Baret) is the image of "our lady with the virgenys afore hire." Several subjects are possible: the betrothal of Mary and Joseph with attending Virgins of the Temple; the Candlemas vision recounted by *The Golden Legend* of Jacobus de Voragine (see Jacobus de Voragine, *The Golden Legend,* trans. and ed. Granger Ryan and Helmut Ripperger [New York and London: Longmans, Green, and Co., 1941; reprint, New York: Arno Press, 1969], 152–53, and the surviving wall-painting on this theme of about 1480 in Eton College chapel); or, a devotional image of Mary surrounded by female saints.

38. Tymms, *Wills and Inventories,* pp. 23, 33.

39. Tymms, *Wills and Inventories,* pp. 35–36.

40. Tymms, *Wills and Inventories,* pp. 35–36.

41. The will of Richard Ferneys (1464) is transcribed in Tanner, pp. 233–34.

42. Tanner, p. 63.

43. See Harrod, pp. 335, 336.

44. *Book of Margery Kempe,* p. 148:

> "& þerfor, as honeste wolde, sche went to þe cherch þer þe lady herd his seruyse, wher þis creatur sey a fayr ymage of owr Lady clepyd a pyte. And thorw þe be- holdyng of þat pete hir mende was al holy ocupyed in þe Passyon of owr Lord Ihesu Christ & in þe compassyon of owr Lady, Seynt Mary, be whech sche was compellyd to cryyn ful lowde & wepyn ful sor, as þei sche xulde a deyd.
>
> Þan cam to hir þe ladys preste seying, "Damsel, Ihesu is ded long sithyn." Whan hir crying was cesyd, sche seyd to þe preste, "Sir, hys deth is as fresch to me as he had deyd þis same day, & so me thynkyth it awt to be to ȝow & to alle Cristen pepil."

45. *Book of Margery Kempe,* p. 94.

46. Tymms, *Wills and Inventories,* p. 17.

47. Tymms, *Wills and Inventories,* p. 42: "And j wil . . . that John Clopton es- quyere be my sup[er]visour and as oon of my executors in eche mat[ter] that lonith to my testement." Baret's wife, Elizabeth Drury, and John Clopton's father's first wife, Margery Drury (who died in childbirth in 1420), were sisters.

48. Woodforde, *Norwich School of Glass-Painting,* pp. 78–79.

49. See Colin Richmond, *John Hopton, A Fifteenth Century Suffolk Gentleman* (Cambridge: Cambridge University Press, 1981), 187–88. John Hopton (not to be confused with John Clopton), was another eminent Suffolk man with important acquaintances. James Hobart was one of Hopton's powerful friends, too, but then, as Richmond notes (p. 188), "James [Hobart] would have known most men in East Anglia who were worth knowing." This rich career lawyer (knighted in 1503) had purchased twenty-eight manors by the time of his death in 1517. A late-fifteenth century painting of Sir James Hobart and his wife can be seen at the church that his fortune built at Loddon, Norfolk, but Hobart is perhaps best known from the *Paston Letters;* he was the man who brought together John Paston and Paston's future wife, Margery Brews. See *Paston Letters and Papers,* 1:628.

50. *Visitation of Suffolke,* 1:38.

51. Richmond, p. 241.

52. See Richmond, pp. 214–16, and Dean Spooner, "The Almshouse Chapel, Hadleigh and the Will of Archdeacon Pykenham," *Proceedings of the Suffolk Institute of Archaeology* 7(1891): 378ff.

53. Parker, *History of Long Melford*, p. 44.

54. Parker, *History of Long Melford*, p. 44.

55. Transcription from Pevsner, *Suffolk*, p. 345.

56. Woodforde, *Norwich School of Glass-Painting*, p. 78. An inscription still present in the St. Edmund window when it was recorded by a seventeenth-century rector of the church asked for prayers for the soul of Hingham, "nuper abbatis de Bury," and "pro bono statu" of Thomas Rattlesden, who succeeded Hyngham in 1479 and who was abbot until 1497 (and hence contemporary with the glazing of the windows).

57. See chapter 5. On Monk Hyngham, see also Donald C. Baker and J. L. Murphy, "The Late Medieval Plays of MS. Digby 133: Scribes, Dates, and Early History," *Research Opportunities in Renaissance Drama* 10(1967):164, and Gail McMurray Gibson, "Bury St. Edmunds, Lydgate, and the *N-Town Cycle*," *Speculum* 56(1981):80.

58. Woodforde, *Norwich School of Glass-Painting*, p. 112.

59. Parker, *History of Long Melford*, p. 170.

60. *Visitation of Suffolke*, 1:37. A 1529 inventory from Long Melford church mentions "A Candlestick of 10 branches before St. Ann" and a hutch and painted altarcloths from St. Anne's chapel. See Parker, *History of Long Melford*, pp. 84–85.

61. See Osbern Bokenham, *Legendys of Hooly Wummen*, ed. Mary Sergeantson, EETS, o.s., 206 (London: Oxford University Press, 1938; reprint, New York: Kraus Reprints, 1971), 40. Katherine Denston's only child was named Anne—as were many of the women in the Clopton clan. John Clopton's will names Anne Drury, Anne Poley, Anne Montgomery, and Anne Gatis. On Katherine Denston, see also note 22 above.

62. The provincial council of Canterbury in the year 1328 attributed the Feast of the Conception to Anselm, although there is evidence that the feast had been celebrated—and subsequently forgotten—in pre-Conquest England. See Edmund Bishop, *Liturgia Historica* (Oxford: Clarendon Press, 1918; reprint, 1962), 238–59, and *The Letters of Osbert of Clare*, ed. E. W. Williamson (London: Oxford University Press, 1929), 11–13.

63. There were three different guilds of St. Anne in Norwich alone by the end of the fifteenth century. See Tanner, p. 349.

64. See, for example, the transcription of the 1470 churchwardens' accounts from Tilney All Saints, Norfolk, in *Records of Plays and Players in Norfolk and Suffolk, 1330–1642*, ed. David Galloway and John Wasson, Malone Society Collections no. 11 (Oxford: Oxford University Press, 1981), 116: "Item . . . in organorum joculatori ad diversa (principalia) ffesta Anni."

65. Controversy has raged for years about whether the Lincoln St. Anne's Day pageants and spectacles were actual dramas or were elaborate floats with images and silent tableaux. Alan Nelson, who is properly, I think, sceptical of the Lincoln St. Anne-plays theory (first advanced by Hardin Craig, who believed that the N-

Town cycle was a lost cycle of St. Anne's Day plays from Lincoln) concludes from his researches in the Lincoln archives that "All records suggest that the liturgical elaborations sponsored by the cathedral at . . . St. Anne's Day were simple or mechanically sophisticated visual displays, or, at most, brief dramatic ceremonies in the manner of liturgical plays." See Nelson, p. 104. The controversy has obscured the real point—that St. Anne's Day was assumed to be an important day for communal celebration and spectacle, civic spectacle that fulfilled a crucial social and religious function in defining the identity of a major English town.

66. Baker, Murphy, and Hall, *Digby Plays*, p. 96 (l. 10).

67. *The Commonplace Book of Robert Reynes of Acle: An Edition of Tanner Ms. 407*, ed. Cameron Louis (New York and London: Garland Publishing Company, 1980), 12, 35. On Weybridge Priory as the meeting place of the Acle St. Anne guild, see also Taylor, p. 27.

68. *Commonplace Book of Robert Reynes*, p. 12.

69. The particularity of the Reynes text and its guild occasion is underscored by another manuscript version of the poem, MS. Harley 4012, that pointedly omits the reference to the guild and replaces "þe worchepe of sent Anne in thys tyme of ȝeere" with the phrase "in any tyme of ȝer." See Roscoe E. Parker, ed., *The Middle English Stanzaic Versions of the Life of Saint Anne*, EETS, o.s., 174 (London: Oxford University Press, 1928), 126 (l. 453).

70. See *Minor Poems of Lydgate*, 1:130–31.

71. *Commonplace Book of Robert Reynes*, p. 200 (l. 57).

72. On the "Trinubium" of St. Anne see *Commonplace Book of Robert Reynes*, pp. 407–9, and Max Forster, "Die Legende von Trinubium der hl. Anna," in *Probleme der englischen Sprache und Kultur: Festscrift Johannes Hoops zum 60 Geburtstag*, ed. Wolfgang Keller (Heidelberg, 1925), 124–30.

73. *Commonplace Book of Robert Reynes*, p. 194.

74. See *Ludus Coventriae*, p. 62, and *N-Town Plays*, fol. 37. Cf. Rosemary Woolf, *The English Mystery Plays* (Berkeley and Los Angeles: University of California Press, 1972), 309: "Learned notes in the margins [of the *N-Town* manuscript] confirm that this was a manuscript made for private reading."

75. Woodforde, *Norwich School of Glass-Painting*, p. 21.

76. See Cautley, *Norfolk Churches*, pp. 233–34, and Lasko and Morgan, p. 49.

77. *Commonplace Book of Robert Reynes*, p. 110.

78. *Commonplace Book of Robert Reynes*, p. 228 (l. 460). Another East Anglian invocation for a feast of St. Anne is found in Trinity College, Cambridge MS. 601, in Parker, *Life of Saint Anne*, pp. 90–109. This studied poem in high rhetorical style provides a striking contrast to the sweetly domestic and popular poem in the Reynes *Commonplace Book*. The Cambridge St. Anne poem appears in a manuscript of Middle English poems, most of them by John Lydgate of Bury, and indeed inscriptions in a sixteenth-century hand (probably that of the antiquary John Stow) attribute the poem to Lydgate. Henry Noble MacCracken, who nearly singlehandedly decreed the Lydgate canon back in 1911, rejected the Lydgate attribution because he thought the verses broke Lydgate's rhyming habits and because he believed the poem was written somewhat later than Lydgate's time (see *Minor Poems of Lydgate*, 1:xxxviii–xl). But as MacCracken admits (p. xl), if the poem was

not written by Lydgate, it is a close and clever imitation of Lydgate's style (cf. especially his *Lyf of Our Lady*). Roscoe Parker, on the strength of the poem's Lydgate connections and dialect, was ready to attribute the poem to Bury St. Edmunds and made the likely suggestion that the poem was used for public recitation by the St. Anne guild of Bury. See Parker, *Life of Saint Anne*, p. xxx). Little more is known about the Bury guild of St. Anne than the guild certificate returns of 1389 can tell us—that it was founded about 1309 (astonishingly early for a dedication to St. Anne, even for Suffolk), that it met in the Bury parish church of St. James, and that its duties included keeping lights before St. Anne's image in the church, attending vespers in torchlight procession on St. Anne's Eve, July 25, and mass on the day of her feast, and honoring the funerals of guild members by guild lights round the body and by giving alms to the needy. It is probable that this guild also had some connection with the "Chapel of St. Anne in the undercroftys" which was in the abbey church at Bury. Indeed, there is striking emphasis upon the the feast of St. Anne in a fifteenth-century psalter and hymnarium from the abbey. This manuscript, now in the possession of the Bury Record Office (Suffolk Record Office E5/91608.7) contains a unique hymn for evensong of St. Anne and a very full series of St. Anne invocations and prayers. St. Anne is listed first in the litany of female saints in the martyrology (see. fol. 224, fols 263–64, irregular pagination). If the Trinity MS St. Anne poem is from Bury, the text itself argues for a connection of some kind between a lay guild and a clerical audience; the audience is addressed simply as "brethren," but a comparatively learned audience and context can be inferred not only from the language and style of the poem but from the poet's appeal (p. 93) to "all masteres that thys shall here or rede" for correction.

79. *Visitation of Suffolke*, 1:38.

80. G. H. Cook, *The English Mediaeval Parish Church* (London: Phoenix House, 1954), 121.

81. Parker, *History of Long Melford*, p. 79, and *The Gentleman's Magazine* 100, no. 2(1830):206–7.

82. See *Victoria History of Suffolk*, 2:340–41. There was a school at Long Melford at least by 1484, when the will of a clothmaker named Robert Harset bequeathed his house to his wife, and, after her death, to the priests of Long Melford church, specifying that the west end "where the children lerne" be retained as a school. In 1670 the Lady Chapel, described as being "much ruinated," was converted into the village school.

83. See Gibson, "Bury St. Edmunds, Lydgate, and the *N-Town Cycle*," pp. 80–81, and J. B. Trapp, "Verses by Lydgate at Long Melford," *Review of English Studies*, n.s., 6(1955):1–11. Trapp mistakenly refers to the *Quis Dabit* poem as *The Lamentation of Mary Magdalene*.

84. Trapp, p. 2. Harley MS. 2255 is a good example of the local East Anglian context of many of Lydgate's lyrics. In this anthology of devotional poems compiled for his abbot, Lydgate includes: a poem celebrating St. Edmund and his "fraunchise" in Bury (*To St. Edmund*, fols. 152–53, printed in *Minor Poems of Lydgate*, 1:124–25); a poem to the seventh-century East Anglian queen St. Osytha (*To St. Ositha*, fol. 116v; *Minor Poems*, 1:137); the poem on the *De Profundis*, fol. 43v,

that Abbot Curteys commissioned for the wall of the abbey church (*Minor Poems,* 1:84); and even what is apparently a topical satire of the Bury Bakers and Weavers guild (fol. 157; *Minor Poems,* 2:448–49). It is significant that the Bury Curteys manuscript also contains Lydgate's translation of *Stella Celi Extirpauit,* the same plague hymn that the shepherds sing in the N-Town "Nativity" play (fol. 103–103f; *Minor Poems,* 1:294–95). On the connections between Lydgate and the N-Town cycle, see chapter 5 and Gibson, "Bury St. Edmunds, Lydgate, and the *N-Town Cycle,*" pp. 56–90.

85. *Victoria History of Suffolk,* 2:71.

86. *Minor Poems of Lydgate,* 1:350 (ll. 575–78).

87. *Minor Poems of Lydgate,* 1:351 (ll. 593–94).

88. *Minor Poems of Lydgate,* 1:361 (l. 874).

89. *Minor Poems of Lydgate,* 1:362 (ll. 890–93).

90. *Visitation of Suffolke,* 1:34.

91. Cf. *Minor Poems of Lydgate,* 1:352–53 (ll. 635–41), and Saint Augustine, *Confessions* (Harmondsworth, England: Penguin Books, 1961), 47–53.

92. Robert Gottfried's assertion that John Baret had both a legitimate and an illegitimate son (pp. 153–59) is almost certainly an error. Gottfried's biographical sketch of Baret (and indeed much of the local and social history of Bury recounted in the book) is plagued by such a number of mistakes as to make it an untrustworthy source; the "sons" apparently come from Gottfried's misunderstanding of Baret's bequests in his will to "my man and my child," i.e., "my manservant and my page." See Tymms, *Wills and Inventories,* p. 34.

93. *Visitation of Suffolke,* 1:36.

94. *Visitation of Suffolke,* 1:36.

95. *Visitation of Suffolke,* 1:38.

96. Parker, *History of Long Melford,* p. 77. In a later Long Melford inventory (of 1541), the "relycke of the pyler" is still listed, but now said to be "in the custodye of Wyll[iam] Mayre. See Parker, p. 88.

97. *Visitation of Suffolke,* 1:47.

98. *Visitation of Suffolke,* 1:48.

99. *Visitation of Suffolke,* 1:48.

100. *Visitation of Suffolke,* 1:48.

101. Parker, *History of Long Melford,* pp. 93–94.

102. See chapter 3, and the visitor's guide to the church, Christopher Sansbury, *Holy Trinity Church, Long Melford* (Norwich: Jarrold and Sons, 1979), 2.

103. Parker, *History of Long Melford,* p. 94.

104. *Visitation of Suffolke,* 1:36.

105. Parker, *History of Long Melford,* pp. 105–7.

106. The text was transcribed in 1692 from Roger Martyn's paper manuscript by Nathaniel Bisbie, rector of Long Melford church. The Martyn reminiscence was printed in somewhat modernized form in Parker, *History of Long Melford,* pp. 70–73; in John Preston Neale, *Views of the Most Interesting Collegiate and Parochial Churches in Great Britain* (London: Longman, Hurst, Rees, Orine, Brown, and Green, 1825), 2:12–14, "Long Melford" section; and in *The Gentleman's Magazine* 100(1830):206–7. Neale reported in 1825 that the transcription was in the collection

of the Reverend William Tylney Spurdens of North Walsham, Norfolk, but the present whereabouts of the transcription is not known. The 1692 transcription indicates that the original manuscript was "lately wasted."

107. On the Harling family see Woodforde, *Norwich School of Glass-Painting,* pp. 43–44; Bennet, pp. 296–99; and Francis Blomefield, *An Essay Towards a Topographical History of the County of Norfolk,* 2d ed. (London: William Miller, 1805), 1:320–23.

108. W. B. Slegg, "History of Harling," MS. 10840 36 F2, Norfolk Public Record Office (1940), *vide* Lord Scrope of Bolton.

109. See Samuel Moore, "Patrons of Letters in Norfolk and Suffolk, c. 1450," *PMLA* 27(1912):203–4, and W. A. Davenport, *Fifteenth-Century English Drama: The Early Moral Plays and Their Literary Relations* (Cambridge: D. S. Brewer; Totowa, N.J.: Rowman and Littlefield, 1982), 134.

110. *Paston Letters,* 1:517.

111. *Testamenta Eboracensia,* 4:152.

112. *Paston Letters,* 1:654.

113. *Paston Letters,* 2:294.

114. According to Slegg, "History of Harling," Anne Harling died of the same unspecified "fatal and infectious" sickness that had killed Lord Scrope.

115. *Testamenta Eboracensia,* 4:154: "In witness whereof to this I have put to my seale of armys and also subscribe it wt myn owne hande."

116. *Testamenta Eboracensia,* 4:153.

117. *Testamenta Eboracensia,* 4:153.

118. See Knowles, *Religious Orders in England,* 2:175–82.

119. *Testamenta Eboracensia,* 2:151.

120. *Visitation of Suffolk,* 4:35.

121. See Harrod, p. 335.

122. *Testamenta Eboracensia,* 4:153.

123. *Testamenta Eboracensia,* 4:154.

124. See, for example, Lloyd de Mause, ed., *The History of Childhood* (New York: Harper and Row, 1975). Except for expressions of tenderness toward the child when it is "non-demanding, especially when the child is either asleep or dead," parental neglect or abuse of children, according to de Mause, characterized most parents' relationships to their offspring until the nineteenth century. The problem, maintains de Mause, was not a failure of love, but rather a failure for parents of the past to achieve "the emotional maturity needed to see the child as a person separate from himself" (p. 17).

125. *Non-Cycle Plays,* p. 56 (ll. 449–59).

126. *Pierce the Ploughman's Crede,* p. 4 (ll. 77–79).

127. Baker, Murphy, and Hale, *Digby Plays,* pp. 111–15.

128. Donald C. Baker, "Is *Wisdom* a Professional Play?" in *The Wisdom Symposium: Papers from the Trinity College Medieval Festival,* ed. Milla Cozart Riggio, AMS Studies in the Middle Ages, no. 11 (New York: AMS Press, 1986), 76.

129. Slegg, "History of Harling," *vide* "Sir William Chamberlaine, K. G."

130. [Gray B. Baker], "Church Ales and Interludes," *The East Anglian* 1(1864): 383. The fifteenth-century churchwardens' accounts, "copied from Tanners' MS

Collections," are quoted at length in this article of 1864, less fully in L. G. Bolin-broke, "Pre-Elizabethan Plays and Players in Norfolk," *Norfolk Archaeology* 11(1892):338 (which seems to be quoting from the article in the *East Anglian*). An inventory of East Harling church books made in 1888 lists "loose churchwardens' accounts dating from 1452," but there is no certain evidence of the existence of the fifteenth-century records after 1888 (or perhaps after Bolinbroke in 1892 if he is not merely quoting from the *East Anglian*). Both John Wasson and I have searched in East Harling and the Norfolk Record Office for the lost East Harling accounts, to no avail. See *Records of Plays and Players in Norfolk and Suffolk*, p. 5. There are no references to the East Harling plays among the Norfolk church notes of Thomas Tanner (bishop of Norfolk, 1674–1735) preserved in the Norfolk Record Office (Tanner Reg. 30, Reg. 31, Reg. 32, and Tanner, Miscellaneous Notes). Many of Bishop Tanner's antiquarian notes, however, were on loose scraps of paper, thrust haphazardly into notebooks. It is difficult to know what became of the Tanner notes that Gray B. Baker—or perhaps the editor of the *East Anglian,* Samuel Tymms—saw in 1864, nor what became of the East Harling fifteenth-century churchwardens' accounts. It should be noted that there is no mention of any fifteenth-century churchwardens' accounts in either W. B. Slegg's manuscript history of East Harling (dated 1940) or in his privately printed *The Gilds and Town Lands of East Harling, Norfolk* (in the local history collection of the Norwich Central Library). Slegg assumes the earliest source of information to be the "book of East Harling parish accounts covering the period 1630 to the latter half of the eighteenth century." Slegg, *Gilds and Town Lands,* p. 28.

131. Baker, "Church Ales," p. 383.

132. The self-conscious purpose with which wealthy laity gave images to enhance and direct the parish's devotional life is underscored in the 1504 testament of Maud Baker, wealthy widow of a Bristol grocer, who bequeathed to her parish church several images, including "an image of the transfiguration of Jesus 'to move and excite the people's devotion.'" See Clive Burgess, "For the Increase of Divine Service: Chantries in the Parish in Late Medieval Bristol," *Journal of Ecclesiastical History* 36(1985):63–64.

133. On the East Harling windows, see especially Woodforde, *Norwich School of Glass-Painting,* pp. 42–55.

134. "A Short Guide to the Parish Church of St. Peter and St. Paul, East Harling" (1981), 2.

135. On the glass of St. Peter Mancroft, see Woodforde, *Norwich School of Glass-Painting,* pp. 16–42.

136. Woodforde, *Norwich School of Glass-Painting,* p. 43.

137. See A. R. Myers, ed., *The Household of Edward IV: The Black Book and the Ordinance of 1478* (Manchester: Manchester University Press, 1959), 253 n. 288, 289.

138. Anne Harling's will specifies that she be buried in this "chapell of Seint Anne, joyned to the chauncell of the churche . . . in Estharlyng, in the tombe w_t my late worshipfull husbond, Sir William Chamberleyn, accordyng to my promyse made unto hym afore this tyme." *Testamenta Eboracensia,* 4:149). The placement of the Chamberlain-Harling tomb is identical to that of the Clopton sepulchre at Long Melford (in a north wall arch separating the chantry chapel from the choir);

like the Clopton tomb, it was probably intended for yearly use as the Easter sepulchre. The 1457 Harling chantry certificate that survives in the Norfolk Record Office (No. 20101) is not for this chapel of St. Anne, but for a chantry priest at the tomb of Anne Harling's father, Sir Robert Harling, in the south aisle of the church.

139. *Victoria History of the County of Norfolk,* ed. William Page (London: Archibald Constable and Co., 1906; reprint, William Dawson and Sons, 1975), 2:459.

140. Bennet, 298.

141. Bennet, 298.

142. Bennet, 372–73.

143. Bennet, 373.

Chapter Five

1. See Woolf, *English Mystery Plays,* pp. 25–38, for a thoughtful discussion of the relationship of medieval drama to the classical inheritance.

2. See Bevington, *Medieval Drama,* p. 38: "Et hunc hymnum canendo revertantur in chorum, plebe conclamante 'Christ ist erstanden.'" ("And singing this hymn, let them return to the choir, while the people sing loudly together [in German] 'Christ has risen'.")

3. Bevington, *Medieval Drama,* pp. 138–54.

4. See Baker, Murphy, and Hall, *Digby Plays,* p. 55: "Here al þe pepull and þe Jewys, Mari and Martha, wyth on woys sey þes wordys: 'We beleve in yow, Savyowr, Jhesus, Jhesus, Jhesus!'"

5. As Marianne G. Briscoe has emphasized, in "Some Clerical Notions of Dramatic Decorum in Late Medieval England," *Comparative Drama* 19 (1985):1–13, clerical antidrama diatribe and legislation was almost always concerned with enforcing dramatic decorum, with criticizing specific abuses, and with outlawing certain kinds of unseemly roles for clergy rather than with challenging the existence of drama or of clerical support of it.

6. See Milla Cozart Riggio, "The Staging of Wisdom," in *The Wisdom Symposium: Papers from the Trinity College Medieval Festival,* ed. Milla Cozart Riggio, AMS Studies in the Middle Ages (New York: AMS Press, 1986), 1–17.

7. See the facsimile edition of *Wisdom* edited by David Bevington, in *The Macro Plays: A Facsimile Edition with Facing Transcription* (Washington, D.C.: Folger Shakespeare Library, 1972), 248–49.

8. Margaret Paston in a letter of about 1459 mentions how Lady Morley, in mourning for her husband, had forbidden the usual Christmas "sportys" of plays ["dysgysynggys"], luting, harping, and singing in the Morley household. See *Paston Letters* 1:257 and Lancashire, p. xxi.

9. See Pamela Sheingorn, *The Easter Sepulchre in England,* Early Drama, Art, and Music Reference Series, no. 5 (Kalamazoo, Michigan: Medieval Institute Publications, 1987), 52–62, for a full description of the function of the Easter sepulchre in parish dramatic ritual.

10. Baker and Murphy, "Late Medieval Plays," p. 164. On the association of the

Macro plays with Abbot Hyngham of Bury, see also Baker, "Is *Wisdom* a 'Professional Play?'" pp. 81–82.

11. Craig, *English Religious Drama,* p. 350.

12. On the textual evidence for the learned and ecclesiastical audience of *Mankind,* see especially Lawrence M. Clopper, "Mankind and Its Audience," *Comparative Drama* 8(1974–75):347–55.

13. Cf. *The Macro Plays,* ed. Mark Eccles, Early English Text Society o.s. 262 (London: Oxford University Press, 1969), ll. 49–52, 109–12:

> Wysdom: The prerogatyff of my loue ys so grett
> þat wo tastyt þerof þe lest droppe sure
> All lustys and lykyngys wordly xall lett;
> They xall seme to hym fylthe and ordure
>
> . . . .
>
> For euery creature þat hat ben or xall
> Was in natur of þe fyrst man, Adame,
> Off hym takynge þe fylthe of synne orygynall
> For of hym all creaturys cam.

14. David M. Bevington, *From Mankind to Marlowe* (Cambridge, Massachusetts: Harvard University Press, 1962).

15. *Macro Plays,* ed. Eccles, p. 168 (l. 461).

16. *Macro Plays,* ed. Eccles, p. 155 (ll. 29–36).

17. Cf. Ephesians 1:19–23; 4:15–24; 1 Corinthians 12:27.

18. *Macro Plays,* ed. Eccles, p. 170 (l. 497).

19. *Macro Plays,* ed. Eccles, p. 162 (ll. 274–76).

20. See Hilton Richard Leslie Beadle, "The Scribal Pattern in the Macro Manuscript," *English Language Notes* 21 (1984):9.

21. See John Marshall, "Marginal Staging Marks in the Macro Manuscript of *Wisdom,*" *Medieval English Theatre* 7(1985):77–82.

22. I have been unable to identify Richard Cake of Bury, but whoever he was, he was not the sixteenth-century "rector of Bradfield near Bury," as Mark Eccles and David Bevington have repeated from a double error in N. R. Ker's *Medieval Libraries of Great Britain.* Ker apparently conflated the names Richard Corke and Edmund Cake which appear consecutively in the Bradfield parish incumbents list—which is, anyway, not from one of the three Suffolk Bradfields near Bury at all, but from Bradfield, Norfolk, near Norwich. A list of the incumbents of Bradfield, Norfolk, appears in volume 2 of the Notes of Bishop Thomas Tanner (1674–1735), Bury and West Suffolk Record Office microfilm J510/2 (acc. 1230).

23. On Cox Macro see Baker and Murphy, "Late Medieval Plays," pp. 163–64, and Gibson, "Bury St. Edmunds, Lydgate, and the *N-Town Cycle,*" pp. 62–63.

24. On Cox Macro's manuscript collection, see Samuel Tymms, "Little Haugh Hall, Norton," *Proceedings of the Suffolk Institute of Archaeology and History* 2(1859):284. Little Haugh Hall is the Georgian manor house built by Cox Macro.

25. Baker and Murphy, "Late Medieval Plays," pp. 163–64, and Baker, Murphy, and Hall, *Digby Plays,* pp. xii–xv.

26. There are a number of other names inscribed in the Macro manuscript which seem to point to Bury. The surname Plandon, for example, which appears in

schoolboy cipher on fol. 104 of *Wisdom*, was the name of a prominent sixteenth-century family (see Tymms, *Wills and Inventories*, p. 98. Robert Oliver, whose name is inscribed and ciphered repeatedly in the manuscript, was perhaps a relative of the Bury physician Thomas Oliver, who donated books to Bury school in 1595. See A. T. Bartholomew and Cosmo Gordon, "On the Library at King Edward VI School, Bury St. Edmunds," *The Library*, 3d ser., vol. 1 no. 1 (1910):8.

27. See *Records of Plays and Players in Norfolk and Suffolk*, p. 166. The subject of Adames' interlude is not specified in Lady Kytson's household accounts, but it must have been an ambitious spectacle. Adames was paid twenty shillings for the performance, although Queen Elizabeth's players who had performed at Hengrave that same year were only paid six shillings.

28. *Late Medieval Religious Plays*, p. xiv.

29. On the Bury school, see Gail McMurray Gibson, "The Play of *Wisdom* and the Abbey of St. Edmund," in *Wisdom Symposium*, ed. Riggio, pp. 41–43, 48; and *Victoria History of Suffolk*, 2:306–18. On the Bury manuscripts of Plautus and Terence, see Rodney M. Thomson, "The Library of Bury St. Edmunds Abbey in the Eleventh and Twelfth Centuries," *Speculum* 47(1972):633.

30. *The Chronicle of Jocelin of Brakelond*, trans. and ed. H. E. Butler (London: Thomas Nelson and Sons, 1949), 92–93. Ian Lancashire (p. 92) assumes the churchyard "spectacula" were plays; Butler suggests "wrestling matches and contests" (p. 92n). It is interesting, in fact, just how closely related plays and wrestling "games," especially Christmas wrestling games, are in medieval performance records. The prioress of Clerkenwell complained to King Edward I about damage to her fields caused by crowds who came to Clerkenwell to watch wrestling matches (*luctas*) and miracle plays. See W. O. Hassall, "Plays at Clerkenwell," *Modern Language Review* 33 (1938):564–70. Forming a ring for wrestling was called "making a place"; the same word, "place" (or in the Latin, *platea*), is the word used in medieval theater for the unlocalized playing area. Wrestling, indeed, seems to have been as much a popular ingredient of medieval drama as the gun fight is in twentieth-century popular films. Wrestling is the subject of a fifteenth-century Robin Hood play fragment that survives from East Anglia. See William Tydeman, *The Theatre in the Middle Ages* (Cambridge: Cambridge University Press, 1978), 19. The Chester Shepherd's play draws on the tradition of Christmas wrestling sports to create a resonant dramatic enactment of Luke 1:52: "He hath put down the mighty from their seat, and hath exalted the humble." See Kolve, pp. 156–59, and compare O. Elfrida Saunders, *A History of English Art in the Middle Ages* (Oxford: Clarendon Press, 1932), 197–98, for carvings of the Adoration of the Magi and of two wrestling figures, both of which support the pedestals of an English Annunciation group from Wells.

31. *Non-Cycle Plays*, pp. cxiv–cxv; 116–17.

32. Public Record Office C. 47/46/401. For text see Karl Young, "An Interludium for a Gild of Corpus Christi," *Modern Language Notes* 48(1933): 85–86.

33. Bury and West Suffolk Record Office B 9/1/2. See Historical Manuscripts of Great Britain, *The Manuscripts of Lincoln, Bury St. Edmunds, and Great Grimsby Corporations: and of the Deans and Chapters of Worcester and Lichfield, &c.*, Four-

teenth report, part 8, ed. William Dunn Macray, Historical Manuscripts Commission, ser. 65 (London: Eyre and Spottiswoode, 1895), 134–36; E. K. Chambers, *The Mediaeval Stage* (Oxford: Oxford University Press, 1903; reprint, 1978), 2:343–44.

34. At the bottom of a note of rents dated 1558 is the heading for an inventory of all movable goods possessed by the guildhall "except for certain pageants." See Margaret Statham, "The Guildhall, Bury St. Edmunds," *Proceedings of the Suffolk Institute of Archaeology* 31(1968):145.

35. Bury and West Suffolk Record Office, Register Pye, fol. 209.

36. Bury and West Suffolk Record Office, Register Pye, fol. 25.

37. A John Basse, draper, requested burial in the north porch of St. Mary's church in his will of 1506. See Samuel Tymms, *An Architectural and Historical Account of the Church of St. Mary, Bury St. Edmunds* (Bury St. Edmunds: Jackson and Frost, 1854).

38. H. F. Westlake, *The Parish Gilds of Mediaeval England* (London: Society for Promoting Christian Knowledge, 1919), 227.

39. Gordon M. Hills, "The Antiquities of Bury St. Edmunds," *Journal of the British Archaeological Association* 21(1865):125.

40. On the abbey refectory and other monastic buildings see A. B. Whittingham, "Bury St. Edmunds Abbey: The Plan, Design, and Development of the Church and Monastic Buildings," *Archaeological Journal* 108(1951):168–89, esp. 176–78. When the abbot was in residence, important secular guests would have been entertained in the great hall of the Abbot's Palace, rather than in the refectory. The palace had been substantially rebuilt in 1433 when Abbot Curteys received word that the young Henry VI was coming to spend the feast of Christmas at the abbey. See Gibson, "Play of *Wisdom*," 51–52.

41. For the role of the abbey in the affairs of the town, see M. D. Lobel, *The Borough of Bury St. Edmunds: A Study in the Government and Development of a Medieval Town* (Oxford: Clarendon Press, 1935), and Gottfried.

42. See Riggio, "Staging of Wisdom," pp. 6–7, 14–16.

43. Samuel Tymms, *A Handbook of Bury St. Edmunds, in the County of Suffolk,* 6th ed. (Bury St. Edmunds: F. T. Groom; London: Simpkin, Marshall, Hamilton, Kent, and Co., 1854), 4–5. The collection of the Museum of London includes a beautiful late medieval ivory crucifix recently found during construction on the site of Bevis Marks House.

44. Tymms, *Wills and Inventories,* p. 98.

45. See Historical Manuscripts Commission, p. 157.

46. Lobel, 123.

47. See Lobel, p. 121.

48. Statham, "Guildhall," 140–41.

49. Lobel, pp. 162–63.

50. Knowles, *Religious Orders,* 1:269.

51. Lobel, p. 168.

52. Lobel, p. 169. Margaret Statham suggests that one reason that Bury may have been slow to appeal for a charter of incorporation is that it had long had an undercover town government in the form of the prestigious Candlemas guild, a lay confraternity that survived the dissolution of chantries by quietly becoming in

fact what it had long been in essence, despite its homage to the abbey's authority—the governing corporate body of the town. See Statham, "Guildhall," 141–46.

53. *Ludus Coventriae*, p. 326 (ll. 1604–5).

54. Such is the popular myth in staunchly Protestant Suffolk today; witness the following personal letter of July 16th, 1981, from my friend and fellow drama historian Stanley Kahrl, who was objecting (he is now more agnostic on this issue) to the argument for joint lay and monastic sponsorship of religious drama at Bury: "Monks paid to see entertainments in their own halls, for sure. But so far I have seen no evidence of their taking an interest in civic religious drama. . . . In King's Lynn, the local people were at legal war with the Bishop of Norwich, an abbot, for most of the fifteenth century. In Bury, I still remember seeing those vast foundations lying open in the air, and asking why so little of the abbey remained. I was told that the local people so hated it that they destroyed it willingly in the Reformation."

55. The building records from Hengrave Hall, Suffolk, begun in the 1530s, clearly document Sir Thomas Kytson's purchases of building stone seized from the former monasteries at Ixworth and Thetford: see John Gage [Rokewode], *The History and Antiquities of Hengrave in Suffolk* (London: James Carpenter; Bury St. Edmunds: John Deck, 1822), 54.

56. Cf. A. Goodwin, *The Abbey of St. Edmundsbury* (Oxford: Basil Blackwell, 1931), 65: "Unfortunately, however, the history of the last eighty or ninety years of the monastery's existence is almost a complete blank."

57. The west doors of the parish churches of St. James and St. Mary of the Assumption opened to the borough streets, but the buildings themselves were constructed within the monastery walls and with separate entrances for the monks within the abbey grounds. It should be noted that unlike other monastic towns, Tewkesbury, for example, Bury St. Edmunds did not need to preserve the monastic church after the Reformation, precisely because the abbey had already supplied the town with two magnificent parish churches of its own.

58. See S. E. Rigold, "The St. Nicholas or 'Boy Bishop' Tokens," *Proceedings of the Suffolk Institute of Archaeology and History* 34(1978):87–101. Payments to "S. Nicholas, the bishop" appear the abbey's account rolls for 1426–27 and 1537–78. See *Victoria History of Suffolk*, 2:312.

59. Historical Manuscripts Commission, p. 124.

60. R. M. Lumiansky and David Mills, *The Chester Mystery Plays: Essays and Documents* (Chapel Hill: University of North Carolina Press, 1983), 166.

61. Salter, p. 41.

62. Salter erroneously calls Francis the abbot of St. Werburgh's. Since his name is the third signatory in the lists, following the subprior, he was not abbot but was evidently a very senior monk of the abbey in the 1370s. He may have written mystery plays as a young monk during the time of Pope Clement VI (1342–52), since "Pope Clement" is mentioned in the Chester cycle "Proclamation" as being pope at the time the cycle was first performed. Pope Clement was also pope, interesting enough, during the time of the residency of Ranulf Higden. Although Higden's name is associated with the Chester cycle only in very late documents, he at

least exerted an indirect influence upon the Chester cycle through the influence of his *Polychronicon* upon *The Stanzaic Life of Christ.* See Lumiansky and Mills, 167–68.

63. Salter, p. 42.

64. Lumiansky and Mills, p. 106.

65. *Records of Early English Drama: Chester,* ed. Lawrence M. Clopper (Toronto: University of Toronto Press, 1979), 21.

66. *Records of Early English Drama: Chester,* p. 84: "Item for a barell of bere to yeue to the pleares to make them to drincke vj s". See also Lumiansky and Mills, p. 185.

67. R. V. H. Burne, *The Monks of Chester* (London: Society for Promoting Christian Knowledge, 1962), 102.

68. Burne, p. 102.

69. See Burne, pp. 129–33.

70. Burne, p. 132: "Nota, nota, nota bene pro libertate nostra contra abbatem tempore Nundinarum."

71. Burne, pp. 119–21.

72. *Records of Plays and Players in Norfolk and Suffolk,* p. 147.

73. Cf. Thomson, *Archives of the Abbey of Bury St. Edmunds,* p. 4, on the paucity even of cartulary records: "The explanation for the low survival ratio of Bury's charters seems to lie sufficiently in the fact of its destruction at the Dissolution instead of its conversion into a secular cathedral. For most of the original documents, excepting the manorial rolls, there was no further use, and those that survive do so largely by accident."

74. See Historical Manuscripts Commission, pp. 123–25.

75. Historical Manuscripts Commission, pp. 124–25.

76. Bury and West Suffolk Record Office A 6/1/17. For the reference to the St. Robert's chapel minstrels (and for several other references to minstrels, entertainments, and players not listed in *Records of Plays and Players in Norfolk and Suffolk*), see Historical Manuscripts Commission, pp. 157–58, and PROE SC 6 Hen. VIII 3397 (not included in the HMC abstracts).

77. See Historical Manuscripts Commission, pp. 123–25, 157–58, and *Records of Plays and Players in Norfolk and Suffolk,* pp. 147–48.

78. *Records of Plays and Players in Norfolk and Suffolk,* p. 148.

79. Historical Manuscripts Commission, p. 157.

80. See Alan Nelson's forthcoming REED edition of the dramatic records of the Cambridge colleges (1:49) for the record in *King's College Mundum Book* 5.2, fol. 108v., of a payment of two shillings on the eve of Epiphany to "vj viris de Bury lude[n]tibu[s] in aula."

81. On the possible association of East Anglian drama with fairs at Bury and at other parishes under the abbey's rectorship, see Gibson, "Bury St. Edmunds, Lydgate, and the *N-Town Cycle*," pp. 75–80.

82. Schirmer, pp. 138–39.

83. Tymms, *Wills and Inventories,* p. 13.

84. For text see James, *Abbey of S. Edmund at Bury,* pp. 204–12.

85. It was the responsibility of the abbey in its status as rector to build and

maintain the chancels and high altars of the town's parish churches; the parishioners took responsibility for funding the naves (see Cook, p. 23). The rebuilding of the present church of St. Mary of the Assumption was begun about 1424, and the high altar was improved and reconsecrated in 1479. See Tymms, *Church of St. Mary*, pp. 19, 55. Although the *Borough of St. Edmundsbury* guide (Norwich: Jarrold and Sons, 1976) says that the Perpendicular-style church of St. James, now St. Edmundsbury Cathedral, dates from the fifteenth century (p. 95), it probably was not begun until the early sixteenth century. Several Bury wills of 1511 and 1512 refer to the "new work" of St. James church (Bury and West Suffolk Record Office, Register Mason, fols. 2, 4, 6, 14, 16, 18). In 1527, Thomas Berewe left a bequest for paving stone for finishing the church of St. James, specifying that the abbot of Bury was to pay the transportation costs of the stone (Bury and West Suffolk Record Office, Register Hoode, fol. 137).

86. See Gibson, "Bury St. Edmunds, Lydgate, and the *N-Town Cycle*", pp. 76–77. The date, however, need not imply the date of actual compilation of the manuscript, which as Martin Stevens has recently argued, may well be "the outcome of a very careful and literate editing that likely took place at the turn of the sixteenth century." See Martin Stevens, *Four Middle English Mystery Cycles: Textual, Contextual, and Critical Interpretations* (Princeton: Princeton University Press, 1987), p. 184.

87. See Gibson, "Bury St. Edmunds, Lydgate, and the *N-Town* Cycle," 85–90.

88. There are even some striking iconographical relationships. Fourteenth-century transcriptions of inscriptions from the paintings and stained glass of the Bury Lady Chapel, for example, tell us that one of those paintings was of that same allegorical meeting of the Four Daughters of God that creates the prologue to the N-Town Annunciation play. See James, *Abbey of St. Edmund*, pp. 126, 142.

89. Craig, *English Religious Drama*, pp. 276–77.

90. The fair of St. James is one of four fairs claimed in the register of Walter Pinchbeck (c. 1330–50) by the abbey of Bury. The other three were fairs of St. Edmund (November 19 to December 24), St. Peter (June 23–29), and St. Matthew (September 20–21). Only the fairs of St. Edmund and St. Matthew seem to have survived the dissolution of the monastery. Both of these fairs were canceled in the year 1665 as a precaution against plague, and afterward St. Matthew's was the sole Bury fair. See Lobel, p. 188, for the text of the Walter Pinchbeck register; for a general history of the Bury fairs see M. P. Statham, "The Bury Fairs," *The Suffolk Review* 4(1974):126–34. By the eighteenth century, Bury Fair meant a single three-week fair held around the feast of St. Matthew, a fair which drew tradesmen and merchants and the likes of Defoe's Moll Flanders from all over England. It also drew actors. Although we can only hypothesize Bury fairs as a likely time of dramatic activity in the late medieval period, there is abundant evidence in the eighteenth century that plays were customarily performed then. In 1734, in fact, the Bury market cross was converted into a playhouse, a purpose for which it was used until 1819. See Tymms, *Handbook of Bury St. Edmunds*, pp. 47–48.

91. See Howard R. Patch, "The *Ludus Coventriae* and the Digby Massacre," *PMLA* 35(1920):324–43.

92. See for the will of John Parfre (or Perfay), Tymms, *Wills and Inventories*, pp.

108–13, and on the Bell Meadow endowment, Tymms, *Church of St. Mary,* pp. 75–76. Since the date 1512 appears three times in the manuscript of the Digby "Killing of the Children" and John Parfre's will was proved in 1509, he could have been author (or sponsor) of the play, but not its scribe. Whoever the reader of the play was who felt compelled, apparently some fifty or more years later, to write John Parfre's name in the Digby Plays manuscript, he almost certainly did not do so because of the importance of the play, but because of the prestige of the name of John Parfre—a name that signaled for several centuries after his death, indeed, even today in Bury St. Edmunds, a civic leader, church patron, and town benefactor of legendary reputation.

93. Cf. Stevens, *Four Middle English Mystery Cycles,* 181–82, on the vexing difficulties of the N-Town cycle: "With all of these very substantial problems in mind, we can be positive about one point: Historical study of this cycle is fraught with difficulty and uncertainty."

94. Cf. Donald C. Baker, "The Drama: Learning and Unlearning," p. 205: "I think that the growing argument for a strong dramatic center or group of centers in East Anglia, focused upon one or more great religious house, is a more likely solution of the problem than the location of *N-Town Plays* in a particular town."

95. Cf. Davenport, p. 3: "Placed with the Chester, York, and Towneley cycles, the N-Town cycle is a cuckoo in the nest; its differences from the other three are repeatedly more interesting than its similarities to them."

96. Taylor, preface.

97. See Knowles, *Religious Orders,* 2:241–43, 287.

98. See Riehle, p. 16.

99. *Minor Poems of Lydgate,* 1:205, (ll. 377–78).

100. See on the issue of the monastic provenance and preoccupations of the play, Riggio, "The Staging of Wisdom," esp. pp. 5–17.

101. See *Ludus Coventriae,* p. 271.

102. David Mills, in "Religious Drama and Civic Ceremonial" (in *Revels History,* ed. Cawley, p. 198), comments upon the importance of the contemplative function of the expositor: "In one sense he is the externalization of Mary's own contemplation as she reads and meditates upon the psalm, and it is her plea for mercy which prompts the ensuing action. But he is also the representative of the collective contemplation of mankind, brooding upon its plight and pleading with God for grace, and as such a spokesman for the audience."

103. *Ludus Coventriae,* p. 62 (ll. 1–8).

104. *Minor Poems of Lydgate,* 1:325 (l. 42).

105. For the best discussion of the complex levels of plays and interpolated plays in the N-Town cycle manuscript, see Stephen Spector, "The Composition and Development of an Eclectic Manuscript: Cotton Vespasian D VIII," *Leeds Studies in English* 9(1977):62–83.

106. See Baker, Murphy, and Hall, *Digby Plays,* pp. 1, 6, 12–13, 23 and pp. 96, 114–15.

107. *Ludus Coventriae,* p. 122 (ll. 7–8).

108. Spector, "Composition and Development," pp. 69–70.

109. We might look for an analogy, for example, to the traditional liturgical play

of the Assumption of the Virgin still performed at the village of Elche in Spain. In that play boys perform the part of the Virgin Mary and all other roles, except for the role of God, which is always played by the parish priest. On the play of Elche see Pamela M. King and Asunción Salvador-Rabaza, "La Festa D'Elx: The Festival of the Assumption of the Virgin, Elche (Alicante)," *Medieval English Theatre* 8(1986):21–50.

110. See Hilton Richard Leslie Beadle, "Plays and Playing at Thetford and Nearby, 1498–1540," *Theatre Notebook* 32(1978):6–7.

111. Beadle, "Plays and Playing," p. 8.

112. Hardin Craig, *English Religious Drama of the Middle Ages* (Oxford: The Clarendon Press, 1955), 280. Craig's argument for the cathedral city of Lincoln as the source of that learning has been seriously questioned in recent years. See Gibson, "Bury St. Edmunds, Lydgate, and *N-Town Cycle*," pp. 56–75, and Baker, "The Drama: Learning and Unlearning," p. 205: "The concrete evidence of the *N-Town Plays* having been the Corpus Christi or Saint Anne's Day play of Lincoln is very slight in spite of Craig's near certainty."

113. Woolf, *English Mystery Plays*, p. 212.

114. Woolf, *English Mystery Plays*, p. 212.

115. *Ludus Coventriae*, p. 183 (l. 157).

116. *Ludus Coventriae*, p. 179 (l. 33).

117. Kathleen M. Ashley, "'Wyt' and 'Wysdam' in N-town Cycle," *Philological Quarterly* 58(1979):123.

118. *Ludus Coventriae*, p. 304 (ll. 950–952).

119. *Ludus Coventriae*, p. 395 (ll. 963–966).

120. *Ludus Coventriae*, p. 13 (l. 430).

121. See Philippe de Mezières, *Figurative Representation of the Presentation of the Virgin Mary in the Temple*, trans. and ed. Robert S. Haller *Lincoln: University of Nebraska Press, 1971)*.

122. See Montague Rhodes James, ed., *The Apocryphal New Testament* (Oxford: Clarendon Press, 1924; reprint, 1980), 41–42, 73.

123. *Ludus Coventriae*, p. 71. Cf. the casting notes in the Avignon "Presentation of the Virgin" by Philippe de Mezières, which specify that Mary be represented by a "very young and very beautiful virgin of around three or four years of age" ("quedm virgo iuuencula et pulcherrima circiter trium aut iiii annorum"). De Mezières, *Figurative Representation*, pp. 6, 30.

124. *Ludus Coventriae*, p. 72 (l. 1).

125. *Ludus Coventriae*, p. 72 (l. 24).

126. *Ludus Coventriae*, p. 74 (l. 58).

127. *Ludus Coventriae*, p. 74 (l. 75).

128. William Durandus, *Rationale divinorum officiorum*, 1: bk. 1, p. 40, cited in De Mezières, *Figurative Representation*, p. xxiv: "The prophets continually show us, in the fifteen psalms, the degrees which a holy man has erected in his heart. Jacob saw this ladder of which the highest part touched the sky. By these degrees are meant, in a manner suitable and clear, the degrees of virtues by which one mounts to the altar, that is to say, to Christ, according to this word of the Psalmist: 'And they shall march and shall elevate themselves from virtue to virtue.'"

129. *Ludus Coventriae*, p. 74 (l. 81).

130. *Ludus Coventriae*, p. 91 (l. 82).

131. See *Ludus Coventriae*, pp. 74–77 (ll. 84–144).

132. *Ludus Coventriae*, p. 75 (ll. 88–91).

133. *Ludus Coventriae*, pp. 79–80 (ll. 226–27).

134. *Ludus Coventriae*, p. 80 (l. 234).

135. On this theme in the parish art of medieval York, see Clifford Davidson, *From Creation to Doom*, pp. 94, 164.

136. *Ludus Coventriae*, pp. 78–79 (ll. 193–95).

137. *Ludus Coventriae*, p. 81 (l. 273).

138. *Minor Poems of Lydgate*, 1:355 (l. 700).

Chapter Six

1. Peter Meredith has recently tried to separate what he believes was originally a single, composite Mary play from the layers of other Marian pageants with which it was interwoven in the N-Town cycle. Despite his assertion that "it is clearly both justifiable and necessary to make the attempt to undo what the scribe was attempting to do, and disentangle the *Mary Play* from its present inappropriate setting" and even with the help of three appendixes of "interpolations," Meredith's premise seems to me problematic and the results often as vexing as the textual contradictions he was attempting to smooth out. Peter Meredith, *The Mary Play from the N-Town Manuscript* (London and New York: Longmans, 1987), 2. See, for example, p. 20: "There are twenty-four stage directions in the *Mary Play*. They seem to be of varying origins since some are Latin and some English; some are centred on the page and were therefore prepared for in the laying-out of the text, while others are squeezed into the margin." In terms of Marian mythology and purpose—and in terms of the scribe-editor's final intention—what Meredith calls the *Mary Play* is now one with the N-Town cycle compilation. "The present inappropriate setting" is no more inappropriate than the setting that brought Grendel monster stories, dragon monster story, and stories of human blood-revenge together in the complexly interlaced poem we now call *Beowulf.*

2. *Ludus Coventriae*, p. 108 (l. 335). "Empress of hell" is a common epithet of the Virgin in John Lydgate's devotional verse. See, for example, "Gloriosa Dicta Sunt De Te," in *Minor Poems of Lydgate*, 1:323 (ll. 225–26): "O blessed lady! qweene of þe heghe heven,/ Whome clerkes calle þemperyse of helle". (Cf. *Minor Poems of Lydgate*, 1:296 (l. 2), 1:261 (l. 29), and 1:284 (l.1). On the close relationships between Lydgate's Marian verse and the N-Town cycle, see Gibson, "Bury St. Edmunds, Lydgate, and the *N-Town Cycle*," esp. pp. 85–90.

3. Cf. John Lydgate's English version of the Marian hymn *Ave Regina Celorum*, which implores Mary to "Entyr in Englond, thy dower with reverence." *Minor Poems of Lydgate*, 1:291–92. The *Gesti Henrici Quinti, Deeds of Henry the Fifth*, trans. and ed. Frank Taylor and John S. Roskell (Oxford: Clarendon Press, 1975), 144–45, compiled in 1416–17, tells how Mary's concern for the people of her dower of England ("genti dotis sue Anglie") led her to send favorable winds for the King of England's naval forces. On the importance of England in the history of Marian

devotion see: Waterton, Hilda Graef, *Mary: A History of Doctrine and Devotion* (London and New York: Sheed and Ward, 1963), vol. 1; and Woolf, *English Religious Lyric,* pp. 116–17.

4. See Roy Strong, *The Cult of Elizabeth: Elizabethan Portraiture and Pageantry* (London: Thames and Hudson, 1977).

5. *Liber de Excellentia* (PL 159: 565B), cited in Graef, *Mary,* 1:216.

6. Hermann of Tournai, died c. 1147 (*PL* 180:30), cited in Graef, *Mary,* 1:234.

7. See Helen Waddell, trans., *Medieval Latin Lyrics,* rev. ed. (New York: W. W. Norton and Company, 1977), 258–61.

8. It is interesting to see what happened to one such riddling song by the time it got, centuries later, to the North Carolina mountains. "The Riddle Song" ("I Gave My Love a Cherry") is a metamorphosed, and by now all but meaningless, Middle English lyric about a cherry without a stain (now a cherry without a "stone"), a dove without a bane (punning on "bone" and on "bane," i.e., "curse") that has shape-shifted from Holy Ghost to chicken filet ("a chicken that has no bone"). Most unlikely of all, the mysterious baby "got" (i.e., conceived and borne) with no pain (or curse or original sin) has become in the American folksong the curious line, "I gave my love a baby with no crying." See Cherrell Guilfoyle, "'The Riddle Song' and the Shepherds' Gifts in *Secunda Pastorum,*" *Yearbook of English Studies* 8(1978):208–19.

9. David Jones, "The Pilgrimage to Walsingham," Norfolk Museums Service Information Sheet (Norwich, 1982).

10. See on the Walsingham pilgrimage John Adair, *The Pilgrim's Way: Shrines and Saints in Britain and Ireland* (London: Thames and Hudson, 1978), 114–20.

11. *Victoria History of Norfolk,* 2:397.

12. *Victoria History of Norfolk,* 2:397.

13. Jones, "Pilgrimage to Walsingham," p. 2.

14. The shrine of Mary in John Clopton's Lady Chapel at Long Melford (see chapter 4), is a good example of a local, apparently fairly short-lived Marian pilgrimage. Only the architecture of the chapel (encircled on four sides within by processional aisles) and an early sixteenth-century inventory of precious gems and gifts once attached to the image of Mary in the chapel survive to testify to what must have once been a Marian shrine attracting pilgrims on their way to Walsingham. See "Ancient Furniture and Utensils in Long Melford Church," *Gentleman's Magazine* 100(1830):352–55, and Parker, *History of Long Melford,* p. 79. On the shrine of Our Lady at Woolpit, see Waterton, 2:249–50; on Our Lady of Ipswich, see Stanley Smith, *The Madonna of Ipswich* (Ipswich: East Anglian Magazine Ltd., 1980). The priory at Thetford mounted what was perhaps the most transparent attempt to compete with Walsingham in the fourteenth-century, when it claimed that a Thetford craftsman had been instructed by the Virgin Mary to build a stone chapel in her honor. As the Department of the Environment billboard for visitors to the Thetford Priory ruins explains:

> Unimpressed by these visions, the Prior at first commissioned a wooden chapel, but when the vision was seen again, he ordered its building in stone.
>   When an old statue of the Virgin was set up in the chapel, the head was found to contain holy relics. These apparently conferred miraculous powers of healing

which soon brought pilgrims flocking to the Priory. At the west end of the Lady Chapel are the remains of spiral stairs which led to a small room where a monk watched over visiting pilgrims.

15. *Paston Letters,* 1:218.

16. *Commonplace Book of Robert Reynes,* p. 323.

17. Tanner, p. 90.

18. Tymms, *Wills and Inventories,* p. 98.

19. Furnivall, pp. 117–18.

20. Adair, p. 118.

21. Adair, p. 118.

22. See Sumptian, p. 50.

23. *Ludus Coventriae,* p. 96 (l. 459).

24. *Homilies of Aelfric,* ed. Benjamin Thorpe, in *The Homilies of the Anglo-Saxon Church* (London, 1844), 1:200: "and heo gelyfde þaes engles bondunge, and swa mid geleafan onfeng on hyre innoð, and hine baer ad middewintresmaesse daeg, and hine ða acende."

25. *Minor Poems of Lydgate,* 1:288 (ll. 1–3) The actual phrase that the most revered of early Christian exegetes, Augustine, had used to describe the mysterious pro-creative faith that "cometh from hearing" (cf. Romans 10:17) was "et virgo per aurem impregnabatur" ("the Virgin through the ear was impregnated"). Augus-tine's metaphor had by the ninth century come to be invoked as a physical *descrip-tion* of the Conception mystery. Christ the Word (cf. John 1:1) had been miracu-lously conceived through the most appropriate orifice—the ear; by the late Middle Ages the doctrine of the *conceptio per aurem* (conception through the ear) was ubiquitous in Marian hymns and devotional poems. One fourteenth-century Middle English poem in the Vernon manuscript even specifies that it was Mary's right ear that conceived God's Son: "Blessed be, Lady, þy Riht Ere:/Þe holygost, he liht in þere/ fflesch and Blod to take." Carl Horstmann, *The Minor Poems of the Vernon Manuscript,* EETS, o.s., 98 (London: Kegal Paul, Trench, Trübner, & Co., 1892), 126 (ll. 211–13). On the *conceptio per aurem* see Yrjo Hirn, *The Sacred Shrine* (Boston: Beacon Press, 1957), 294–98, and J. Vriend, S. J., *The Blessed Virgin Mary in the Medieval Drama of England* (Purmerend, Holland: J. Muusses, 1928), 150–59.

26. Mills, "Religious Drama and Civic Ceremonial," in *Revels History,* ed. Caw-ley, 1:199. Cf. the beautiful fifteenth-century lyric "I Sing of a Maiden," which praises Mary who freely chose to bear Christ: "to here sone che ches." Brown, *Religious Lyrics of the XVth Century,* p. 119 (l. 2).

27. *Ludus Coventriae,* p. 106.

28. The desending dove was nearly inevitable in depictions of the Annunciation in medieval art after the twelfth century (see Schiller, 1:43–52) and appears to have been commonly used in medieval drama as well. There are no instructions for staging the Conception in the other English Annunciation plays, but a rubric from a fourteenth-century church drama from the cathedral of Padua in Italy explains that a dove was to be lowered from the roof of the cathedral as Gabriel spoke the words "Spiritus Sanctus superveniet in te"; Mary was then to cover the dove with her cloak to symbolize the Conception. See Karl Young, *The Drama of the Medieval*

Church, (Oxford: Clarendon Press, 1962), 2:249. The rubric from the Conception episode in the Bibliothèque St. Geneviève *Nativité* says simply: "Here descends a dove which is made in a goodly manner" ("Cy descende un coulom qui soit fait par bonne maniere"); see *La Nativité et le Geu des Trois Roys: Two Plays from MS. 1131 of the Bibliothèque Sainte Geneviève, Paris* ed. Ruth Whittredge (Richmond, Virginia: William Byrd Press, 1944), 133.

29. *Ludus Coventriae,* p. 107.

30. According to Louis Réau, *Iconographie de l'art chrétien* (Paris: Presses Universitaires de France, 1955–59), 2: pt. 2, p. 92), statues of this type first appeared in the late thirteenth century and occurred with increasing frequency in the four- teenth and fifteenth centuries, especially in France and Germany. No English sculptures of this type managed to survive the rage of the Reformers—and indeed even the Catholic Counter-Reformation found them heretical (cf. John Gerson, *Opera,* ed. L. Ellies du Pin (Antwerp, 1706), 3:947; "quae in ventribus earum unam habent Trinitatem, veluti si tota Trinitas in Virgine Maria carnem assumpisset hu- manum . . . bea namque sententia nulla in eis est pulchritudo, nec devotia, et possunt esse causa erroris et indevotionis"). That there *were* medieval English Vierges ouvrantes statues, however, we know from a description of a cult image called "the Lady of Boultone" that appears in a sixteenth-century reminiscence, "Ancient Monuments, Rites, and Customes belonginge within the Monastical church of Durham before the Suppression," printed in Chambers, 2:311. Douglas Gray has attempted to excuse the "unorthodoxy" and "bad taste" of such images by explaining them as "the expression of a fervent popular devotion." Douglas Gray, *Themes and Images in the Medieval English Religious Lyric* (London and Bos- ton: Routledge and Kegan Paul, 1972), 36. But such criticism misreads both the significance of the image and the historical evidence. The crest of a noble family adorned the base of the Lady of Boultone; Blanche of Castille, powerful widow of King Louis VIII (and granddaughter of Henry II of England) gave a Vierge ouvrante statue to the Cistercian abbey of Maubisson (Réau, 2:pt. 2, p. 93); and the inventory of the treasures of the great Dukes of Burgundy lists not one but two such images "on which the womb of Our Lady opens, where inside is the Trinity." See X[avier] Barbier de Montault, *Traité d'Iconographie chrétienne* (Paris: Louis Vives, 1890), 2:220.

31. *Ludus Coventriae,* p. 108 (l. 333).

32. *Ludus Coventriae,* p. 120 (l. 116).

33. M. D. Anderson, *Drama and Imagery in English Medieval Churches* (Cam- bridge: Cambridge University Press, 1963), 132.

34. On the Christ Child of the Annunciation see especially David M. Robb, "The Iconography of the Annunciation in the Fourteenth and Fifteenth Centu- ries," *Art Bulletin* 18 (1936):524–26. Several English alabasters in the Hildburgh Collection of the Victoria and Albert Museum in London contain the Christ Child—or mutilated remains of the Christ Child—in the scene of the Annuncia- tion, and there is a Christ Child descending with the dove in the Annunciation illumination from the Bolton Hours (York Add. MS. 2), a York psalter of about 1420 that once belonged to John Bolton, chamberlain and sheriff of York.

35. *Ludus Coventriae,* p. 181 (ll. 97–100).

36. Woodforde, *Norwich School of Glass-Painting*, p. 24.

37. See Woodforde, *Norwich School of Glass-Painting*, pp. 23–24.

38. David King has argued that the surviving St. Peter Mancroft windows representing the Life of Mary and the Infancy of Christ were originally above an altar in the north aisle dedicated to the Holy Name of Jesus. See David King, "New Light on the Medieval Glazing of the Church of St. Peter Mancroft, Norwich," in *Crown in Glory: A Celebration of Craftsmanship—Studies in Stained Glass*, ed. Peter Moore (Norwich: Jarrold and Sons, 1982), 18–19.

39. See Franz Kieslinger, *Gotische Glasmalerei in Osterrich bis 1450* (Zurich: Amalthea Verlag, n.d.), pl. 81.

40. See Schiller, *Iconography of Christian Art*, 1:fig. 105.

41. *Ludus Coventriae*, p. 109 (ll. 15–16). Cf. *Glossa ordinaria*, "In Matthaeum I, 25" (*PL* 114:72): "Dicitur quod Joseph Mariam facie ad faciem videre non poterat quam Spiritus Sanctus a conceptione impleverat penitus. Et ideo non cognoscebat facie ad faciem quam desponsaverat, donec uterus evacuaretur: de quo hic non agitur."

42. Bonaventure, *Lignum vitae*, 1.3, *The Works of Bonaventura: Mystical Opuscula*, vol. 1, ed. and trans. José de Vinck (Paterson, New Jersey: St. Anthony Guild Press, 1960), 105.

43. *Ludus Coventriae*, p. 109 (l. 16).

44. "Sabbato Office of the Fourth Sunday in Advent," in *The Sarum Missal Edited from Three Early Manuscripts*, ed. J. Wickham Legg (Oxford: Clarendon Press, 1969), 21.

45. Tydeman, p. 169.

46. *Ludus Coventriae*, p. 107 (ll. 293–98). Cf. *Meditations on the Life of Christ*, p. 19:

> The spirit was created and placed into the sanctified womb as a human being complete in all parts of His body, though very small and child-like. He was then to grow naturally in the womb like other children, but the infusion of the soul and the separation of the limbs were not delayed as in others. Thus He was a perfect God as well as a perfect man and as wise and powerful then as now.

47. Robb, "Iconography of the Annunciation," p. 526, quotes St. Antoninus of Florence (1389–1459) and his *Summa hist.* 3, tit. 8, 4.11: "Represensibiles sunt pictores, cum pingunt . . . in Annunciatione Virginis parvulum puerum formatum, scilicet Jesum, mitti in uterum Virginis, quasi non esset ex substantia Virginis corpus eius assumptum."

48. York Add. MS. 2.

49. Joan Evans, *English Art, 1307–1461*, Oxford History of Art, no. 5 (Oxford: Oxford University Press, 1949), 112. The abbot's order for his new pastoral staff specified that it be crafted with a figure of St. Edmund in a tabernacle in the crook of the staff, surmounted on one side by the image of the Annunciation to the Virgin and on the other by the final glorification of the virginal conception, the Virgin's Assumption.

50. See W. H. Sewell, "The Sexton's Wheel and the Lady Fast," *Norfolk Archaeology* 9(1884):201–14.

51. See on the medieval plays of Joseph's Doubt and their iconographic tradi-

tions, Gail McMurray Gibson, "The Images of Doubt and Belief: Visual Symbolism in the Middle English Plays of Joseph's Troubles about Mary" (Ph.D. dissertation, University of Virginia, 1975).

52. *Ludus Coventriae*, p. 109 (ll. 1–16).

53. Eleanor Prosser, *Drama and Religion in the English Mystery Plays* (Stanford: Stanford University Press, 1961), 96.

54. On the tradition of the porta clausa in medieval thought, see Gail McMurray Gibson, "'Porta Haec Clausa Erit': Comedy, Conception, and Ezekiel's Closed Door in the *Ludus Coventriae* Play of 'Joseph's Return,'" *Journal of Medieval and Renaissance Studies* 8(1978):137–56.

55. Jerome, *In Hiezechielem* 13:44, 1–3 (*Corpus Christianorum*, 75, 646): "Pulchre quidam portam clausam, per quam solus Dominus Deus Israel ingreditur et dux cui porta clausa est, Mariam virginem intellegunt, quae et ante partum et post partum virgo permansit."

56. See Gibson, "'Porta Haec Clausa Erit,'" esp. pp. 144–50.

57. *Ludus Coventriae*, p. 59 (ll. 42–46):
A vysion of þis fful veryly
I Ezechiel haue had also
Of a gate þat sperd [locked] was trewly
And no man but a Prince myght þer-in go.

Cf. *Chester Cycle*, p. 477 (ll. 313–28), where Ezekiel's vision of the locked door is glossed by the Expositior as
that way the Holy Ghost in went
when God tooke flesh and bloode
in that sweet mayden Mary.
Shee was that gate wytterly
ffor in her he light graciouslie
Mankind to doe good.

58. The *Glossa Ordinaria* reveals that Mary so shone with light after she had conceived Christ that no man could stand to look directly upon her, and even suggests the possibility that it was for this reason impossible for Joseph to have intercourse with Mary after their marriage. (*Glossa ordinaria*, in Matthaeum, I. 25 [*PL* 114:72]. On the medieval tradition of the radiance on Mary's face after the Conception, see Gibson, "'Porta Haec Clausa Erit,'" pp. 154–55.

59. *Ludus Coventriae*, p. 111 (ll. 64–66).

60. Augustine, *De civitate dei* XIII.xxiii.3 (*PL* 41:398): "quia de coelo venit ut terrenae mortalitatis corpore vestiretur, quod coelesti immortalitate vesiret."

61. William Durandus, *Rationale divinorum officiorum*, I [1503]: "Sacrarium siue locus in quo sacra reponuntur siue in quo sacerdos sacras vestes induit uterum sacratissime marie significat: in quo christus se sacra veste carnis induit. Sacerdos a loco in quo vestes induit ad publicum procedit quia christus ex utero virginis procedens in mundum venit." For a discussion of the symbolism of the sacristy in the Annunciation panel of the fifteenth-century Ghent Altarpiece by Jan and Hubert van Eyck, see Carol J. Purtle, *The Marian Paintings of Jan van Eyck* (Princeton: Princeton University Press, 1982), 25–29.

62. Lydgate, *Life of Our Lady*, p. 344 (l. 480).

63. *The Towneley Plays*, ed. George England and Alfred W. Pollard, Early English

Text Society, e.s., 71 (London: Oxford University Press, 1897; reprint, 1966), 270 (ll. 386–389). Pollard and England gloss these lines "she sees the robe she gave Jesus all rent," but that is certainly an error since the whole point of the following "Play of the Talents" is that Christ's seamless tunic *cannot* be torn and so must be gambled for by the soldiers. On this passage see also Theresa Coletti, "Devotional Iconography in the N-Town Marian Plays," *Comparative Drama* 11 (1977):25–26.

64. See *Vita Beatae Virginis Mariae et Salvatoris Rhythmica,* ed. A. Vogtlin, Bibliothek des Litterarischen Vereins, Stuttgart 180 (Tübingen: Bibliothek des Litterarischen Vereins, 1888), 105 (ll. 3046–61):

> Mater Jesu fecerat opere textili
> Tunicam, quam texuit arte tam subtili,
> Quod in tota tunica nulla consutura
> Fuit, sed in sarciendo fiebat nec scissura.
> Cum adhuc infantulus esset, adaptata
> Tunc fuit ista tunica Jesuque parata . . .

The *Vita Rhythmica* was the source for the popular vernacular life of Mary written about 1400 by Wernher the Swiss (who falsely credits Ignatius as the authority for the strange legend of the magic tunic). See *Das Marienleben des Schweizers Wernher,* ed. Max Papke and Arthur Hübner, Deutsche Texte des Mittelalters 27 (Berlin, 1920), 89–90. The story of Mary making the seamless tunic also is alluded to in the *Marienleben* of Walters von Rheinau (*Das Marienleben,* ed. Edit Perjus in Acta Academiae Aboensis, Humaniora 17, vol. 1 [1949], 131, 234); the verse life of Mary by Brother Philip the Carthusian (*Bruder Philipps des Carthausers Marienleben,* ed. Heinrich Ruckert, Bibliothek der Deutschen National-Literatur, no. 24 [Amsterdam, 1966], 99–100); and the *Vita Christi* of Ludolphus of Saxony (*Vita Christi,* 2, 63 [Lugduni, 1557), 664–65).

65. See Stephen Spector, "Composition and Development," pp. 62–83.

66. *Ludus Coventriae,* p. 144 (l. 291).

67. *Ludus Coventriae,* p. 145.

68. *Ludus Coventriae,* p. 145 (ll. 297–99).

69. *Ludus Coventriae,* p. 149 (l. 109).

70. *Ludus Coventriae,* p. 148 (l. 59).

71. *Ludus Coventriae,* p. 153 (l. 64).

72. *Ludus Coventriae,* pp. 153–54 (ll. 70, 82).

73. *Ludus Coventriae,* p. 192 (ll. 131–34).

74. Although none of the English plays contain stage directions for the labors, it is certain from visual and documentary evidence and from the language of the plays themselves that shovel and distaff would have been essential stage properties. In the Chester cycle, Eve refers to "this wool" that she "will spyn threede by threede" (*Chester Cycle,* p. 33 [l. 503]), and "adams spade Ives distaffe" appear in the properties list of the accounts of the Cappers guild from Coventry. See W. W. Ingram, *Records of Early English Drama: Coventry* (Toronto and Buffalo: University of Toronto Press, 1981), 334. In a French mystery play by Arnoul Greban, Eve speaks of finding an artful tool ("ung engin subtil") with which she can make thread. *Le Mystère de la Passion d'Arnoul Greban,* ed. Omer Judogne, Koninklijke Academie van Belgie, Klasse der Letteren, Verhandelingen 12, part 3 (Brussells:

Palais Academies, 1965), 1: 21 (ll. 684–87). The most industriously spinning Eve in medieval theater must be the Eve of the Bibliothèque St. Geneviève *Nativité*, who sits down to spin "cloths and kerchiefs, / Tablecloths, napkins and pillowcases" (p. 105 [ll. 286–92]):

> Il me convient aussy entendre
> Sanz delay a faire besoigne,
> Et filler, tantost ma queloigne
> Pour faire draps et cravechiez
> Nappes, touailles, et oreilliez
> Faire le fault quant le convient,
> Car tel ouvraige m'apartient.

75. Steven May, "A Medieval Stage Property: The Spade," *Medieval English Theatre* 4(1982): 88.

76. Eccles, *Macro Plays,* p. 176 (l. 676).

77. *Ludus Coventriae,* p. 28 (ll. 408–11).

78. *Ludus Coventriae,* p. 104 (ll. 217–20).

79. On the historical development of the iconography of the Annunciation to Mary, see Schiller, 1: 33–52.

80. Schiller, 1: 42.

81. Cf. the fifteenth-century translation of the *Meditationes vitae Christi* by Nicholas Love, which reveals that as the angel appeared to Mary in her house in Nazareth she was "in hire prive chambre that tyme closed and in here prayers or in hire meditaciouns peradventure redynge the prophecies of yfaire touchynge the Incarnation." Nicholas Love, *The Mirrour of the Blessed Lyf of Jesus Christ,* pp. 24–25.

82. Panofsky, *Early Netherlandish Painting,* 1:131; 2: fig. 104.

83. See, for example, the illumination of the Virgin in the Temple in the *Grandes Heures of Jean de Berry* (Paris: BN MS lat. 919, fol. 34) of 1409, reproduced in Millard Meiss, *French Painting in the Time of Jean de Berry: The Late Fourteenth Century and the Patronage of the Duke* (London: Phaidon Press, 1967), 2: fig. 234, which shows the crowned and nimbed Virgin Mary interrupted at her weaving work in the Temple by an angel who brings her a basket of food. The *Meditationes vitae Christi* attributes to St. Jerome (a letter claiming that Jerome had translated the text circulated with some manuscripts of the *Pseudo-Matthew*) the information that the Virgin Mary's life in the Temple before her marriage to Joseph followed this routine: "In the morning she prayed until the third hour, from the third to the ninth hour she was busy spinning, and from the ninth she again prayed, continuing until the appearance of the angel from whose hands she received her food." (*Meditations on the Life of Christ,* p. 12).

84. The popularity in the fourteenth and fifteenth centuries of the Doubting-Joseph theme, like that of the doubting midwife, is surely not unrelated to the philosophical revolution wrought by the nominalists like William of Ockham, who insisted that knowledge was necessarily limited by sense experience. The collision of faith and sense experience implicit in Joseph's doubting of the miracle of the virgin birth confronts—and mimetically resolves—what was for the late Middle Ages a disturbing and profoundly serious philosophical issue. On the phil-

osophical backgrounds of the Joseph's Doubt theme, see Gibson, "Images of Doubt," pp. 48–74.

85. On the symbolic interiors of fifteenth-century Annunciation paintings, see Schiller, 1:48–52.

86. See *Pseudo-Matthew* in *The Ante-Nicene Fathers,* 8:372–73.

87. Lydgate, *Life of Our Lady,* p. 305 (ll. 813–19).

88. The pun survives in the modern French term *fils de la Vierge,* meaning the filmy cobwebs that in English are called "gossamer." See *Mansion's Concise French and English Dictionary,* ed. J. E. Mansion (Boston: D. C. Heath and Company), 487. Emile Mâle (*Gothic Image,* p. 244) observes that *fils de la Vierge* ("the Virgin's threads") is a survival in folklore of the medieval spinning iconography, but he does not note the pun. On the importance of puns in medieval theological thought and in the Latin hymn tradition, see Walter J. Ong, "Wit and Mystery: A Revaluation in Mediaeval Latin Hymnody," *Speculum* 22 (1947): 310–41.

89. *Pseudo-Matthew* in *The Ante-Nicene Fathers,* vol. 8, ed. Alexander Roberts and James Donaldson, rev. A. Cleveland Coxe. (Buffalo: Christian Literature Company, 1886), 372: "Then Joseph received [Mary] with the other five virgins who were to be with her in Joseph's house. These virgins were Rebecca, Sephora, Susannah, Abigea, and Cael; to whom the high priest gave the silk, and the blue, and the fine linen, and the scarlet, and the purple, and the fine flax." Cf. Lydgate, *Life of Our Lady,* p. 302 (ll. 771–74). In the N-Town "the Betrothal of Mary" (*Ludus Coventriae,* p. 93 [ll. 350–56]), Susanne, Rebecca, and Sephore are sent with Mary by Episcopus to be guardians of Mary's chastity.

90. *Ludus Coventriae,* p. 109 (l. 26).

91. Phythian-Adams, *Crisis and Order.*

92. On the doctrine of the Assumption, see Warner, p. 92, and Raymond Winch and Victor Bennett, *The Assumption of Our Lady and Catholic Theology* (London: Society for Promoting Christian Knowledge, 1950).

93. See *Records of Early English Drama: Chester,* pp. 20–21, 23–24.

94. Cf. *Ludus Coventriae,* p. 361 (rubric and l. 170): "hic [John] pulsavit super portam intrante domum marie sibi dicente, 'heyl moder mary mayden perpetuall'."

95. But see Woolf, in *Mystery Plays,* p. 287, who dismisses this astonishing pageant as "the work of an inferior writer," a judgment with which Martin Stevens' recent book on the mystery plays agrees. Cf. Stevens, *Four Middle English Mystery Cycles,* p. 254.

96. *Ludus Coventriae,* p. 372 (l. 483).

97. Tymms, *Wills and Inventories,* p. 18.

98. On the rood lofts and canopies of honor in fifteenth-century East Anglian churches, see Cautley, *Suffolk Churches,* pp. 137–43.

99. Tymms, *Wills and Inventories,* p. 39.

100. Clive Paine, *St. Mary's, Bury St. Edmunds* (1986), 4.

101. On Rougham Church, see Cautley, *Suffolk Churches,* p. 343, and Pevsner, *Suffolk,* p. 407. The same Bury mason, William Layer, who is thought to have designed the nave of Bury St. Mary may have designed the angel roofs of both the Bury and the Rougham churches of St. Mary, for Layer left a generous bequest to

Rougham Church in his will of 1444. See Harvey, *English Medieval Architects,* p. 158.)

102. Although this church was (and is) commonly referred to simply as "St. Mary's," it is clear from the medieval historian William Worcestre, who visited the church and carefully recorded its dimensions in his *Itineraries* of 1478–80, that the actual dedication was to "The Assumption of the Blessed Mary." Cf. William Worcestre, *Itineraries,* ed. John H. Harvey (Oxford: Clarendon Press, 1969), 171.

103. See J. B. L. Tolhurst, "The Hammer-Beam Figures of the Nave Roof of St. Mary's Church, Bury St. Edmunds," *Journal of the British Archaeological Association,* 3d ser., 25 (1962): 67.

104. On the late medieval iconographic convention of representing angels as subministers of a Mass "in which Christ himself is the celebrant vested in the chasuble of his flesh", see M. B. McNamee, "The Origin of the Vested Angel as a Eucharistic Symbol in Flemish Painting," *Art Bulletin* 54 (1972): 263–78.

105. See Tolhurst, pp. 68–70, and Paine, p. 3: "The last . . . pairs of figures will probably always be subject to speculation and re-interpretation."

106. See Caroline Feudale, "The Iconography of the Madonna del Parto," *Marsyas* 7 (1957): 10.

107. Tolhurst, pp. 69–70.

108. On the Lancastrian collar, see Tymms, *Wills and Inventories,* pp. 234, 249. The only known extant Lancastrian collar of *SS* was recently given to the collection of the Museum of the City of London.

109. The long-standing tradition of royal patronage at Bury St. Edmunds was at no time as important as in the first half of the fifteenth century, when Abbot Curteys developed a close, even fatherly, relationship to the child-king Henry VI. As a boy of 12, Henry VI spent the months from Christmas 1433 to Easter 1434 as a houseguest at the monastery of Bury and at the abbot's country estate at Elmswell. This unusually lengthy visit was recognized as an extraordinary sign of the king's favor, favor that was formalized at the end of the famous visit by a solemn ceremony in the chapter house of the abbey, in which the king and his courtiers were admitted to lay-confraternity status in the abbey of St. Edmund. (See Dugdale, 3:113 and Schirmer, pp. 144–46.) After the 1433–34 visit, Abbot Curteys commissioned from John Lydgate a verse account of the life and miracles of St. Edmund and had it splendidly illuminated. Lydgate's *Life of St. Edmund* was presented to King Henry VI, says Lydgate's poem, in hope and expectation that Henry would be the embodiment of the ideal Christian king, the guardian and defender of the Church—and especially the guardian of the church of St. Edmund. Lydgate continued to wage a one-man propaganda campaign for Henry VI and for the Lancastrian dynasty, writing political poems in which Henry is extravagantly praised as both glorious king of England and rightful king of France. (Schirmer, pp. 163–64). Henry VI was repeatedly a visitor to the abbey of Bury St. Edmunds; there are records of visits in 1436, 1446, and 1448 (Taylor, p. xx)— and a letter survives in the fifteenth-century register of Abbot Curteys (another manuscript in the Cox Macro collection) in which Henry VI appeals to his old friend Abbot Curteys for a loan to help finance the elaborate royal pageantry

deemed necessary to bring Margaret to her 1445 coronation in London "in such wise as it shall be according to the state and worshipe of us, of hir, and of this oure reaume, and, that doone, to purveye for the solemnite of hir coronation in maner and fourme accusumed." Thomas Arnold, ed., *Memorials of St. Edmunds Abbey* (London, 1896), 3:245).

110. As Richard Osberg observes, in "The Jesse Tree in the 1432 London Entry of Henry VI: Messianic Kingship and the Rule of Justice," *Journal of Medieval and Renaissance Studies* 16(1986): 215, the theme of Henry VI's royal entry into London in 1432 was "the advent of the virtuous king whose reign of justice will recreate the lost order of the prelapsarian world."

111. See Gibson, "Play of *Wisdom,*" pp. 53–55.

112. See Kathryn Horste, "'A Child is Born': The Iconography of the Portail Ste.-Anne at Paris," *Art Bulletin* 69(1987): 204–10.

113. For the argument that the figure of Wisdom in the East Anglian play by that name personifies not only Christ's just kingship but is figural compliment to the Yorkist King Edward IV (who had emerged as supporter of the abbey of St. Edmund after some hasty political realignment at the monastery), see Gibson, "Play of *Wisdom,*" pp. 55–60.

114. On the convention of representing Ecclesia as a crowned queen and on the allegorical meaning of Mary as the Church, see Adolf Katzenellenbogen, *The Sculptural Programs of Chartres Cathedral* (New York: W. W. Norton and Company, 1959), 59–65.

115. Augustine, *Expositions on the Book of Psalms,* quoted in Purtle, p. 32.

116. For text of the Margaret entry, see Carleton Brown, "Lydgate's Verses on Queen Margaret's Entry into London," *Modern Language Review* 7(1912): 225–34, and Robert Withington, "Queen Margaret's Entry into London, 1445," *Modern Philology* 13(1915–16): 53–57. The Bury poet and monk John Lydgate has traditionally been credited with writing the pageant speeches for Margaret of Anjou. A recent article by Gordon Kipling, "The London Pageants for Margaret of Anjou: A Medieval Script Restored," *Medieval English Theatre* 4(1982): 5–25, refutes that tradition, but does not challenge, I think, the real truth of the tradition, that the names of Bury St. Edmunds and of Lydgate were automatically associated with acts of public support for the Lancastrian dynasty.

117. *Ludus Coventriae,* p. 358 (ll. 81–84).

118. Cf. the speech of the child Jesus in the N-Town play of Christ and the Doctors (*Ludus Coventriae,* p. 183 [ll. 161–64]).

> Ffor be my ffadyr kynge celestyall
> With-out begynnyng I am endles
> but be my modyr þat is carnall
> I am but xii ȝere of age

119. *Minor Poems of Lydgate,* 1:287 (ll. 77–78).

120. *Ludus Coventriae,* p. 373 (l. 493).

Select Bibliography

Drama Texts and Other Published Primary Sources

Arnold, Thomas, ed. *Memorials of St. Edmunds Abbey.* 3 vols. London, 1896.

Augustine, Saint. *Confessions.* Harmondsworth, England: Penguin Books, 1961.

Bede. *A History of the English Church and English People.* Translated by Leo Sherley-Price and revised by R. E. Latham. Harmondsworth, England: Penguin Books, 1955. Reprint. 1979.

Bevington, David, ed. *Medieval Drama.* Boston: Houghton Mifflin, 1975.

Bokenham, Osbern. *Legendys of Hooly Wummen.* Edited by Mary Sergeantson. Early English Text Society, o.s., 206. London: Oxford University Press, 1938. Reprint. New York: Kraus Reprints, 1971.

Bonaventure, Saint. *The Works of Bonaventura: Mystical Opuscula.* Vol. 1. Edited and translated by José de Vinck. Paterson, New Jersey: St. Anthony Guild Press, 1960.

Brown, Carleton, ed. *Religious Lyrics of the XVth Century.* Oxford: Clarendon Press. Reprint. 1967.

The Chester Mystery Cycle. Vol. 1. Edited by R. M. Lumiansky and David Mills. Early English Text Society, s.s., 3. Oxford: Oxford University Press, 1974.

Cook, G. H. *Letters to Cromwell and Others on the Suppression of the Monasteries.* London: John Barker, 1965.

The Dance of Death. Edited by Florence Warren and Beatrice White. Early English Text Society, o.s., 181. London: Oxford University Press, 1931.

Darlington, Ida, ed. *London Consistory Court Wills, 1492–1547.* London Record Society Publications, no. 3. London: London Record Society, 1967.

de Mezières, Philippe. *Figurative Representation of the Presentation of the Virgin Mary in the Temple.* Translated and edited by Robert S. Haller. Lincoln: University of Nebraska Press, 1971.

DeWald, E[rnest] T[heodore], ed. *The Illustrations of the Utrecht Psalter.* Princeton: Princeton University Press, n.d.

Dives and Pauper. Vol. 1. Edited by Priscilla Heath Barnum. Early English Text Society, o.s., 275. London: Oxford University Press, 1976.

Dowsing, William. *The Journal of William Dowsing of Stratford, Parliamentary Visitor, Appointed Under a Warrant from the Earl of Manchester for Demolishing the Superstitious Pictures and Ornaments of Churches, Within the County of Suffolk, in the Years 1643–1644.* Edited by Rev. C. H. Evelyn White. Ipswich: Pawsey and Hayes, 1885.

Froning, Richard, ed. *Das Drama des Mittelalters,* Darmstadt: Wissenschaftliche Buchgesellschaft, 1964.

Furnivall, Frederick J., ed. *The Fifty Earliest English Wills in the Court of Probate, London.* Early English Text Society, o.s., 78. London: Trübner and Company, 1882.

Gesti Henrici Quinti, Deeds of Henry the Fifth. Translated and edited by Frank Taylor and John S. Roskell. Oxford: Clarendon Press, 1975.

Greban, Arnoul. *Le Mystère de la Passion d'Arnoul Gréban.* Edited by Omer Judogne. Koninklijke Academie van Belgie, Klasse der Letteren, Verhandelingen 12, Part 3. Brussels: Palais Academies, 1965.

Herrick, Robert. *The Poetical Works of Robert Herrick.* Edited by L. C. Martin. London: Clarendon Press, 1956.

Historical Manuscripts Commission of Great Britain. *The Manuscripts of Lincoln, Bury St. Edmonds, and Great Grimsby Corporations: and of the Deans and Chapters of Worcester and Lichfield, &c.* Fourteenth Report, part 8. Edited by William Dunn Macray. Historical Manuscripts Commission, ser. 65. London: Eyre and Spottiswoode, 1895.

Hoccleve, John. *Selections from Hoccleve.* Edited by M. C. Seymour. Oxford: Clarendon Press, 1981.

Holkam Bible Picture Book, Edited by W. O. Hassall. London: Dropmore Press, 1954.

Hrabanus Maurus. *De laudibus sancta crucis: Studien zur Uberlieferung und Geistesgeschichte mit dem Faksimile-Textabdruck aus Codex Reg. Lat. 124 der vatikanischen Bibliothek.* Edited by Hans-Georg Muller. Miltellateinischen Jahrbuch 11. Ratingen: A. Henn Verlag, 1973.

Jacobus de Voragine. *The Golden Legend.* Translated and edited by Granger Ryan and Helmut Ripperger. New York and London: Longmans, Green, 1941. Reprint. New York: Arno Press, 1969.

James, Montague Rhodes, ed. *The Apocryphal New Testament,* Oxford: Clarendon Press. 1924. Reprint. 1980.

Jocelin of Brakelond. *The Chronicle of Jocelin of Brakelond concerning the acts of Samson, Abbot of the Monastery of St. Edmund.* Translated and edited by H. E. Butler. London: Thomas Nelson and Sons, 1949. Reprint. 1951.

Julian of Norwich. *A Book of Showings to the Anchoress Julian of Norwich.* 2 vols. Edited by Edmund Colledge and James Walsh. Toronto: Toronto University Press, 1978.

Kempe, Margery. *The Book of Margery Kempe.* Edited by Sanford Brown Meech and Hope Emily Allen. Early English Text Society, o.s., 212. London: Oxford University Press, 1940. Reprint. 1961.

The Late Medieval Religious Plays of Bodleian Mss. Digby 133 and E. Museo 160. Edited by Donald C. Baker, John L. Murphy, and Louis B. Hall, Jr. Early English Text Society o.s. 283. Oxford: Oxford University Press, 1982.

La Livre de Conduite du Régisseur et la compte des dépenses pour le mystère de la passion joué à Mons en 1501. Edited by Gustave Cohen. Paris: Librairie Ancienne Honoré Champion, 1925.

Love, Nicholas, trans. *The Mirrour of the Blessed Lyf of Jesus Christ*. Edited by Lawrence Powell. Oxford: Clarendon Press, 1908.

Ludus Coventriae; or, the Plaie Called Corpus Christi. Edited by K. S. Block. Early English Text Society, e.s., 120. London: Oxford University Press, 1922. Reprint. 1960.

Lydgate, John. *A Critical Edition of John Lydgate's Life of Our Lady*. Edited by Joseph A. Lauritis, Ralph A. Klinefelter, and Vernon T. Gallagher. Duquesne Philological Series, no. 2. Pittsburgh: Duquesne University Press. 1961.

———. *The Minor Poems of John Lydgate*. Part 1, *Lydgate Canon and Religious Poems*, edited by Henry Noble MacCracken. Early English Text Society, e.s., 107. London: Kegan Paul, 1911. Part 2, *Secular Poems*, edited by Henry Noble MacCracken and Merriam Sherwood. Early English Text Society, o.s., 192. London: Oxford University Press, 1934. Reprint. 1961.

———. and Benedict Burgh. *Lydgate and Burgh's Secrees of Old Philisoffres*. Edited by Robert Steele. Early English Text Society, e.s., 66. London: Kegan Paul, Trench, Trubner and Co., 1894.

The Macro Plays. Edited by Mark Eccles. Early English Text Society, o.s., 262. London: Oxford University Press, 1969.

The Macro Plays: A Facsimile Edition with Facing Transcription. Edited by David Bevington. Washington, D.C.: Folger Shakespeare Library, 1972.

Meditations on the Life of Christ. Translated by Isa Ragusa and edited by Isa Ragusa and Rosalie B. Green. Princeton: Princeton University Press, 1961.

Migne, J[acques] P[aul], ed. *Patrologiae cursus completus: series graeca*. 162 vols. Paris: J. P. Migne, 1857–66.

———. *Patrologiae cursus completus: series latina*. 221 vols. Paris: J. P. Migne, 1844–66.

Mirk, John. *Mirk's Festial: A Collection of Homilies*. Part 1. Edited by Theodore Erbe. Early English Text Society, o.s., 96. London: Oxford University Press, 1905.

Myers, A. R., ed. *The Household of Edward IV: The Black Book and the Ordinance of 1478*. Manchester: Manchester University Press, 1959.

La Nativité et le Geu des Trois Roys: Two Plays from MS. 1131 of the Bibliothèque Sainte Geneviève, Paris. Edited by Ruth Whittredge. Richmond: William Byrd Press, 1944.

Non-Cycle Plays and Fragments. Edited by Norman Davis. Early English Text Society, s.s., 1. London: Oxford University Press, 1970.

The N-Town Plays: A Facsimile of British Library MS Cotton Vespasian D. VIII. Edited by Peter Meredith and Stanley J. Kahrl. Leeds Texts and Monographs, Medieval Drama Facsimiles, no. 4. Ilkey, England: Scholar Press, 1977.

Osbert of Clare. *The Letters of Osbert of Clare, Prior of Westminster*. Edited by E. W. Williamson. London: Oxford University Press, 1929.

Parker, Roscoe E., ed. *The Middle English Stanzaic Versions of the Life of Saint Anne*, Early English Text Society, o.s., 174. London: Oxford University Press, 1928.

Paston Letters and Papers of the Fifteenth Century. Parts 1 and 2. Edited by Norman Davis. Oxford: Clarendon Press, 1971 and 1976.

Select Bibliography

Pierce the Ploughman's Crede. Edited by Walter W. Skeat. Early English Text Society, o.s., 30. London: N. Trübner, 1873.

Queen Mary's Psalter: Miniatures and Drawings by an English Artist of the 14th Century, Reproduced from Royal MS. 2b.VIII in the British Museum. Edited by George Warner. London: Oxford University Press, 1912.

Pseudo-Matthew in *The Ante-Nicene Fathers,* vol. 8. Edited by Alexander Roberts and James Donaldson and revised by A. Cleveland Coxe. Buffalo, New York: Christian Literature Company, 1886.

Records of Early English Drama: Chester. Edited by Lawrence M. Clopper. Toronto: University of Toronto Press, 1979.

Records of Early English Drama: Coventry. Edited by R. W. Ingram. Toronto and Buffalo: University of Toronto Press, 1981.

Records of Early English Drama: York. 2 vols. Edited by Alexandra F. Johnston and Margaret Rogerson. Toronto and Buffalo: University of Toronto Press, 1979.

Records of Plays and Players in Norfolk and Suffolk, 1330–1642. Edited by David Galloway and John Wasson. Malone Society Collections, no. 11. Oxford: Oxford University Press, 1981.

Reyce, Robert. *Suffolk in the XVII Century: The Breviary of Suffolk.* Edited by Lord Francis Hervey. London: J. Murray, 1902.

Reynes, Robert. *The Commonplace Book of Robert Reynes of Acle: An Edition of Tanner MS. 407.* Edited by Cameron Louis. New York and London: Garland Publishing Company, 1980.

Rites of Durham, being a Description or Brief Declaration of all the Ancient Monuments, Rites, and Customs belonging or being within the Monastical Church of Durham Before the Suppression, written 1593. Surtees Society Publications, no. 107. Durham, England: Andrews and Company, 1903.

Rogers, Thomas. *The Catholic Doctrine of the Church of England: An Exposition of the Thirty-Nine Articles. 1586.* Edited by J. J. S. Perowne. Parker Society, no. 40. Cambridge, England, 1854.

Ross, Woodburn O., ed. *Middle English Sermons.* Early English Text Society, o.s., 209. London: Oxford University Press, 1940.

The Sarum Missal Edited from Three Early Manuscripts. Edited by J. Wickham Legg. Oxford: Clarendon Press, 1969.

Stow, John. *A Survey of London.* Edited by Charles Lethbridge Kingsford. Oxford: Clarendon Press, 1908. Reprint. 1971.

Testamenta Cantiana: East Kent. Edited by Arthur Hussey. London: Mitchell Hughes and Clarke, 1907.

Testamenta Cantiana: West Kent. Edited by Leland L. Duncan. London: Mitchell Hughes and Clarke, 1906.

Testamenta Eboracensia: A Selection of Wills from the Register at York. Vol. 4. Edited by James Raine. Surtees Society, no. 53. Durham: Andrew and Company, 1869.

The Towneley Plays. Edited by George England and Alfred W. Pollard. Early English Text Society, e.s., 71. London: Oxford University Press, 1897. Reprint. 1966.

Select Bibliography

Tymms, Samuel, ed. *Wills and Inventories from the Registers of the Commissary of Bury St. Edmunds and the Archdeacon of Sudbury.* Camden Society, ser. 1, no. 49. London: J. B. Nichols and Son, 1850. Reprint. New York: AMS Press, 1968.

The Visitation of Suffolke made by William Hervey, Clarenceux King of Arms, 1561, with Additions from Family Documents, Original Wills, Jermyn, Davy, and Other MSS. 2 vols. Edited by Joseph Jackson Howard. Lowestoft and London: Samuel Tymms and Whittaker and Company, 1866.

Vita Beatea Virginis Mariae et Salvatoris Rhythmica. Edited by A. Vogtlin. Bibliothek des Litterarischen Vereins, Stuttgart 180. Tübingen: Bibliothek des Litterarischen Vereins, 1888.

Waddell, Helen, trans. *Medieval Latin Lyrics.* Rev. ed. New York: W. W. Norton and Company, 1977.

Wernher the Swiss. *Das Marienleben des Schweizers Wernher.* Edited by Max Papke and Arthur Hübner. Deutsche Texte des Mittelalters 27. Berlin, 1920.

Worcestre, William. *Itineraries.* Edited by John H. Harvey. Oxford: Clarendon Press, 1969.

Scholarly Studies

Adair, John. *The Pilgrim's Way: Shrines and Saints in Britain and Ireland.* London: Thames and Hudson, 1978.

Almack, Richard. "Some Account of Melford Church." *Proceedings of the Suffolk Institute of Archaeology* 2(1859):73–83.

———. "Three Kings of Cologne, Melford Church." *Gentleman's Magazine* 100(1830):204–5.

"Ancient Furniture and Utensils in Long Melford Church." *Gentleman's Magazine* 100(1830):352–55.

Anderson, M. D. *Drama and Imagery in English Medieval Churches.* Cambridge: Cambridge University Press, 1963.

Armstrong, C. A. J. "The Piety of Cicely, Duchess of York: A Study in Late Medieval Culture." In *For Hilaire Belloc: Essays in Honor of His 71st Birthday,* edited by Douglas Woodruff. New York: Sheed and Ward, 1942.

Ashley, Kathleen M. "'Wyt' and 'Wysdam' in N-town Cycle." *Philological Quarterly* 58(1979):121–35.

Aston, Margaret. "Huizinga's Harvest: England and the *Waning of the Middle Ages.*" *Medievalia et Humanistica,* n.s., 9(1979):1–24.

Baker, Alan R. H. "Changes in the Later Middle Ages." In *A New Historical Geography of England,* edited by H. C. Darby. Cambridge: Cambridge University Press, 1973.

Baker, Donald C. "The Drama: Learning and Unlearning." In *Fifteenth-Century Studies: Recent Essays,* edited by Robert F. Yeager. Hamden, Connecticut: Shoe String Press, 1984.

———. "Is *Wisdom* a Professional Play?" In *The Wisdom Symposium: Papers from the Trinity College Medieval Festival,* edited by Milla Cozart Riggio. AMS Studies in the Middle Ages, no. 11. New York: AMS Press, 1986.

———— and J. L. Murphy. "The Books of Myles Blomefylde." *The Library* 31(1976):377–85.

Baker, Donald C., and J. L. Murphy. "The Late Medieval Plays of MS Digby 133: Scribes, Dates, and Early History." *Research Opportunities in Renaissance Drama* 10(1967):153–66.

Baker, Gray B. "Church Ale-games and Interludes: Bungay Holy Trinity." *The East Anglian* 1(1864):291–92, 304, 334–36. Also "Church Ales and Interludes," 383.

Bannister, Ann. "The Introduction of the Cultus of St. Anne in the West." *English Historical Review* 43(1903):107–12.

Bartholomew, A. T., and Cosmo Gordon. "On the Library at King Edward VI School, Bury St. Edmunds." *The Library,* 3d ser., 1(1910):1–27.

Baxandall, Michael. *Painting and Experience in Fifteenth-Century Italy.* London: Oxford University Press, 1974.

Beadle, Hilton Richard Leslie. "The Medieval Drama of East Anglia: Studies in Dialect, Documentary Records and Stagecraft." 2 vols. D. Phil. dissertation, University of York, Centre for Medieval Studies, 1977.

————. "Plays and Playing at Thetford and Nearby, 1498–1540." *Theatre Notebook* 32(1978):4–11.

————. "The Scribal Pattern in the Macro Manuscript." *English Language Notes* 21(1984):1–13.

Bennet [Edward Kedington]. "Notes on the Original Statutes of the College of St. John Evangelist of Rushworth, Co. Norfolk, Founded by Edmund Gonville, A.D. 1342." *Norfolk Archaeology* 10(1888):50–64, 277–382.

Bennett, H. S. *Chaucer and the Fifteenth Century.* Oxford: Clarendon Press, 1947.

Bennett, Jacob. "The Language and Home of the Ludus Coventriae." *Orbis: Bulletin international de documentation linguistique* 22(1973):43–63.

Bevan, Beckford. "Foundation Deed of S. Saviour's Hospital, Bury St. Edmunds." *Proceedings of the Suffolk Institute of Archaeology and History* 6(1888):296–301.

Bevington, David M. *From Mankind to Marlowe.* Cambridge, Massachusetts: Harvard University Press, 1962.

Bishop, Edmund. *Liturgica Historica.* Oxford: Clarendon Press, 1918. Reprint. 1962.

Blomefield, Francis. *An Essay Towards a Topographical History of the County of Norfolk.* 2d ed. London: William Miller, 1805.

Boglioni, Pierre. "Some Methodological Reflections on the Study of Medieval Popular Religion." *Journal of Popular Culture* 11(1977):697–705.

Bolingbroke, L. G. "Pre-Elizabethan Plays and Players in Norfolk." *Norfolk Archaeology* 11(1892):332–51.

Bouman, Cornelius A. "The Immaculate Conception in the Liturgy." In *The Dogma of the Immaculate Conception: History and Significance,* edited by Edward D. O'Connor. South Bend, Indiana: University of Notre Dame Press, 1958.

Brewer, Derek. *English Gothic Literature.* New York: Schocken Books, 1983.

Briscoe, Marianne G. "Some Clerical Notions of Dramatic Decorum in Late Medieval England." *Comparative Drama* 19(1985):1–13.

Brown, Arthur. "The Study of English Medieval Drama." In *Franciplegius: Medie-*

val and Linguistic Studies in Honor of Francis Peabody Magoun, Jr. New York: New York University Press, 1965.

Brown, Carleton. "Lydgate's Verses on Queen Margaret's Entry into London." *Modern Language Review* 7(1912):225–34.

Burgess, Clive. "For the Increase of Divine Service: Chantries in the Parish in Late Medieval Bristol." *Journal of Ecclesiastical History* 36(1985):46–65.

Burne, R. V. H. *The Monks of Chester,* London: Society for Promoting Christian Knowledge, 1962.

Bynum, Caroline Walker. *Holy Feast and Holy Fast: The Religious Significance of Food to Medieval Women.* Berkeley: University of California Press, 1987.

Calderhead, Iris G. "Morality Fragments from Norfolk." *Modern Philology* 14(1916):1–9.

Cameron, Kenneth, and Stanley J. Kahrl. "The N-Town Plays at Lincoln." *Theatre Notebook* 20(1965):61–69.

Cautley, H. Munro. *Norfolk Churches.* Ipswich: Boydell Press, 1949. Reprint. 1979.

———. *Suffolk Churches and Their Treasures.* 4th ed. Ipswich: Boydell Press, 1975.

Caviness, Madeline Harrison. *The Early Stained Glass of Canterbury Cathedral, circa 1175–1220.* Princeton: Princeton University Press, 1977.

Cawley, A. C., Marion Jones, Peter F. McDonald, and David Mills, *The Revels History of Drama in English.* Vol. 1, *Medieval Drama.* London: Methuen, 1983.

Chambers, E. K. *The Mediaeval Stage.* 2 vols. Oxford: Oxford University Press, 1903. Reprint. 1978.

Cheetham, Francis. *English Medieval Alabasters.* Oxford: Phaidon and Christie's Limited, 1984.

Clopper, Lawrence M. "The History and Development of the Chester Cycle." *Modern Philology* 75(1978):219–46.

———. "Mankind and Its Audience." *Comparative Drama* 8(1974–75):347–55.

Cohen, Kathleen. *Metamorphosis of a Death Symbol: The Transi Tomb in the Late Middle Ages and the Renaissance.* Berkeley and Los Angeles: University of California Press, 1973.

Cohn, Norman. *The Pursuit of the Millenium.* Rev. ed. New York: Oxford University Press, 1970.

Coldewey, John. "The Digby Plays and the Chelmsford Records." *Research Opportunities in Renaissance Drama* 18(1975):103–21.

———. "The Last Rise and Final Demise of Essex Town Drama." *Modern Language Quarterly* 36(1975):239–60.

———. "Plays and Play in Early English Drama." *Research Opportunities in Renaissance Drama* 28(1985):181–88.

Coletti, Theresa. "Devotional Iconography in the N-Town Marian Plays." *Comparative Drama* 11(1977):22–44.

Condor, E. Lauriston. *Church of the Holy Trinity, Long Melford, Suffolk,* London: Dryden Press, 1876.

Cook, G. H. *The English Mediaeval Parish Church.* London: Phoenix House, 1954.

Cooke, William. *The College or Chantry of Denston.* London: John Murray, 1898.

Cornell, Henrik. *The Iconography of the Nativity of Christ.* Uppsala Universitets Arsskrift. Uppsala: A. B. Lundequistska Bokhandeln, 1924.

Coulton, G. G. "The Plain Man's Religion in the Middle Ages." *The Hibbert Journal* 14(1915–16):592–603.

Craddock, Lawrence. "Franciscan Influences on Early English Drama." *Franciscan Studies* 10(1950):383–417.

Craig, Hardin. *English Religious Drama of the Middle Ages*. Oxford: The Clarendon Press, 1955.

———. "Mystery Plays at Lincoln—Further Research Needed." *The Lincolnshire Historian* 11, no. 2 (1964):37–41.

Crossley-Holland, Kevin. *The Green Children*. London, 1966.

Cutts, Cecilia. "The Croxton Play: An Anti-Lollard Piece." *Modern Language Quarterly* 5(1944):45–60.

Davenport, W. A. *Fifteenth-Century English Drama: The Early Moral Plays and Their Literary Relations*. Cambridge: D. S. Brewer; Totowa, New Jersey: Rowman and Littlefield, 1982.

Davidson, Clifford. *Drama and Art: An Introduction to the Use of Evidence from the Visual Arts for the Study of Early Drama*. EDAM Monograph Series, no. 1. Kalamazoo, Michigan: The Medieval Institute, 1977.

———. *From Creation to Doom: The York Cycle of Mystery Plays*. New York: AMS Press, 1984.

———. "Northern Spirituality and the Late Medieval Drama of York." In *The Spirituality of Western Christendom*, edited by E. Rozanne Elder. Kalamazoo, Michigan: Cistercian Publications, Inc., 1976.

Davis, Sister Marian. "Nicholas Love and the N-Town Cycle." Ph.D. dissertation, Auburn University, 1979.

Davis, Natalie Zemon. "Some Tasks and Themes in the Study of Popular Religion." In *The Pursuit of Holiness in Late Medieval and Renaissance Religion*, edited by Charles Trinkaus and Heiko A. Oberman. Leiden: E. J. Brill, 1974.

Deanesly, Margaret. *The Lollard Bible and Other Medieval Biblical Versions*. Cambridge: Cambridge University Press, 1920.

———. "Vernacular Books in England in the Fourteenth and Fifteenth Centuries." *Modern Language Review* 15(1920):349–58.

de Coo, Josef. "In Josephs Hosen Jhesus Ghewonden Wert: Ein Weihnachtsmotiv in Literatur und Kunst." *Aachener Kunstblatter* 30(1965):144–84.

de Mause, Lloyd, ed. *The History of Childhood*. New York: Harper and Row, 1975.

Denny, Neville, ed. *Medieval Drama*. Stratford-upon-Avon Studies, no. 16. London: Edward Arnold, 1973.

Dickman, Susan. "Margery Kempe and the Continental Tradition of the Pious Woman." In *The Medieval Mystical Tradition in England: Papers Read at Dartington Hall, July, 1984*, edited by Marion Glasscoe. Cambridge: D. S. Brewer, 1984.

Dodd, Kenneth Melton. "Another Elizabethan Theater in the Round." *Shakespeare Quarterly* 21(1970):125–56.

Dodds, Madeleine Hope. "The Problem of the Ludus Coventriae." *Modern Language Review* 9(1914):79–91.

Dugdale, William. *Monasticon Anglicanum*. Revised edition. Vol. 3. Translated by John Caley et al. London: James Bohn, 1846.

Select Bibliography

Dunn, E. Catherine. "Popular Devotion in the Vernacular Drama of Medieval England." *Medievalia et Humanistica*, n.s., 4(1973):55–68.

Dutka, Joanna. "Mystery Plays at Norwich: Their Formation and Development." *Leeds Studies in English*, n.s. 10(1978):107–20.

Dyde, W. *The History and Antiquities of Tewkesbury*. 2d ed. Tewkesbury: W. Dyde, 1798.

Earl, James W. "Typology and Iconographic Style in Early Medieval Hagiography." *Studies in the Literary Imagination* 8(1975):15–46.

Eccles, Mark. "Ludus Coventriae: Lincoln or Norfolk?" *Medium Aevum* 40(1971):135–41.

Ellis, Deborah S. "Margery Kempe and the Virgin's Hot Caudle." *Essays in Arts and Sciences* 14(1985):1–11.

Erickson, Carolly. *The Medieval Vision: Essays in History and Perception*. New York: Oxford University Press, 1976.

Evans, Joan. *English Art, 1307–1461*. Oxford History of Art, no. 5. Oxford: Oxford University Press, 1949.

Farrow, M. A. *Index to Wills Proved in the Consistory Court of Norwich, 1370–1550*. British Record Society, no. 69. London: British Record Society, 1945.

Feudale, Caroline. "The Iconography of the Madonna del Parto." *Marsyas* 7(1957):8–24.

Flanigan, Clifford. "The Medieval English Mystery Cycles and the Liturgy." Paper delivered at the Seventeenth Medieval Studies Congress at Western Michigan University, Kalamazoo, Michigan, May, 1982.

Fleming, John. *An Introduction to the Franciscan Literature of the Middle Ages*. Chicago: Franciscan Herald Press, 1977.

Forrest, Sister M. Patricia. "Apocryphal Sources of the St. Anne's Day Plays in the Hegge Cycle." *Medievalia et Humanistica* 17(1966):38–50.

Friedmann, Herbert. *The Symbolic Goldfinch: Its History and Significance in European Art*. Washington, D.C.: Pantheon, 1946.

Gardiner, Harold C., S. J. *Mysteries End: An Investigation of the Last Days of the Medieval Religious Stage*. New Haven and London: Yale University Press, 1946.

Gibson, Gail McMurray. "Bury St. Edmunds, Lydgate, and the *N-Town Cycle*." *Speculum* 56(1981):56–90.

———. "East Anglian Drama and the Dance of Death: Some Second Thoughts on the 'Dance of Paul's.'" *Early Drama, Art, and Music Newsletter* 5(1982):1–9.

———. "The Images of Doubt and Belief: Visual Symbolism in the Middle English Plays of Joseph's Troubles about Mary." Ph.D. dissertation, University of Virginia, 1975.

———. "Long Melford Church, Suffolk: Some Suggestions for the Interdisciplinary Study of English Medieval Drama and the Visual Arts." *Research Opportunities in Renaissance Drama* 21(1978):105–15.

———. "The Play of *Wisdom* and the Abbey of St. Edmund." In *The Wisdom Symposium: Papers from the Trinity College Medieval Festival*, edited by Milla Cozart Riggio. New York: AMS Press, 1986.

———. "'Porta Haec Clausa Erit.' Comedy, Conception, and Ezekiel's Closed

Door in the *Ludus Coventriae* Play of 'Joseph's Return.'" *Journal of Medieval and Renaissance Studies* 8(1978):137–57.

Gillett, H. M. *Famous Shrines of Our Lady*. 2 vols. London: Samuel Walker, 1950.

Gillingwater, Edmund. *An Historical and Descriptive Account of St. Edmund's Bury, in the County of Suffolk*. Bury St. Edmunds: J. Rackham, 1804.

Gilyard-Beer, R. "The Eastern Arm of the Abbey Church at Bury St. Edmunds." *Proceedings of the Suffolk Institute of Archaeology and History* 36 (1969):256–62.

Goodwin, A. *The Abbey of St. Edmundsbury*. Oxford: Basil Blackwell, 1931.

Gottfried, Robert S. *Bury St. Edmunds and the Urban Crisis: 1290–1539*. Princeton: Princeton University Press, 1982.

Graef, Hilda. *Mary: A History of Doctrine and Devotion*. 2 vols. London and New York: Sheed and Ward, 1963.

Gransden, Antonia. "The Legends and Traditions Concerning the Origin of the Abbey of Bury St. Edmunds. *English Historical Review* 394(1985):1–24.

Gray, Douglas. *Themes and Images in the Medieval English Religious Lyric*. London and Boston: Routledge and Kegan Paul, 1972.

Guilfoyle, Cherrell. "'The Riddle Song' and the Shepherds' Gifts in *Secunda Pastorum*." *Yearbook of English Studies* 8(1978):208–19.

Hall, Donald J. *English Mediaeval Pilgrimage*. London: Routledge and Kegan Paul, 1965.

Hardison, O. B. *Christian Rite and Christian Drama in the Middle Ages*. Baltimore: Johns Hopkins University Press, 1965.

Harrod, Henry. "Extracts from Early Wills in the Norwich Registries." *Norfolk Archaeology* 4(1855): 317–39.

Hart, Richard. "The Shrines and Pilgrimages of the County of Norfolk." *Norfolk Archaeology* 6(1864):277–94.

Hartung, Albert E., ed. *A Manual of the Writings in Middle English, 1050–1500*. Vol. 5. New Haven: Connecticut Academy of Arts and Sciences, 1975.

Harvey, John. *English Medieval Architects: A Biographical Dictionary Down to 1550*. London: B. T. Batsford, 1954.

Haslewood, Francis. "Our Lady of Ipswich." *Proceedings of the Suffolk Institute of Archaeology and Natural History* 10(1898):53–55.

Hassall, W. O. "Plays at Clerkenwell." *Modern Language Review* 33(1938):564–70.

Heimann, Adelheid. "Trinitas Creator Mundi." *Journal of the Warburg and Courtauld Institutes* 2(1938):42–52.

Henshaw, Millett. "The Attitude of the Church toward the Stage to the End of the Middle Ages." *Medievalia et Humanistica* 7(1952):3–17.

Hillen, Henry J. *History of the Borough of King's Lynn*. 2 vols. Norwich: East of England Newspaper Company, 1907.

Hills, Gordon M. "The Antiquities of Bury St. Edmunds." *Journal of the British Archaeological Association* 21(1865):32–56, 104–40.

Hirn, Yrjö. *The Sacred Shrine*. Boston: Beacon Press, 1957.

Horste, Kathryn. "'A Child is Born': The Iconography of the Portail Ste.-Anne at Paris." *Art Bulletin* 69(1987):204–10.

Hoskins, W. G. *The Age of Plunder: King Henry's England, 1500–1547*. London and New York: Longmans, 1976.

Huizinga, J[ohan]. *The Waning of the Middle Ages.* London: Edward Arnold, 1927.

Hunt, Percival. *Fifteenth Century England.* Pittsburgh: University of Pittsburgh Press, 1962.

Jacob, E. F. *Essays in Later Medieval History.* New York: Barnes and Noble; Manchester: Manchester University Press, 1968.

James, Montague Rhodes. "Bury St. Edmunds Manuscripts." *English Historical Review* 41 (1926):251–60.

———. *On the Abbey of S. Edmund at Bury.* 2 vols. in 1. Cambridge Antiquarian Society, Octavo Publications, no. 28. Cambridge: Cambridge Antiquarian Society, 1895.

———. *The Sculptures in the Lady Chapel at Ely.* London: D. Nutt, 1895.

———. *Suffolk and Norfolk: A Perambulation of the Two Counties with Notices of Their History and Their Ancient Buildings.* London: J. M. Dent, 1930. Reprint. 1939.

Jaynes, Julian. *The Origin of Consciousness in the Breakdown of the Bicameral Mind.* Boston: Houghton Mifflin, 1976.

Jenney, F. G. "The Comic in German-Folk-Christmas Plays." *Poet Lore* 27(1916): 680–99.

Jones, David. "The Pilgrimage to Walsingham." Norfolk Museums Service Information Sheet. Norwich: 1982.

Jones, Ernest. "The Legend of the Madonna's Conception through the Ear." *Essays in Applied Psychoanalysis* 2(1957):268–357.

Jones, W. R. "Lollards and Images: The Defense of Religious Art in Later Medieval England." *Journal of the History of Ideas* 34(1973):27–50.

Jordan, W. K. *The Charities of Rural England, 1480–1660.* New York: Russell Sage Foundation, 1962.

Kahrl, Stanley J. "The Brome Hall Commonplace Book." *Theatre Notebook* 22(1968):157–61.

———. *Traditions of Medieval English Drama.* Pittsburgh, Pennsylvania: University of Pittsburgh Press, 1975.

Katzenellenbogen, Adolf. *The Sculptural Program of Chartres Cathedral.* New York: W. W. Norton and Company, 1959.

Kelley, Michael R. *Flamboyant Drama: A Study of "The Castle of Perseverance," "Mankind," and "Wisdom."* Carbondale and Edwardsville, Illinois: Southern Illinois University Press, 1979.

King, David. "New Light on the Medieval Glazing of the Church of St. Peter Mancroft, Norwich." In *Crown in Glory: A Celebration of Craftsmanship—Studies in Stained Glass,* edited by Peter Moore. Norwich: Jarrold and Sons, 1982.

King, Pamela M., and Asunción Salvador-Rabaza. "La Festa D'Elx: The Festival of the Assumption of the Virgin, Elche (Alicante)." *Medieval English Theatre* 8(1986):21–50.

Kingsford, C. L. *Prejudice and Promise in XVth Century England.* Oxford: Clarendon Press, 1925.

Kipling, Gordon. "The London Pageants for Margaret of Anjou: A Medieval Script Restored." *Medieval English Theatre* 4(1982):5–25.

Klapisch-Zuber, Christiane. *Women, Family, and Ritual in Renaissance Italy.* Translated by Lydia Cochrane. Chicago: University of Chicago Press, 1985.

Select Bibliography

———. *The Religious Orders in England.* 3 vols. Rev. ed. Cambridge: Cambridge University Press, 1979.

Kolve, V. A. *The Play Called Corpus Christi.* Stanford: Stanford University Press, 1966.

Lancashire, Ian. *Dramatic Texts and Records of Britain: A Chronological Topography to 1558.* Studies in Early English Drama, no. 1. Toronto: University of Toronto Press, 1984.

Lasko, P., and N. J. Morgan, eds. *Medieval Art in East Anglia, 1300–1520.* Norwich: Jarrold and Sons, 1973.

Linnell, C. L. S. "The Commonplace Book of Robert Reynys of Acle." *Norfolk Archaeology* 32(1961):111–27.

Lloyd, T. H. *The English Wool Trade in the Middle Ages.* Cambridge: Cambridge University Press, 1977.

Lobel, M[ary] D[oreen]. *The Borough of Bury St. Edmunds.* Oxford: Clarendon Press, 1935.

Lochrie, Karma. "The Book of Margery Kempe: The Marginal Woman's Quest for Literary Authority." *Journal of Medieval and Renaissance Studies* 16 (1986):33–55.

Lumiansky, R. M. and David Mills. *The Chester Mystery Plays: Essays and Documents.* Chapel Hill: University of North Carolina Press, 1983.

McClenaghan, Barbara. *The Springs of Lavenham and the Suffolk Cloth Trade in the XV and XVI Centuries.* Ipswich: W. E. Harrison, 1924.

McFarlane, K. B. *Lancastrian Kings and Lollard Knights.* Oxford: Clarendon Press, 1972.

McNamee, M. B. "The Origin of the Vested Angel as a Eucharistic Symbol in Flemish Painting." *Art Bulletin* 54(1972):263–78.

Malden, Henry C. "Lavenham Church Tower." *Proceedings of the Suffolk Institute of Archaeology and History* 9(1897):370–72.

Mâle, Emile. *The Gothic Image: Religious Art in France of the Thirteenth Century.* Translated by Dora Nussey. New York: Harper and Row, 1958.

Mander, R. P. "Bury Fair." *East Anglian Magazine* 9(1949): 12–17.

Marshall, John. "Marginal Staging Marks in the Macro Manuscript of *Wisdom*." *Medieval English Theatre* 7(1985):77–82.

Martin, Roger. "The State of Melford Church and Our Ladies' Chapel at the East End, as I Did Know It." *Gentlemen's Magazine* 100(1830):206–7.

May, Steven. "A Medieval Stage Property: The Spade." *Mediaeval English Theatre* 4(1982):77–92.

Meiss, Millard. *French Painting in the Time of Jean de Berry: The Late Fourteenth Century and the Patronage of the Duke.* London: Phaidon Press, 1967.

———. *French Painting in the Time of Jean de Berry: The Limbourgs and Their Contemporaries.* 2 vols. New York: George Braziller, 1974.

Mepham, W. A. "The Chelmsford Plays of the 16th Century." *Essex Review* 56(1947):148–52, 171–78.

Meredith, Peter. *The Mary Play from the N-Town Manuscript.* London and New York: Longmans, 1987.

Select Bibliography

Messent, Claude J. W. *The Monastic Remains of Norfolk and Suffolk.* Norwich: H. W. Hunt, 1934.

Mills, David. "Approaches to Medieval Drama." *Leeds Studies in English,* n.s., 3 (1969):47–61.

Moore, Samuel. "General Aspects of Literary Patronage in the Middle Ages." *The Library,* n.s., 4(1913):369–92.

———. "Patrons of Letters in Norfolk and Suffolk, c. 1450." *PMLA* 27(1912): 188–207; 28(1913):79–105.

Myers, A. R. *England in the Late Middle Ages.* 8th ed. Harmondsworth, England, and New York: Penguin Books, 1979.

Neale, John Preston. *Views of the Most Interesting Collegiate and Parochial Churches in Great Britain.* Vol. 2. London: Longman, Hurst, Rees, Orine, Brown, and Green, 1825.

Nelson, Alan H. *The Medieval English Stage: Corpus Christi Pageants and Plays.* Chicago: University of Chicago Press, 1974.

Newton, Francis. *St. Francis and His Basilica Assisi.* Assisi: Casa editrice Francescana, 1926.

Nilgen, Ursula. "The Epiphany and the Eucharist: On the Interpretation of Eucharistic Motifs in Medieval Epiphany Scenes." Translated by Renate Franciscono. *Art Bulletin* 49(1967):311–16.

Osberg, Richard. "The Jesse Tree in the 1432 London Entry of Henry VI: Messianic Kingship and the Rule of Justice." *Journal of Medieval and Renaissance Studies* 16(1986):213–31.

Pächt, Otto. *The Rise of Pictorial Narrative in Twelfth-Century England.* Oxford: Clarendon Press, 1962.

Paine, Clive. *St. Mary's, Bury St. Edmunds.* 1986.

Panofsky, Erwin. *Early Netherlandish Painting: Its Origins and Character.* 2 vols. New York: Harper and Row, 1971.

Parker, Sir William. *The History of Long Melford.* London: Wyman and Sons, 1873.

Patch, Howard R. "The *Ludus Coventriae* and the Digby Massacre." *PMLA* 35(1920):324–43.

Pearsall, Derek. *John Lydgate.* Charlottesville: University Press of Virginia, 1970.

Perrow, Eber Carle. "The Last Will and Testament as a Form of Literature." *Transactions of the Wisconsin Academy of Sciences, Arts, and Letters* 17, no. 1 (1914): 682–753.

Pettitt, Thomas. "Approaches to the Medieval Folk Drama." *Early Drama, Art, and Music Newsletter* 7(1985):23–27.

Pevsner, Nikolaus. *North-East Norfolk and Norwich.* Buildings of England Series. Harmondsworth, England, and New York: Penguin Books. Reprint. 1979.

———. *North-West and South Norfolk.* Buildings of England Series. Harmondsworth, England, and New York: Penguin Books. Reprint. 1977.

———. *Suffolk.* 2d ed. Revised by Enid Radcliffe. Buildings of England Series. Harmondsworth, England, and New York: Penguin Books, 1974.

Pfaff, R. W. *New Liturgical Feasts in Later Medieval England.* Oxford: Clarendon Press, 1970.

Phillips, John. *The Reformation of Images: Destruction of Art in England, 1535–1660.* Berkeley: University of California Press, 1973.

Phythian-Adams, Charles. *Crisis and Order in English Towns, 1500–1700: Essays in Urban History.* Toronto: University of Toronto Press, 1972.

Prosser, Eleanor. *Drama and Religion in the English Mystery Plays.* Stanford: Stanford University Press, 1961.

Purtle, Carol J. *The Marian Paintings of Jan van Eyck.* Princeton: Princeton University Press, 1982.

Réau, Louis. *Iconographie de l'art chrétien.* 3 vols. in 6 parts. Paris: Presses Universitaires de Frances, 1955–59.

Redstone, Lilian J. "First Minister's Account of the Possessions of the Abbey of St. Edmund." *Proceedings of the Suffolk Institute of Archaeology and History* 13(1909):311–66.

———. "The Liberty of St. Edmund." *Proceedings of the Suffolk Institute of Archaeology and History* 15(1913):200–11.

Redstone, Vincent B., ed. *Calendar of Pre-Reformation Wills, Testaments, Probates, Administrations Registered at the Probate Office, Bury St. Edmunds, 1354–1535.* Ipswich: W. E. Harrison, 1907.

Richmond, Colin. *John Hopton, A Fifteenth Century Suffolk Gentleman.* Cambridge: Cambridge University Press, 1981.

Riehle, Wolfgang. *The Middle English Mystics.* London: Routledge and Kegan Paul, 1981.

Riggio, Milla Cozart. "The Staging of Wisdom." *Research Opportunities in Renaissance Drama* 27(1984):169–75.

———, ed. *The Wisdom Symposium: Papers from the Trinity College Medieval Festival.* AMS Studies in the Middle Ages. New York: AMS Press, 1986.

Rigold, S. E. "The St. Nicholas or 'Boy Bishop' Tokens." *Proceedings of the Suffolk Institute of Archaeology and History* 34(1978):87–101.

Ringbom, Sixten. "Devotional Images and Imaginative Devotions: Notes on the Place of Art in Late Medieval Private Piety." *Gazette des Beaux Arts* 6th ser., 73(1969):159–70.

Robb, David M. "The Iconography of the Annunciation in the Fourteenth and Fifteenth Centuries." *Art Bulletin* 18(1936):480–526.

[Rokewode], John Gage. *The History and Antiquities of Hengrave in Suffolk.* London: James Carpenter; Bury St. Edmunds: John Deck, 1822.

Ronan, Myles V. *S. Anne, Her Cult and Her Shrines.* London: Sands and Company, 1927.

Rosenau, Helen. "A Study in the Iconography of the Incarnation." *Burlington Magazine* 85(1944):176–79.

Rosenthal, Joel T. *The Purchase of Paradise: Gift Giving and the Aristocracy, 1307–1485.* London: Routledge and Kegan Paul; Toronto: University of Toronto Press, 1972.

Ross, Thomas W. "Five Fifteenth-Century 'Emblem' Verses from British Museum Additional MS. 37049." *Speculum* 32(1957):274–82.

Rowe, Joy. "The Medical Hospitals of Bury St. Edmunds." *Medical History* 2, no. 4(1958):253–363.

Select Bibliography

Salter, F. M. *Medieval Drama in Chester.* Toronto: Toronto University Press, 1955.

Sansbury, Christopher. *Holy Trinity Church, Long Melford.* Norwich: Jarrold and Sons, 1979.

Saunders, O. Elfrida. *A History of English Art in the Middle Ages.* Oxford: Clarendon Press, 1932.

Scarfe, Norman. *The Suffolk Landscape.* London: Hodder and Stoughton, 1972.

Schapiro, Meyer. "The Image of the Disappearing Christ: The Ascension in English Art Around the Year 1000." *Gazette des Beaux Arts* 6th ser., 23(1943): 135–52.

Schiller, Gertrud. *Iconography of Christian Art.* 2 vols. Translated by Janet Seligman. Greenwich, Connecticut: New York Graphic Society, 1971.

———. *Ikonographie der christlichen Kunst.* Vol. 3. Gütersloh: Gütersloher Verlagshaus G. Mohn, 1971.

Schirmer, Walter F. *John Lydgate: A Study in the Culture of the XVth Century.* Translated by Ann E. Keep. London: Methuen and Company, 1961.

Scott, Kathleen. "Lydgate's Lives of Saints Edmund and Fremund: A Newly Located Manuscript in Arundel Castle." *Viator* 13(1982):335–66.

Sewell, W. H. "The Sexton's Wheel and the Lady Fast." *Norfolk Archaeology* 9(1884):201–14.

Sheehan, Michael M. *The Will in Medieval England from the Conversion of the Anglo-Saxons to the End of the Thirteenth Century.* Pontifical Institute of Mediaeval Studies, Studies and Texts, no. 6. Toronto: Pontifical Institute of Mediaeval Studies, 1963.

Sheingorn, Pamela. *The Easter Sepulchre in England.* Early Drama, Art, and Music Reference Series, no. 5. Kalamazoo, Michigan: Medieval Institute Publications, 1987.

Shorr, Dorothy C. *The Christ Child in Devotional Images in Italy During the XIV Century.* New York: George Wittenborn, 1954.

Slegg, W. B. *The Gilds and Town Lands of East Harling, Norfolk.* Local History Collection, Norwich Central Library.

———. "History of Harling" MS. 10840 36 F2, Norfolk Record Office. 1940.

Smith, Edwin, Graham Hutton, and Olive Cook. *English Parish Churches.* London: Thames and Hudson, 1976.

Smith, Stanley. *The Madonna of Ipswich.* Ipswich: East Anglian Magazine, Ltd., 1980.

Spector, Stephen. "The Composition and Development of an Eclectic Manuscript: Cotton Vespasian D VIII." *Leeds Studies in English* 9(1977):62–83.

———. "Paper Evidence and the Genesis of the Macro Plays." *Medievalia* 5 (1979):217–32.

———. "The Provenance of the N-Town Codex." *The Library,* 6th ser., no. 1 (1979):25–33.

———. "Symmetry in Watermark Sequences." *Studies in Bibliography* 31 (1978):162–78.

Statham, Margaret. "The Guildhall, Bury St. Edmunds." *Proceedings of the Suffolk Institute of Archaeology* 31(1968):117–57.

———. *The Book of Bury St. Edmunds.* Buckingham, England: Barracuda Books, 1987.

Statham, M[artin] P. "The Bury Fairs." *Suffolk Review* 4(1974):126–34.

Stephens, W. B. *Sources for English Local History.* Manchester: Manchester University Press, 1973.

Stevens, Martin. *Four Middle English Mystery Cycles: Textual, Contextual, and Critical Interpretations.* Princeton: Princeton University Press, 1987.

Strong, Roy. *The Cult of Elizabeth: Elizabethan Portraiture and Pageantry.* London: Thames and Hudson, 1977.

Sumption, Jonathan. *Pilgrimage: An Image of Mediaeval Religion.* Totowa, New Jersey: Rowman and Littlefield, 1975.

Swales, T. H. "Opposition to the Suppression of the Norfolk Monasteries; Expressions of Discontent, The Walsingham Conspiracy." *Norfolk Archaeology* 33(1962):254–65.

Symonds, William. "The Booke of Subscriptions, 1663–1702." *Proceedings of the Suffolke Institute of Archaeology and History* 13(1909):44–56.

Tanner, Norman P. *The Church in Late Medieval Norwich, 1370–1532.* Pontifical Institute Studies and Texts, no. 66. Toronto: Pontifical Institute of Mediaeval Studies, 1984.

Taylor, Richard. *Index Monasticus; or, the Abbeys and Other Monasteries, Alien Priories, Friaries, Colleges, Collegiate Churches and Hospitals with their Dependencies formerly established in the Diocese of Norwich and the Ancient Kingdom of East Anglia.* London: Richard and Arthur Taylor, 1821.

Thomas, Keith. *Religion and the Decline of Magic.* London: Weidenfeld and Nicolson, 1971.

Thomson, John A. F. *The Later Lollards, 1414–1520.* 2d ed. London: Oxford University Press, 1967.

Thomson, Rodney M. *The Archives of the Abbey of Bury St. Edmunds.* Suffolk Records Society, no. 21. Bury St. Edmunds: St. Edmundsbury Press, 1980.

———. "The Library of Bury St. Edmunds Abbey in the Eleventh and Twelfth Centuries." *Speculum* 47(1972):617–45.

Tobin, Mary Lampland. "A Study of the Formation and Auspices of the Ludus Coventriae." Ph.D. dissertation, Rice University, 1973.

Tolhurst, J. B. L. "The Hammer-Beam Figures of the Nave Roof of St. Mary's Church, Bury St. Edmunds." *Journal of the British Archaeological Association,* 3d ser., 25(1962):66–70.

Trapp, J. B. "Verses by Lydgate at Long Melford." *Review of English Studies,* n.s., 6(1955):1–11.

Travis, Peter. *Dramatic Design in the Chester Cycle.* Chicago: University of Chicago Press, 1982.

Trenholme, Norman Maclaren. *The English Monastic Boroughs.* University of Missouri Studies, no. 2. Columbia,: University of Missouri Press, 1927.

Trinkaus, Charles, and Heiko A. Oberman, eds. *The Pursuit of Holiness in Late Medieval and Renaissance Religion.* Studies in Medieval and Reformation Thought, no. 10. Leiden: E. J. Brill, 1974.

Tydeman, William. *The Theatre in the Middle Ages.* Cambridge: Cambridge University Press, 1978.

Select Bibliography

Tymms, Samuel. *An Architectural and Historical Account of the Church of St. Mary, Bury St. Edmunds.* Bury St. Edmunds: Jackson and Frost, 1854.

———. "Cupola House, Bury St. Edmunds." *Proceedings of the Suffolk Institute of Archaeology and History* 3(1863):375–85.

———. *A Handbook of Bury St. Edmunds, in the County of Suffolk.* 6th ed. Bury St. Edmunds: F. T. Groom; London: Simpkin, Marshall, Hamilton, Kent, and Co., 1854.

———. "Little Haugh Hall, Norton." *Proceedings of the Suffolk Institute of Archaeology and History* 2(1859):279–87.

Victoria History of the County of Norfolk, 2 vols. Edited by William Page. London: Archibald Constable and Co., 1906. Reprint. William Dawson and Sons, 1975.

Victoria History of the County of Suffolk. 2 vols. Edited by William Page. London: Archibald Constable and Co., 1907. Reprint. William Dawson and Sons, 1975.

Vloberg, Maurice. "The Iconography of the Immaculate Conception." In *The Dogma of the Immaculate Conception: History and Significance,* edited by Edward Dennis O'Connor. South Bend, Indiana: University of Notre Dame Press, 1958.

Vriend, J., S. J. *The Blessed Virgin Mary in the Medieval Drama of England.* Purmerend, Holland: J. Muusses, 1928.

Wallace, R. Hedger. "White Cattle in British Folktales and Customs." *Folk-Lore* 10(1899):352–57.

Warner, Marina. *Alone of All Her Sex: The Myth and the Cult of the Virgin Mary.* New York: Alfred A. Knopf, 1976.

Wasson, John. "Corpus Christi Plays and Pageants at Ipswich." *Research Opportunities in Renaissance Drama* 19(1976):99–108.

Waterton, Edmund. *Pietas Mariana Britannica.* 2 vols. in 1 part. London: St. Joseph's Catholic Library, 1879.

Welch, Edwin. "Some Suffolk Lollards." *Proceedings of the Suffolk Institute of Archaeology and History* 29(1963):154–65.

Westlake, H. F. *The Parish Gilds of Mediaeval England.* London: Society for Promoting Christian Knowledge, 1919.

Whittingham, A. B. "Bury St. Edmunds Abbey: The Plan, Design, and Development of the Church and Monastic Buildings." *Archaeological Journal* 108(1951): 168–87.

Winch, Raymond, and Victor Bennett. *The Assumption of Our Lady and Catholic Theology.* London: Society for Promoting Christian Knowledge, 1950.

———. "Queen Margaret's Entry into London, 1445." *Modern Philology* 13(1915–16):53–57.

Woodforde, Christopher. *The Norwich School of Glass-Painting in the Fifteenth Century.* London: Oxford University Press, 1950.

———. "The Stained and Painted Glass in Hengrave Hall, Suffolk." *Proceedings of the Suffolk Institute of Archaeology and History* 22(1936):1–16.

———. "Two Unusual Subjects in Ancient Glass in Long Melford Church." *Proceedings of the Suffolk Institute of Archaeology and History* 21(1931):63–66.

Wood-Legh, K. L. *Perpetual Chantries in Britain.* Cambridge: Cambridge University Press, 1965.

Select Bibliography

Woolf, Rosemary. *The English Mystery Plays*. Berkeley and Los Angeles: University of California Press, 1972.

———. *The English Religious Lyric in the Middle Ages*. Oxford: Clarendon Press, 1968.

Wright, A. R. *British Calendar Customs: England*. London: William Glaisher, 1938.

Wright, Richard. "Community Theatre in Late Medieval East Anglia." *Theatre Notebook* 28(1974):24–38.

———. "Medieval Theatre in East Anglia: A Study of Drama and the Community in Essex, Suffolk and Norfolk, 1200–1580 with special reference to Game, Interlude and Play in the late 15th and early 16th century." D. Phil. dissertation, University of Bristol, 1971.

Yates, Richard. *History and Antiquities of the Abbey of St. Edmund's Bury*. London: J. B. Nichols and Sons, 1843.

Young, Abigail Ann. "Plays and Players: The Latin Terms for Performance." *REED Newsletter* 9, no. 2 (1984):56–62; 10, no. 1 (1985): 9–16.

Young, Karl. *The Drama of the Medieval Church*. 2 vols. Oxford: Clarendon Press, 1962.

———. "An Interludium for a Gild of Corpus Christi." *Modern Language Notes* 48(1933):84–86.

Index

Index